Judaism:

Basis – Past – Present – Future

Part 2

Judaism:

Basis - Past - Present - Future
Part 2

Manfred Davidmann

Social Organisation Limited

Published by Social Organisation Limited
30-34 New Bridge Street, London, EC4V 6BJ, United Kingdom
Contact: books@socialorganisation.eu
www.socialorganisation.eu

Manfred Davidmann shows that the Pentateuch's God-given social rules and social system are the very foundation of Judaism, Christianity and Islam and underlie freedom, liberty, independence and well-being. He proves that what these main religions have in common is that in each case a ruling elite succeeded in bypassing or overturning the religion's essential God-given benevolent social provisions and human rights, in this way exposing their communities and whole populations to oppression and exploitation.

The author reveals for each religion the controversies and conflicts between church and state, between beliefs and practice. He examines the root causes of major social problems and shows how to resolve the problems by dealing with their basic causes.

And Manfred Davidmann shows how to apply and put into practice the essential benevolent and egalitarian social provisions and human rights of the Pentateuch under modern conditions.

Published by Social Organisation Limited in 2019

ISBN 978-0-85192-061-0

Printed and bound by Witley Press Ltd
24-26 Greevegate, Hunstanton, Norfolk, PE36 6AD, United Kingdom

Cover design by Dr. Angelika Schaumberg

CONTENTS

"Freedom and independence of mind and person and the quality of life depend on one's behaviour. The consequences of one's behaviour are inevitable, inescapable. Keeping or disregarding the Pentateuch laws has consequences which cannot be avoided. Whole communities prosper or suffer (are 'persecuted') as a consequence of their individual and thus collective behaviour.

Those who behave according to the law have good and satisfying lives, gain social and military strength. Behaviour which is contrary to the law lowers the quality of life, increases internal stress and conflict to the point of social disruption and military weakness.

If we want freedom, independence, good life of high quality, then we have to follow these laws. If we do not, then we lose freedom, independence, good life and the country in which we live. The consequences of our behaviour cannot be avoided but we can change the course of events by changing our behaviour."

Manfred Davidmann

In accordance with Manfred Davidmann's will and wishes his works are published in form of books.

Manfred Davidmann is the author of this book's content (Chapter 2 to Chapter 17).

These chapters were selected from Manfred Davidmann's publications on the solhaam.org website and in books, considering as well the author's notes about this book's content and title.

Following the author's wording and style, the description on page 4, 'Contents', 'Overview' (Chapter 1) and the text for the cover's back page have been added in order to complete the book for publication. Additions to the author's original text are stated and marked *.

In loving memory of Manfred Davidmann who taught people worldwide to live by the social laws and social system of the Pentateuch which underlie Judaism, Christianity, Islam and Democracy.

Dr. Angelika Schaumberg, Social Organisation Limited, 2019

Overview

2   CHURCH AND STATE, GOVERNMENT AND RELIGION

2.1   The God-given Human Rights, Social Laws and Social System

This chapter is a comprehensive statement of the God-given human rights and obligations which underlie freedom, liberty, independence and well-being. They underlie and determine a good life of high quality. People at all stages of development are struggling to achieve these rights and benefits, all over the planet.

Directly relevant to today's social and economic problems, these rights and obligations determine the quality of life in areas such as social and economic security, social responsibility and accountability, ownership and decision-making, government and management, humane behaviour, teamwork and trustful cooperation.

These human rights, these social rules and this social system, are the very foundation of the three main religions of Judaism, Christianity and Islam.

What these religions have in common is that in each case a ruling elite succeeded in bypassing or overturning the religion's essential God-given benevolent social provisions and human rights, in this way exposing their communities and whole populations to oppression and exploitation.

What Manfred Davidmann has done with his works on the Pentateuch and the Bible, on religion and church-state relations, is to expose and correct the misinterpretations and mistranslations of the past. His works are major breakthroughs, constituting essential information for understanding the meaning and significance of the Pentateuch and the Bible.

2.2 Church and State, Government and Religion: Judaism, Christianity and Islam

Shows that underlying Judaism, Christianity and Islam are the Pentateuch's benevolent and egalitarian social laws and social system. Reveals for each religion the controversies and conflicts between church and state, between beliefs and practice.

2.3 Church and State, Government and Religion: Religion, Government and Education

Illustrates conflicting aims and interests of state and church with reference to teaching evolution (creationism) and teaching immorality (state-condoned promiscuity). Relative authority of Bible, common law, case law, religious leaderships, judges.

2.4 Creationism and Intelligent Design, Evolution, Education or Indoctrination

Conflicts have arisen because parts of Genesis have been mistranslated or misinterpreted.

The 'Creationism' hypothesis apparently assumes that the resulting erroneous text correctly states God's deeds. And the 'Intelligent Design' hypothesis apparently assumes that the same erroneous text correctly states the deeds of some other supernatural being.

Manfred Davidmann's research and discoveries showed and proved that the source text of Genesis corresponds in the major steps to the order in which the earth and life are known to have been formed and developed. Described is the formation of the earth and early plant life, and evolution by the 'survival of the fittest'. The evolution from reptilian to mammalian instincts, feelings and behaviour is clearly stated, as is the evolution and corresponding behaviour, feeling and thinking of human beings from humanoids (animals resembling humans) through Homo erectus (early man) to Homo sapiens (human beings, ourselves).

There is no conflict or contradiction between what is recorded in the source Genesis text and our scientific knowledge about evolution of human beings and of our planet.

3   Family, Community, Sex and the Individual

This work examines root causes of what are now major social problems and shows how to resolve the problems by dealing with their basic causes.

Human beings work primarily for their family and members of a family stand by, support and help each other in times of need. The family is the basic unit of society and it looks after the interests of all its members, as individuals as well as collectively. This gives great strength to each member of the family in the struggle for daily bread, security and happiness.

Manfred Davidmann exposes the causes of what seems to be progressive breaking down of family life and of social strength. This report is an unprecedented and comprehensive overview, states new insights, proves basic underlying causes.

For example, in a comprehensive review, Manfred Davidmann defines the role of the family as being:

To struggle as a family to survive.

To protect and support mother and children until children become mature and independent adults capable of providing for themselves.

To provide a good standard of living and a life of high quality. Which includes struggling against oppression and exploitation - and sometimes one has to fight to preserve a good way of life.

To serve the interests of, and to support, each member of the family. In turn, each member of the family supports the family.

Here he also covers and reports on the impact of casual sexual relations and its effects on individuals, family and community, on the social strength of individuals and communities.

Manfred Davidmann was the first to clearly describe and show, the effects of increasing life spans on the family, on its members and on their responsibilities. He also illustrated the underlying basis of teamwork within the family, stating the various roles and responsibilities and functional relationships of its members for effective teamwork within the family.

4   Kibbutzim

Kibbutzim are successful co-operative communities now experiencing both practical and ideological problems. So the study looks at what is taking place to find reasons for success and causes of problems.

5   Quotable Quotes about Judaism

The struggle for the right to take decisions. Manipulated elections. Secretive top-level multinational meetings and agreements. Misuses of economics, statistics and experts. Human rights, social responsibility, social costs and much more.

6   Using Words to Communicate Effectively

Shows how to communicate more effectively, covering aspects of thinking, writing, speaking and listening as well as formal and informal communications.

Consists of guidelines found useful by university students and practising middle and senior managers.

7   The Way Ahead: Policies for a Better Future

This work contains findings and conclusions based on extensive research reported over a period of time by Manfred Davidmann in other publications which are relevant to individuals, communities, countries and the whole planet, and it summarises what needs to be achieved.

Manfred Davidmann shows that the Torah contains a statement of scientific social laws of behaviour and of community and social organisation, such as:

Money has to be lent by the community, free of interest.

Outstanding loans have to be cancelled after a period of time.

A country's wealth belongs to its inhabitants.

He proves that keeping the social laws of the Torah guarantees human rights. They apply to all people alike and have the force of law. He also explains how the application of these social laws affects not only the standard of living of all members of society, but the future of the planet as a whole.

8   Faith and Trust in God, No Matter by What Name called

A statement of belief and request for support and aid, to God no matter by what name called, in the worldwide struggle for a better and more secure life. Combined with a description of mutual responsibilities and care, of corresponding guidance and protection.

9   The choice is yours:
Unemployment, Charitable Social Security and Today's
Religious Teachings
or
High Standard of Living, Satisfying Work and a Good Life,
as God-given rights.

About social and economic security, government and management, equality and ownership, the role of biblical prophets and their warnings, and now.

This theme brings together in one place relevant material on core problems of our times, drawn from Manfred Davidmann's published works. Essential reading for quickly absorbing the substance of his teachings, for those aiming to make this a better world.

10   The Meaning of Genesis

10.1   Meaning and Significance of the Names of God in Genesis

Manfred Davidmann describes and proves the meaning and significance of the different names of God which are used in Genesis, which had been lost and which are of the greatest importance for understanding the meaning of the text of the Bible.

10.2   Essential Notes on Hebrew Grammar

Here Manfred Davidmann states the fundamental rules which were ignored at time of translation because required background knowledge was not available at that time, with consequent mistranslations. He lists and illustrates the grammatical rules which help to differentiate between references to individuals and references to groups or life forms. Essential information for understanding the meaning of Genesis.

10.3 Bible Translations, Versions, Codes and Hidden Information in Bible and Talmud

Manfred Davidmann shows how changes made in the past obscured the original intended meaning. He also describes the ways in which hidden information has been encoded and labeled so that its original meaning could not be misunderstood or misinterpreted.

11   The Social Laws and Social System of the Pentateuch: (Ha Mim) The Word of Allah as Taught by Mohammed

12   Creationism and Intelligent Design, Evolution, Education or Indoctrination.
And
Reading, Interpreting, Translating of Ancient Consonantal Texts like the Bible or the Koran.

13   Judaism at the Crossroads, at the Final Parting of the Ways

14   Israel and The Social Laws and Social System of the Pentateuch

15   Muslims and Jews

Includes a comprehensive summary table of the struggles of the Muslims while Mohammed was alive, primarily against the Meccan ruling elite but also including their conflicts with the Jewish Medinan clans.

The unexpected but convincing conclusions are directly relevant to understanding present tensions and conflicts within Islam.

16   The Global (Worldwide) Struggle for a Better Life
and
The Root of all Evil, the Source of All Good, and the Messianic Struggle

Combines major advances in human knowledge and key findings, from Manfred Davidmann's published works and teachings, into a comprehensive but detailed overview of the life we lead, of life's problems and struggles, of the (worldwide) struggle for a better life, and of the Messianic struggle of good against evil.

In this report, Manfred Davidmann exposes humanity's innermost secrets to the light of day.

As you read the report, you are brought ever closer to humanity's hidden core confrontations and the reality of the struggle for a better life. That is, you will see what humankind is struggling against; you will see the fundamental cause. You will see the core and source of evil, corruption, brutality, perversion, oppression and enslavement.

This report is about past and present struggles, achievements and defeats, about whole communities betrayed and misled, about religious teachings distorted and even turned upside down. And it is about how to achieve our own well-being, about our ensuring that we as individuals have good and satisfying lives.

And you will see how that which is good arises from the selfless and unstinting efforts of human beings cooperating for the common good.

'And if the facts are unexpected or if you do not like the facts then don't blame me. I am merely recording them', says Manfred Davidmann.

17   About the Author

Chapter 2

CHURCH AND STATE, GOVERNMENT AND RELIGION

This series of works together lays bare the controversies between church and state, between religious belief and practice on the one hand, and the government on the other. Each work is self-standing but together they provide the knowledge needed for understanding the causes of conflicts and point to solving them.

The works in this series bring together findings and conclusions from Manfred Davidmann's published reports and provide new knowledge and insights, exploring their subject in depth, generally in advance of current knowledge.

Chapter 2.1:

> **The God-given Human Rights, Social Laws and Social System**

Chapter 2.2:

> **Church and State, Government and Religion: Judaism, Christianity and Islam**

Chapter 2.3:

> **Church and State, Government and Religion: Religion, Government and Education**

Chapter 2.4:

> **Creationism and Intelligent Design, Evolution, Education or Indoctrination**

The God-given Human Rights, Social Laws and Social System

Introduction

This report is a comprehensive statement of the God-given human rights which underlie all human freedom, liberty and independence, and which underlie and determine a good life of high quality. People at all stages of development are struggling to achieve these rights and benefits, all over the planet.

Directly relevant to today's social and economic problems, these rights and obligations determine the quality of life in areas such as social and economic security, social responsibility and accountability, ownership and decision-making, government and management, humane behaviour, teamwork and trustful cooperation.

These human rights, these social rules and this social system, are the very foundation of the three main religions of Judaism, Christianity and Islam.

When the Pentateuch <1> was written, people had but little knowledge about science or evolution compared with what is known today. So concepts for which we now have precise terms were described rather than stated. Instead of the term 'scientific law' being used, for example, we see described that 'what is written applies to all people, present or absent, past or future, will happen regardless of how one feels about it, that the results of certain actions are reversed if the actions are reversed'. <2>

And concepts and descriptions were expressed in religious terms so that they could be understood and followed by the population.

What these religions have in common is that in each case a ruling elite succeeded in bypassing or overturning the religion's essential God-given benevolent social provisions and human rights {1, 2, 14-15, 6-9}, in this way exposing their communities and whole populations to oppression and exploitation.

Now that our technological progress so vastly exceeds our social organisation and behaviour, the survival of our species is in doubt. Hence the urgency of the need to apply these rules of behaviour in our daily lives. Here the aim is to show what needs to be done and how it can be achieved.

What Manfred Davidmann has done with his works on the Pentateuch and the Bible, on religion and church-state relations, is to expose and correct the misinterpretations and mistranslations of the past. His works are major breakthroughs, constituting essential information for understanding the meaning and significance of the Pentateuch and the Bible.

In his "Meaning and Significance of the Names of God in Genesis" (see chapter 10.1)*, Manfred Davidmann proved the meaning and significance of the different names of God which had been lost. In

"Meaning and Intent of Genesis: Essential Notes on Hebrew Grammar" (see chapter 10.2)*, he stated the fundamental rules which were ignored at time of translation because required background knowledge was not available, with consequent mistranslations. And in "Bible Translations, Versions, Codes and Hidden Information in Bible and Talmud" (see chapter 10.3)*, he showed how changes made in the past obscured the intended meaning.

Further, the Pentateuch records and details the Social Cause-and-Effect Relationship, a fundamental scientific law which is stated as such and which was discovered there by Manfred Davidmann. This states that the consequences of keeping or not keeping the social laws are inescapable, that what happens to one is in the end the inevitable result of one's own behavior. It is stated to enable people to benefit from knowing the effects of their behavior.

Ignorance of these rules of behavior is no excuse and the relationship applies to all. History and social science confirm it, the prophets knew and understood it and predicted accordingly. Jesus confirmed it; the Koran records Prophet Mohammed repeatedly confirming the Pentateuch, referring to it both as a guide and as a warning.

Whole communities prosper or suffer as a consequence of their collective behavior. Manfred Davidmann says, "The consequences of our behavior cannot be avoided but we can change the course of events by changing our behavior."

Good and Evil and the Difference between Them   {3}

The first volume of the Pentateuch (Genesis) describes how plants and animals were formed, evolved and populated the planet. It describes how the behaviour of successive life forms changed as they evolved into human beings. {3}

Evolution had turned into a bitter struggle for the survival of the fittest, where the most fittest was the most vicious and violent. The most 'advanced' species was the species which was the most vicious. Life was brutal and dominated by evil. This is how reptiles came to dominate the earth.

Then mammals evolve from reptiles, and develop feelings of care and affection towards others. Genesis describes {3} that from them evolved a mammalian human-like life form (homo erectus) whose behaviour was more beast-like than human, without knowledge of good and evil and unable to distinguish between them.

Genesis states {3} that if there is to be further development towards good then there has to be knowledge of and understanding of good and evil and of the difference between them so that people can choose between them. And that consequently the human brain evolved from the mammalian brain.

The increased brain capacity and the evolution of the neocortex {10} enable humans (Homo sapiens) to know the difference between good and evil and human beings with their larger brains spread across the planet and replaced Homo erectus.

In this way the Pentateuch, in religious language, records {3} the evolution (creation) and behaviour of human beings who know of, can distinguish between and can choose between, good and evil.

The human brain underlies free will, enabling us to decide independently whether to do good or evil, that is what to do or not to do.

But this needs to be supplemented with the ability to think clearly, to assess and evaluate on the basis of knowledge of good and evil and of the essential need for behaving humanely, for following (doing) good instead of evil.

It is here that the relevance and importance of the Pentateuch's social laws and teachings <3> become apparent. The Pentateuch adds to mere mechanistic and chance processes the knowledge that human beings need to, and have to, behave humanely if they wish to prosper and succeed. Stating clearly what is, and is not, humane behaviour, clearly defining the difference between good (including human rights and justice) and evil, adding that human beings stand or fall by the way they behave. {12}

And it is the God-given social laws and social system of the Pentateuch which define and state human rights and behaviour which people need to follow if they wish to prosper and succeed, if they wish to have a high standard of living and a life of high quality.

Unavoidable Consequences of One's Behaviour (Social Cause-and-Effect Relationship <2> {12})

A covenant is an agreement in which each of the parties undertakes duties and obligations towards the other. And the Pentateuch records God's promise that human beings will have a good life of high quality as long as human beings fulfil their obligations under the covenant, as long as human beings follow God's laws, as long as they behave like human beings. <4>

This is also recorded in the Pentateuch as a fundamental scientific law, the Social Cause-and-Effect Relationship {12} <2>, in the language of religion. This states that the consequences of keeping or not keeping the Pentateuch's laws are inescapable, that what happens to one is in the end the inevitable result of one's own behaviour. Also clearly stated is that this is a scientific law which was defined and stated using the language of religion so that people would benefit from knowing the effects (consequences) of their behaviour. The relationship is stated in precise terms. History {2} and social science {21} confirm it.

We are told that the relationship applies to all without exception and at all times, wherever one may be, regardless of type of government, form of religion or social system or country. It applies whether you like it or not, agree or disagree.

The consequences of one's behaviour are detailed both ways, clearly and powerfully illustrating intermediate stages between the two ends of the scale, and we are told that the process is reversible: Increasingly disregarding the laws (rules of behaviour) results in greater suffering and oppression, increasingly behaving according to the laws results in greater freedom, liberty, independence and a better life.

The relationship applies to all. Ignorance is no excuse, not knowing the law does not prevent consequences of one's behaviour, and the relationship is stated in a way which enables people to benefit from knowing the effects of their behaviour, even if they do not understand the underlying relationship.

The relationship is clearly stated in the Pentateuch {12}, confirmed by Jesus {1} and then by Mohammed. The Koran records Mohammed repeatedly confirming the Pentateuch, referring to it both as a guide and as a warning {9}, and Arab and Muslim history illustrates the working of the cause-and-effect relationship.

Freedom and independence of mind and person and the quality of life depend on one's behaviour. The consequences of one's behaviour are inevitable, inescapable. Keeping or disregarding the Pentateuch laws has consequences which cannot be avoided. Whole communities prosper or suffer (are 'persecuted') as a consequence of their individual and thus collective behaviour.

Those who behave according to the law have good and satisfying lives, gain social and military strength. Behaviour which is contrary to the law lowers the quality of life, increases internal stress and conflict to the point of social disruption and military weakness.

If we want freedom, independence, good life of high quality, then we have to follow these laws. If we do not, then we lose freedom, independence, good life and the country in which we live. The consequences of our behaviour cannot be avoided but we can change the course of events by changing our behaviour.

Planet-wide Danger

By the end of the twentieth century a new factor had entered the equation. {21}

Up to now when some people suffered, when a village was wiped out in a war fought for the benefit of another establishment, when a whole country and its people were devastated, it did not mean the end of humanity. The point is that as a result of the impact of technology and increasing speed of transport and communication it is possible for the first time in the history of human beings on this planet for just one or only a very few socially irresponsible persons to do something or to introduce changes which could destroy us all as human beings or else make this planet uninhabitable for human beings.

I showed twenty years ago in 'Social Responsibility, Profits and Social Accountability' {21} that we were experiencing a sequence of accidents and catastrophes which were occurring more and more frequently and were affecting more and more people.

Since then most people have become aware of this. But I also showed what could and should be done about this trend of events.

So now we do not have a choice. If we do not now observe and put into effect the social laws (rules) and social system of the Pentateuch and its code of behaviour then the planet will become uninhabitable for human beings.

Humane Behaviour

Trustful Co-operation (Ten Commandments)

The Ten Commandments <5> are so important and are so well known because it is behaviour in accordance with these rules of behaviour which is the basis for people trusting each other and so for people co-operating and working well with each other. They underlie freedom, independence and strength to oppose and resist oppression. Wherever there is any independence of the mind and material freedom today it exists because people followed these rules of behaviour and it exists to the extent to which they do so. To free ourselves from mental manipulation, conditioning and brainwashing we need to follow them. {12}

In other words, following the provisions of the law results in freedom and ensures it, ensures strength and security. {17}

Take these two commandments (principles of behaviour):
> You must not steal.
> You must not desire anything which belongs to your neighbour.

Much trust and community friendliness is gained when people follow these principles.

But look around you. These principles are at times applied ruthlessly to protect the possessions of the rich from the starving poor who see no other way to survive apart from stealing some scraps of food.

I may be overstating the case so as to make a point. But consider that these laws apply equally to the rich and powerful. It is also the rich and powerful who must not steal from the poor even the little which the poor have. It is the rich and powerful who must not cast longing glances at what little the rest of us possess, it is the rich and powerful who must not aim to gain at our expense.

And now consider this {24}:

> Shareholders would not even consider handing their moneys over to a corporation without in return becoming an owner of a corresponding part of the corporation, without getting a corresponding number of shares in return.

> But customers are not given a choice. Corporations (their owners) simply take their customers' moneys
> > (a) for getting back money already spent on the business and
> > (b) for expanding the business
> without in return giving customers (or the community) corresponding ownership rights.

> To 'rob' is to take unlawfully. But we are here looking at moneys being taken legally and largely without the owners' (customers') knowledge or agreement.

> What is taking place is perhaps best described as 'legalised robbery'.

> What we see is a people divided against each other, conflict and struggle.

We are resisting oppression and exploitation and building a better world for ourselves and our children. Our strength depends on co-operation between men and women, on the family, on developing our human potential by controlling the sexual urge, on being able to trust each other and rely on each other. Consider these commandments {12}:

You must not commit murder.

You must not bear false witness against your neighbour.

You must not commit adultery.

People who behave promiscuously (permissively) have sexual relations before marriage, or after marriage with a person other than their spouse. Promiscuity turns men against women, and women against men, and robs both of the support of their family {13, 16}. Hence this prohibition of promiscuous behaviour. <6>

Another commandment <5> is

Honour your father and your mother and willingly accept the stated principles of behaviour, and the tradition, knowledge and life experience of your parents so that you will progress and advance in understanding and in life and so that you will have long and secure lives of high quality in the land in which you live.

In other words, when your parents believe in the principles stated here, and apply them in their daily lives, then one must learn and respect these teachings. One must not be led astray, no matter how plausible the persuading voices or images in one's social environment seem to be. In one's impressionable years one must not be led astray from the principles of behaviour stated here as these principles underlie freedom and independence and a good and secure life of high quality.

Morality (Men and Women, Family and Family Purity)   {16}

Genesis <7> shows human beings becoming aware of the existence of good and evil and of the difference between them, shows human beings learning to choose that which is good and gaining social strength and good lives of high quality as a result. It is about human beings struggling to stop behaving like our beastlike primitive ancestors and instead doing what is good, learning to behave like human beings, to behave humanely.

And underlying humane behaviour is the need, the necessity, to control and overcome the brutalising influences we are struggling against, to control the sex impulse, so as to achieve good lives of high quality.

And what we have in the Pentateuch are rules of behaviour which point to the essence of humane behaviour. We know that ignoring them results in social corruption, oppression and exploitation of the many by the few. And we know that following these rules ensures social strength and a good life for all. {12}

Normal for human beings is an exclusive sexual relationship between husband and wife within a monogamous single life-long relationship (family) which ensures the young are protected for the many years before they reach maturity, and which protects and supports husband and wife as they grow old. On marriage the male accepts responsibility for the resulting family for life. {3, 13}

> For a comprehensive review of the role of the family and of a family's members, of the impact of casual sexual relations on individuals, family and community, on the effect of increasing lifespans, on dominance, oppression and exploitation within and without the family, on teamwork within the family, on the effects of promiscuous behaviour on social strength of individuals and communities, see {13}.

Those who behave humanely, morally, can trust each other, cooperate with each other, grow, gain strength together, prosper.

All other sexual relations are abnormal and we are told {16} the effects (consequences) of inhuman beastlike (unrestrained, uncontrolled) sexual behaviour.

Those who behave immorally weaken their family and social strength. Those who initiate moral behaviour, who behave morally and humanely, gain strength and standing, and those who support them in this are supported in return. Confirmed by history {12, 2}, we see it taking place all around us.

And sexual relations outside marriage are prohibited before and during marriage.

A clear way of stating
> the importance of chastity,
> that human beings can and do control their sexual urges,
> the importance and necessity for the human male to control the beastlike sexual urge lurking at the border of the conscious.

Sodomy, having sexual relations between persons of the same sex, is unnatural and abnormal, corrupting and destructive of human society and humane behaviour, is punished with utmost severity.

And incest, having sexual relations between members of a close or extended family, is abnormal, corrupting and destructive of family trust, family life and family strength. Incest is primitive beastlike behaviour and perpetrators are punished with utmost severity.

The Pentateuch contains detailed statements about what constitutes abnormal, promiscuous, adulterous sexual relations and prostitution, with associated comments and severe penalties. <8>

Morality and family, individual and social strength, are interrelated. Morality more than any other factor determines the strength and well-being of individuals, families and communities. So morality is of determining importance and these laws of behaviour need to be protected, applied and enforced.

Social and Moral Problems of Our Times

The consequences of immorality cannot be avoided. {12} <2>

The Pentateuch's warnings, punishments and penalties concerning morality are in most cases to the male. It is males who are behind the corrupting of family morality and who are attempting to brutalise women so as to make women more readily available for sex. Even brainwashing and manipulating women into making themselves available. With consequent weakening and breaking up of family, society and quality of life. {13}

Conditioning, persuading, inducing or compelling a person to have sex before marriage, person to person or through the media, is in my opinion an act of rape. The younger the person, the worse is the offence.

Morality has to be protected by punishing immorality, by protecting women and punishing men and women who behave immorally. By punishing those who spread immorality and seduce others into immoral behaviour.

In democracies or when people are struggling for their liberty, authoritarians condone and promote promiscuity so as to weaken the family and weaken the population. People are subjected to conditioning towards immorality to weaken the working population to make them easier to exploit, to weaken the society and democracy. <9>

But when in control, dictatorships of left or right or religious absolutist hierarchies then pedal back to gain strength for their people, so that they will fight for and protect, and slave for, their manipulating rulers. <10>

Hence the importance of morality, of Pentateuch morality and laws of behaviour, of protecting communities and people by restraining immoral behaviour, conditioning and propaganda, by appropriately punishing the perpetrators.

Social Strength

The Pentateuch states what has to be done and what is prohibited, by positive and negative rules of behaviour. {2}

Positive rules state what has to be done so as to create a just and strong society. And point the way ahead towards greater strength, freedom, liberty and a good way of life.

Negative rules (prohibitions) state what must not be done and such rules protect the people from oppression and exploitation, from the antisocial behaviour of others, safeguard the people's strength and freedom.

But support and co-operation have to be two-way flows. The community supports the individual but only if the individual supports the community. Those supported by the community are under obligation to support others in need of support, when able to do so, to share with others who are in need. Where 'need' includes the need for capital to secure their operation, to achieve the general standard of living and quality of life.

Which means that benefits and support from the community are given only to those who believe in its benevolent principles and live accordingly. 'Supporting the community' includes helping to spread knowledge and understanding of its principles. <11>

Throughout, it is only those who themselves keep and apply the benevolent social laws given in this report in their daily lives who are entitled to these rights. Otherwise, to give but one example, funds provided by the community free-of-interest to a non-member (stranger) might be used by the stranger to exploit people by lending funds to others and charging interest so as to enrich himself.

Social and Economic Security

All persons have the right to be free and independent masters of their own fate and no person may oppress or exploit another. Because people can be exploited through their needs there has to be a system of social and economic security which guarantees freedom from needs and so protects people from becoming dependent on others for essential income, protects against loss of material independence and which protects them from losing their spiritual independence.

Every community member is entitled as a matter of right to social security <12>. This means that community members are entitled to be supported by the community not only when they fall on hard times but also to maintain their independence as independent breadwinners for their families. For example, the community has to provide backup funds to those who need them and they have to be provided as and when required.

To prevent people being exploited through their need these funds have to be provided without charging interest. They are called 'loans' because the recipient is under moral obligation to repay them to the community if he can do so. However, such 'loans' are cancelled every seventh calendar year if the borrower has been unable to repay them. <11>

These essential social provisions of the Pentateuch are clear and to the point. This is what is laid down as a matter of law {12}:

1. The community has to provide ('lend') money to those who need it, free of interest.
2. All such loans, if outstanding, are to be cancelled every seventh year.

Work and Leisure

Weekly Day of Rest

Every seventh day is a day of rest for all, for those who are employed as well as for those who employ. Work stops on the weekly day of rest, the Sabbath, to let those who labour have a regular day of rest. On this day the servant is as free as the master, the worker is as free as the employer. The weekly day of rest has spread and benefits almost all the civilised world. {12} <11>

Sabbatical Year

Community members are entitled to a sabbatical year every seventh year. During this year they are entitled to be freed from work at the expense of the community. <13> {12}

Academics already enjoy regular sabbatical years. During this period they are paid their salaries. {19}

Free to travel, train for more skilled or better work, update knowledge, study, gain greater understanding, qualify. Those on a sabbatical must not work for pay, or produce to sell, during that year but receive the average rate earned by community members during the previous calendar year. <11>

Consider what sabbatical years would mean. For you and for others who would during such a year be free to do as they pleased. We could have much more satisfying lives, we could do much for our own communities, could do much for those in need, for those who are underdeveloped and unable to afford our own expert skills. {19} <14>

Freedom, Liberty and Independence

The words freedom, liberty and independence are usually given subtly different meanings, as follows:

Freedom	The right and power to act, speak, or think freely.
Liberty	The state of being free from oppression or imprisonment.
Independence	Self governing and not depending on another for livelihood or subsistence.

Freedom, liberty and independence go hand-in-hand, support and complement each other. Liberty includes being free from slavery or despotic control by others, means being free from social, economic, political, mental or physical control by others, means being free from antisocial control or manipulation by others. And independence includes not being dependent on, and not being controlled by, another person, group, organisation, or thing.

But it is the social rules and social system of the Pentateuch which in effect state that all are equal, that no person may exploit another or oppress so as to exploit. All have the right to be free and independent masters of their own fate and there has to be a system of social security which guarantees not just freedom from need but also protection against loss of material and spiritual independence.

Government and Management

Here we are looking at the laws of the Pentateuch which control the behaviour and limit the power {12, 2} of government, of top executives and of the establishment, of those in positions of trust, responsibility or authority. The Pentateuch {11} leaves little doubt about what they must not do.

We saw already that

> Positive laws state what has to be done so as to create a just and strong society. And point the way ahead towards greater strength, freedom, liberty and a good way of life.

> Negative laws (prohibitions) state what must not be done and such laws protect the people from oppression and exploitation, from the antisocial behaviour of others, safeguard the people's strength and freedom.

And so the laws quoted here protect people, safeguard their strength and freedom, and need to be applied.

These laws of government relate to 'rulers', apply to all in positions of trust, responsibility or authority, no matter whether secular, religious or military, no matter what the hierarchy or organisation.

Such people may not amass servants and may not oppress the people for their own benefit. They may not amass possessions and wealth, may not grasp power or behave promiscuously.

In other words, they may not put themselves above others by grasping power, may not satisfy personal desires at the expense of others.

And a ruler (person in position of trust, responsibility or authority) has to follow these laws and abide by them every day if he wishes 'to prolong his days in his kingdom, he and his children'. For 'kingdom' read 'position' and include 'influence'.

So the Pentateuch laws quoted here protect people and safeguard their strength and freedom by laying down that those in positions of trust, responsibility or authority may not grasp power, may not oppress the people, may not behave promiscuously, may not enrich themselves. Those in authority must not oppress people so as to increase their own possessions and power, must not form enforcing squads or organisations so as to multiply their own power, must not behave promiscuously, must not gain wives or wealth. {12}

Equality and Ownership

Ownership {24} is the right to possess something and to decide what is to be done with it. If I own something it belongs to me and I decide what is to be done with it. An example would be owning a house.

Possession is having something in one's custody as distinct from owning it. If I possess something it belongs to another but I can decide how to use it. An example would be renting a house.

Another example would be deciding what to do with my money (ownership) or deciding and controlling the use of money belonging to someone else (possession).

And considering the right to ownership, two questions need to be considered. Namely where does the right come from and how is it exercised.

The right to own property varies among societies. Ownership laws which assign ownership 'rights' to owners have been devised by the owners themselves or by those who serve them. {20}

Ownership of land and means of production, of funds and wealth, has always been accumulated at someone else's expense. All belonged to the community, belonged to all alike. And this is what Chapter 5 of Genesis appears to be saying {18}.

A human right is a something one may legally or morally claim, is the state of being entitled to a privilege or immunity or authority to act. Human rights are those held to be claimable by any living person, apply to all living people. Every living person is entitled to them.

So ownership of land and means of production, of funds and wealth, rightfully belongs to the community, belongs to all alike, is a human right. Those who have accumulated them have only possession, which means they can use and apply them but may do so only on behalf of, and for the benefit of, the community and that they are accountable to the community for the way in which they do so. {19}

Hence we have the use of possessions as long as we use them to provide a good living for our family, and beyond that for the benefit of the community. For the benefit of others less able or fortunate, for the benefit of the community around us and then for the benefit of communities abroad.

But we may only support those who themselves genuinely support our benevolent ideals and principles and their application and who themselves live and act accordingly, who behave humanely. {12} <15>

A maximum differential of two, the maximum gross earnings being twice the minimum earnings, within a country and also between countries, would seem a reasonable target to achieve under present more extreme circumstances. {19}

Bearing this in mind, the country's wealth, and this includes productive assets and capital, including land, enterprise and corporation ownership, property, bank deposits and reserves, belongs equally to all community members and needs to be shared out <16>.

To be shared out family by family {12}, where 'family' is a life-long single union {13} between husband and wife. With shares updated at regular intervals of between three and not more than five calendar years <17>. Each receives a share of the community's total net assets <18>, their 'Asset Share'. An Asset Share cannot be sold but the owner has the right to determine its use and to the resulting benefits.

The Worldwide Struggle for God-given Human Rights {17, 13}

Freedom, Liberty and Independence {17}

Humane behaviour is aimed at survival of the young and of the family, and then is for the good of one's family, other people and the community. It is based on feelings of care and affection for others. From this emerges a sense of social responsibility: people matter and are important, need to be treated well and looked after, are entitled to share equally. Backed up by knowledge, understanding and reason. {10}

We know that dominating others is conditioned, that is unnatural, behaviour which is destructive of humane behaviour. A throw-back to the level of the unthinking unfeeling primitive animal. {10}

Genesis says much in chapters 5 and 6. About inhuman behaviour, about possessions, ownership and riches, about domineering, oppression and misusing people by force.

And knowledge of good and evil enables us to choose that which is good (humane) and to overcome that which is inhumane (beast-like, evil).

These themes are continued in Genesis and in the other four volumes (books) of the Pentateuch. We are told about the obligatory social laws and social system which have to be kept if evil is to be overcome, are told about consequent reward and punishment, justice and retribution, so that human beings can have good lives of high quality.

Those who follow and keep the benevolent social laws of the Pentateuch have in the past been opposed by dictatorships of both right and left, by those who wish to establish and support such dictatorships, by those who wish to oppress so as to exploit people. Openly under dictatorship and in more hidden ways under other forms of government.

Dictatorships both of the left and of the right, or those who approve or condone such systems, have also attempted to discredit and wipe out from human memory that which God's prophets teach us, namely the social laws and social system of the Pentateuch. {1, 2, 4, 5}

What we see in the working environment is a worldwide struggle to achieve a humane way of life, each person, family or community struggling to advance at their own level of development, struggling against those who wish to dominate, exploit, oppress. A struggle whose successful outcome depends on trustful cooperation, companionship and teamwork. {13, 23, 22}

The struggle is against those who wish to dominate other people. Against those who want primitive power over others, against those who wish to exploit, against those who may brutally and without feeling oppress human beings so as to exploit them. And 'to exploit' includes the whole range of antisocial decisions and activities of those who put profit before people and community. {21}

Human rights are based on controlling primitive dominant behaviour, on concern, care and affection for our young, for our families, people and communities, and express themselves in cooperation and teamwork between men and women to achieve a good life of high quality.

Defence {13}

Sometimes one has to fight to preserve a good way of life, to prevent others from taking what has been achieved. Or one may be expected to fight on behalf of those who dominate and exploit.

Our primitive animal ancestors behaved instinctively. Hunt for food, kill or be killed, fight or flee. Self before others, regardless of needs of others, marking out and defending territory, might being right.

Later mammals tend to have feelings, care and affection for their young. Human beings think as well as feel, and care for and look after their young for many years.

Having to fight, maim and kill amounts to a throwback to primitive animal behaviour, to behaviour which puts self before others. A throwback to beast-like behaviour for those who attack, to beast-like behaviour to counter beast-like behaviour for those who defend.

But one way of countering viciousness is by greater strength. If attacked, we have to defend ourselves.

Authoritarian organisations are much less effective than participative ones. In authoritarian organisations morale is low, people cease to care and tend to work against each other instead of cooperating with each other for the benefit of the organisation. {25-26}

Human beings cooperate well and achieve effective teamwork. Reason and evaluation can temper (add to, or change) emotional and instinct-motivated behaviour and combine with cooperation and teamwork so as to counter, and overcome, threats.

One has to be stronger than the enemy, socially as well as militarily. Essential is greater social as well as military strength. But the authoritarian mind (which includes the military) has to be balanced to prevent it from taking over, has to be motivated towards 'good'.

So we must not allow ourselves to be corrupted by what has to be done when fighting to preserve and secure that which is good, our way of life. Those who fight on our communities' behalf need to know, believe in, and practice, the word of God every day of their lives.

Responsibility and Accountability

Human beings found an effective defence against antisocial manipulations, namely the basic principle that we are responsible and accountable for what we do and how we do it. Obeying an order is no excuse. It does not matter whether the order comes from a secular or religious source or whether it pops up in one's mind. The person taking the decision, the person giving the order, the person carrying out the order, are each responsible for what they do or omit to do, and for the consequences.

Conclusion

So what one aims to achieve is

> to apply in our lives, and in the communities in which we live, the God-given benevolent social laws and social system of the Pentateuch,

> so as to achieve a good and secure life of high quality,

> by working for the benefit of the community, and

> by taking part in the struggle for a better life.

And we need to co-operate with each other as individuals, families and communities, supporting each other in this common struggle for a better life.

It appears that hurt and pain, oppression and exploitation, suffering and hardship, can and should be transformed and countered by an applied sense of social responsibility, by a sense of common purpose and cooperation between people working together in teams. That is by a sense of, and by the satisfaction of, achievement in locating, countering and overcoming the source of the suffering.

Colloquially speaking, there is enough food here for everyone. Pick your ground, pick whichever you think is most important and then use your knowledge, abilities and skills to achieve the good way of life portrayed in this report.

Your life is likely to be a much more rewarding life of higher quality.

Notes <..>

    < 1>   Also known as the 'Five Books of Moses' and as 'Torah'.

    < 2>   In {12} see section on 'The Social Cause-and-Effect Relationship'.

            The Social Cause-and-Effect Relationship is also listed (in biblical language and in plain English) in Appendix 4 of {12}, with references to the Pentateuch text.

    < 3>   The Pentateuch (Five Books of Moses, at times called 'Torah') consists only of the five books of Moses.

            Those wishing to give other writings an appearance of greater authority refer to these other writings as if they were part of 'Torah'. Those doing so appear to be spreading a kind of misleading political propaganda.

    < 4>   In {18} see 'Behaviour and Consequences (Genesis Chapter 9)'

    < 5>   For a full listing of the Ten Commandments, in biblical and plain English, see Appendix 5 of {12}. For a good discussion of its provisions see {12}.

< 6>   Normal for human beings is an exclusive sexual relationship between a husband and a wife who joined together to form a life-long family so as to ensure that their children are protected for the many years before they reach maturity. And the family protects and supports husband and wife as they grow old. {3, 13}

People who behave humanely, morally, can trust each other, co-operate with each other, grow, gain strength together, prosper.

All other sexual relations are abnormal, immoral. Those who behave immorally weaken their family and social strength. Those who initiate moral behaviour, who behave morally and humanely, gain strength and standing. {16}

Hence the
> importance of chastity,
> of human beings controlling their sexual urges,
> and for the human male to control the sexual urge lurking at
> the border of the conscious.

And on marriage the male accepts responsibility for the resulting family for life. {13}

< 7>   First volume of the Pentateuch (Five Books of Moses).

< 8>   Largely in Leviticus.

< 9>   See {13}

<10>   See {17}

<11>   For more information about, and other listings of, the Pentateuch's social rules of behaviour and about its social system, see {12, 17, 16, 4}

<12>   Social security also includes provision covering unemployment, ill health and old age, provided cooperatively {19}. <19>

<13> At present people would take their sabbatical year in turn, one-seventh of the community in any one year, including one-seventh from each of the different occupations.

<14> It must be up to the individual to select and choose what he wants to do. Sabbaticals are not an opportunity for the government, the state, a political party, a religious hierarchy or the management of an organisation to direct or train its employees, to condition through some kind of educational scheme, to pressurise one way or another. {19}

<15> In {18} see 'Social Laws, Social System'

<16> Companies and corporations present annual accounts to their shareholders including Funds Flow statements. Community accounts should be made available also in form of a 'Funds Flow' statement, as these can show clearly in meaningful terms where the funds have come from and what has been done with them. In terms such as 'Received from Income Tax', 'Received from Corporation Tax', 'Spent on Unemployment Benefit', 'Spent on Payments to Corporations', and so on.

<17> At the time the Pentateuch was written, the sharing out of assets was to be updated after every 49 years. At present, updating at regular intervals of between three and not more than five calendar years is more appropriate.

<18> 'Net assets' is the amount of money which would be left for distributing among the owners if everything belonging to an enterprise were sold and all its debts paid.

<19> The level of support (such as what proportion of the community's income is to be spent on health care) needs to be decided by the population, for example by referendum on basis of valid clearly-stated information compiled by concerned community groups.

References {..}

{ 1}   'Origin of Christianity and Judaism:
What Actually Happened, What Jesus Actually
Taught and Later Changes'
Manfred Davidmann
www.solhaam.org

{ 2}   In 'Judaism: Basis - Past - Present - Future, Part 1'
Manfred Davidmann
ISBN 978-0-85192-060-3
see chapter 2.2: 'History Speaks: Monarchy,
Exile and Maccabees'

{ 3}   In 'God and People:
The Social Laws and Social System Underlying
Judaism, Christianity, Islam and Democracy'
Manfred Davidmann
ISBN 978-0-85192-054-2
see chapter 6.1: 'The Meaning of Genesis:
Creation, Evolution and the Origin of Evil'

{ 4}   In 'Judaism: Basis - Past - Present - Future, Part 1'
Manfred Davidmann
ISBN 978-0-85192-060-3
see chapter 4: 'Causes of Antisemitism'

{ 5}   In 'Islam: Basis - Past - Present - Future'
Manfred Davidmann
ISBN 978-0-85192-053-5
see chapter 2: 'Prophet Mohammed's Struggle
for a Better Life for All'

{ 6}   In 'Islam: Basis - Past - Present - Future'
Manfred Davidmann
ISBN 978-0-85192-053-5
see chapter 4: 'The Divine Right to Rule'

{ 7}   In 'Islam: Basis - Past - Present - Future'
Manfred Davidmann
ISBN 978-0-85192-053-5
see chapter 5: 'Compiling the Koran: Hadiths
(Traditions) State the Underlying Reality'

{ 8}   In 'Islam: Basis – Past – Present – Future'
Manfred Davidmann
ISBN 978-0-85192-053-5
see chapter 6: 'Uthman's Rearrangement of the
Chronological (as revealed) Koran's Chapters'

{ 9}   In 'Islam: Basis – Past – Present – Future'
Manfred Davidmann
ISBN 978-0-85192-053-5
see chapter 7: 'Prophet Mohammed's Word of
Allah and the Voice of the Ruling Elite'

{10}   In 'The Human Mind and How it Works:
Group Minds in Action:
How the Human Group Mind Shapes
the Quality of Our Life and Living'
Manfred Davidmann
ISBN 978-0-85192-055-9
see chapter 2: 'How the Human Brain
Developed and How the Human Mind Works'

{11}   Pentateuch, Deuteronomy 17: 14-20

{12}   In 'Judaism: Basis – Past – Present – Future, Part 1'
Manfred Davidmann
ISBN 978-0-85192-060-3
see chapter 2.1 : 'Struggle for Freedom:
The Social Cause-and-Effect Relationship'

{13}   See chapter 3:
'Family, Community, Sex and the Individual'

{14}   In 'Judaism: Basis – Past – Present – Future, Part 1'
Manfred Davidmann
ISBN 978-0-85192-060-3
see chapter 2.3: 'At the Time of Jesus,
This is What Actually Happened in Israel:
The Truth about Hillel and his Times'

{15}   In 'Judaism: Basis – Past – Present – Future, Part 1'
Manfred Davidmann
ISBN 978-0-85192-060-3
see chapter 2.4: 'One Law for All:
Freedom Now, Freedom for Ever'

{16}   In 'God and People:
The Social Laws and Social System Underlying
Judaism, Christianity, Islam and Democracy'
Manfred Davidmann
ISBN 978-0-85192-054-2
see chapter 6.3: 'The Meaning of Genesis:
Morality, Sexual Behaviour and Depravity'

{17}   In 'God and People:
The Social Laws and Social System Underlying
Judaism, Christianity, Islam and Democracy'
Manfred Davidmann
ISBN 978-0-85192-054-2
see chapter 6.4: 'The Meaning of Genesis:
Nephilim, Dominance and Liberty'

{18}   In 'God and People:
The Social Laws and Social System Underlying
Judaism, Christianity, Islam and Democracy'
Manfred Davidmann
ISBN 978-0-85192-054-2
see chapter 6.2: 'The Meaning of Genesis:
Pre-flood Evils and the Social Problems of Our
Time'

{19}   In 'Cooperatives and Cooperation:
Causes of Failure, Guidelines for Success'
Manfred Davidmann
ISBN 978-0-85192-056-6
see chapter 3: 'Causes of Failure,
Guidelines for Success'

{20}   In 'The Real World in Which We Live:
The Social Rules and Social System under
Which We Suffer, Struggle, Survive and Prosper'
Manfred Davidmann
ISBN 978-0-85192-058-0
see chapter 10: 'What People are Struggling
Against: How Society is Organised for
Controlling and Exploiting People'

{21}   In 'Messianic Struggle:
        The Worldwide Struggle for a Good and
        Secure Life for All, Here and Now'
        Manfred Davidmann
        ISBN 978-0-85192-059-7
        see chapter 2: 'Social Responsibility,
        Profits and Social Accountability'

{22}   In 'The Human Mind and How it Works:
        Group Minds in Action:
        How the Human Group Mind Shapes
        the Quality of Our Life and Living'
        Manfred Davidmann
        ISBN 978-0-85192-055-9
        see chapter 7: 'Motivation Summary'

{23}   In 'The Real World in Which We Live:
        The Social Rules and Social System under
        Which We Suffer, Struggle, Survive and Prosper'
        Manfred Davidmann
        ISBN 978-0-85192-058-0
        see chapter 16: 'The Will to Work:
        What People Struggle to Achieve'

{24}   In 'The Real World in Which We Live:
        The Social Rules and Social System under
        Which We Suffer, Struggle, Survive and Prosper'
        Manfred Davidmann
        ISBN 978-0-85192-058-0
        see chapter 12: 'Understanding How Society is
        Organised for Controlling and Exploiting People'

{25}   In 'Management and Leadership:
        Local, National, Multinational (Global),
        Principles and Practice'
        Manfred Davidmann
        ISBN 978-0-85192-057-3
        see chapter 2: 'Style of Management and
        Leadership'

{26}   In 'Management and Leadership:
        Local, National, Multinational (Global),
        Principles and Practice'
        Manfred Davidmann
        ISBN 978-0-85192-057-3
        see chapter 3: 'Role of Managers under Different
        Styles of Management'

Press Notice

**'The God-given Human Rights, Social Laws and Social System':
A Report by Manfred Davidmann.   (Los Angeles Times)**

What Manfred Davidmann has done with his works on the Pentateuch and the Bible, on religion and church-state relations, is to expose and correct the misinterpretations and mistranslations of the past. His works are major breakthroughs, constituting essential information for understanding the meaning and significance of the Pentateuch and the Bible.

In his report "Meaning and Significance of the Names of God in Genesis" (see chapter 10.1)*, Manfred Davidmann proved the meaning and significance of the different names of God which had been lost. In "Meaning and Intent of Genesis: Essential Notes on Hebrew Grammar" (see chapter 10.2)*, he stated the fundamental rules which were ignored at time of translation because required background knowledge was not available, with consequent mistranslations. And in "Bible Translations, Versions, Codes and Hidden Information in Bible and Talmud" (see chapter 10.3)*, he showed how changes made in the past obscured the intended meaning.

And so Manfred Davidmann's report "The God-given Human Rights, Social Laws and Social System" is a comprehensive statement of the human rights and obligations which underlie freedom, liberty, independence and well-being, and which are largely unknown or ignored.

Directly relevant to today's social and economic problems, these rights and obligations determine the quality of life in areas such as social and economic security, social responsibility and accountability, ownership and decision-making, government and management, humane behaviour, teamwork and trustful cooperation.

Further, the Pentateuch records and details the Social Cause-and-Effect Relationship, a fundamental scientific law which is stated as such and which was discovered there by Manfred Davidmann. This states that the consequences of keeping or not keeping the social laws are inescapable, that what happens to one is in the end the inevitable result of one's own behavior. It is stated to enable people to benefit from knowing the effects of their behavior.

Ignorance of these rules of behavior is no excuse and the relationship applies to all. History and social science confirm it, the prophets knew and understood it and predicted accordingly. Jesus confirmed it; the Koran records Prophet Mohammed repeatedly confirming the Pentateuch, referring to it both as a guide and as a warning.

Whole communities prosper or suffer as a consequence of their collective behavior. Manfred Davidmann says, "The consequences of our behavior cannot be avoided but we can change the course of events by changing our behavior."

He states "A new factor has entered the equation. It is now possible for the first time in the history of human beings on this planet for just one or only a few socially irresponsible persons to do something or to introduce changes which could destroy us all or else make this planet uninhabitable for human beings ..."

... and that "if we do not now observe and put into effect the social rules and social system first described in the Pentateuch, then the planet is likely to become uninhabitable for human beings."

When a scientist of Manfred Davidmann's proven track record (of achievement and objectivity) and international standing makes such a statement, this needs to be taken seriously.

See chapter 2.1:
'The God-given Human Rights, Social Laws and Social System'
Manfred Davidmann

* Added by the Editor

Church and State, Government and Religion: Judaism, Christianity and Islam

Introduction

The world in which we live at present is in turmoil, in a mess. So we want to know why and what can be done about it.

We begin by looking at church and state, government and religion, at their aims and purpose, at the conflicts and confrontations between them. And start by describing what words such as state and religion mean and imply, as follows:

Government
> The group or organisation ruling a country or conducting its affairs. It can also refer to the government's style of management (authoritarian or participative, dictatorship or democracy).

Religion
> A system of faith and worship, based on belief in the existence of a benevolent God, usually expressed by believers living according to its doctrine (principles, rules of behaviour, customs).

State
> Somewhat vague term which refers to the combination of government and the community (country, population) being governed. Its use ignores important distinctions between people, government and the government's style of management, and their often conflicting interests. For example it does not distinguish between a government which serves its people and one which serves a country's rulers.

Church
> Refers to the religion's clergy, or to its hierarchy. It can also refer to the religion's organisation, its decision-taking processes, the doctrine it follows and the policies it applies.

But then there are different kinds of states and different kinds of churches {10}:

> Some states consist of governments which serve the rulers by oppressing the people so that they can be exploited and such states stifle opposition and protest. Here those at the top and their experts tell people what they should do and have to do.

> Other states consist of governments where those who govern serve the people and are accountable to them, where decisions are made at the lowest possible level by referendum with experts explaining the consequences both ways when a decision has to be made.

> Similarly some churches serve rulers and in effect condition their people into gladly serving the rulers, into gladly allowing themselves to be exploited, the general approach then being 'gladly accept the tough life you are leading, the reward will come in a next life'.

And other churches preach that it is the will of God that all people are equal, that no person may exploit another, that it is the role of the establishment to serve the people.

The history of the religions of Judaism, Christianity and Islam illustrates the underlying conflict and the present-day confrontations between church and state, government and religion, and points to ways of solving (healing) them.

Pentateuch {3}

What stands out is that human beings, guided by God, learned the difference between the brutal behaviour of their beastly ancestors, and the humane socially-responsible behaviour of human beings.

Following a fundamental revelation, their struggles and achievements were recorded in the Pentateuch <1>, as were the social system and social rules of behaviour which underlie a good life of high quality combining freedom, independence and liberty <2>. Positive and constructive, rewarding what is good, punishing that which is inhuman, providing social security and a good life of high quality.

The whole history of the people and the essential social laws of behaviour and social system, were then recorded in the Pentateuch which has been handed down unaltered to this day. <1>

The beliefs of Judaism, Christianity and Islam include the social laws and social system of the Pentateuch and each of these religions experienced major conflicts and strife between church and state, religion and government. The struggle between them is about the application in our everyday lives of the social provisions of the Pentateuch.

So first we look at some key social laws of the Pentateuch, and describe its social system, to illustrate what the confrontation between 'church' and 'state' is about. <3>

Social and Economic Security

All persons have the right to be free and independent masters of their own fate and no person may oppress or exploit another. Because people can be exploited through their needs there has to be a system of social and economic security which guarantees freedom from needs and so protects people from becoming dependent on others for essential income, protects against loss of material and spiritual independence.

This is what is laid down as a matter of law {6}:

1. The community has to provide ('lend') money to those who need it, free of interest.
2. All such loans, if outstanding, are to be cancelled every seventh year.

Trustful Co-operation (Ten Commandments)

The Ten Commandments <4> are so important and are so well known because behaviour in accordance with these rules is the basis for people trusting each other and so for people co-operating and working well with each other. The Ten Commandments underlie freedom, independence and strength to oppose and resist oppression. Wherever there is any independence of the mind and material freedom today it exists because people followed these rules of behaviour and it exists to the extent to which they do so. {6}

Take these two commandments (principles of behaviour):

You must not steal.

You must not desire anything which belongs to your neighbour.

Much trust and community friendliness is gained when people follow these principles.

But consider that these laws apply equally to the rich and powerful. It is also the rich and powerful who must not steal from the poor even the little which the poor have. It is the rich and powerful who must not cast longing glances at what little the rest of us possess, it is the rich and powerful who must not aim to gain at our expense.

Government and Management

The laws of the Pentateuch control the behaviour and limit the power of 'rulers', that is of government, of top executives and of the establishment, of those in positions of trust, responsibility or authority, no matter whether secular, religious or military, no matter what the hierarchy or organisation. {6-7}. The Pentateuch {11} states clearly what they must not do.

They may not amass servants and may not oppress the people. They may not amass possessions and wealth, may not grasp power or behave promiscuously. In other words, they may not put themselves above others by grasping power, may not satisfy personal desires at the expense of others.

And a ruler (person in position of trust, responsibility or authority) has to follow these laws and abide by them every day if he wishes 'to prolong his days in his kingdom, he and his children'. For 'kingdom' read 'position' and include 'influence'.

These Pentateuch laws lay down that those in positions of trust, responsibility or authority must not oppress people so as to increase their own possessions and power. These laws forbid personal gain from the misuse of authority, wealth or position. Those in positions of trust, responsibility or authority may not grasp power, may not oppress the people, may not behave promiscuously, may not gain wives or wealth. {6}

Equality and Ownership

The country's wealth <5> belongs equally to all community members and needs to be shared out family by family {6}, where 'family' is a life-long single union {4} between husband and wife. With shares updated at regular intervals of between three and not more than five calendar years <6>. Each receives a share of the community's total net assets <7>, their 'Asset Share'. An Asset Share cannot be sold but the owner has the right to determine its use and to the resulting benefits.

But only those are supported who themselves genuinely support the Pentateuch's benevolent ideals and principles and their application and who themselves live and act accordingly, who behave humanely. {6}

Liberation Theology   {5}

According to Liberation theologians, Christian belief and practice ranges along a continuous scale between two kinds, one at each end of the scale.

At one end is the kind which in effect serves the rulers and their establishment, those in authority such as a government or multinational, those who oppress and exploit. It teaches that the reward for this life's hardships will be a better life in a life to come.

At the other end is another kind of Christianity which bases its belief and practice on compassion for the poor and according to Christian texts which side with the poor against the rich, with the poor against the oppressor.

Liberation theologians advocate the second kind of Christianity which is one of compassion and leadership in the struggle against oppressors, in the struggle for a better life here and now in this life.

How come there are such widely differing kinds of belief and practice?

Among deprived Christian communities such as disadvantaged African negroes, South American indians, Indian indians and Filipinos, we now hear voices which distance themselves from ruler-serving Christian beliefs. We see them arguing for a Christian belief which puts equality and independence among their most important goals. And wherever there is extreme poverty and suffering and pain you are likely to find Christians who are struggling on the side of the oppressed. Such as priests who provide encouragement and guidance to oppressed and suffering people in their struggle for a better life against the ruling establishment, against established ruling oppressors, doing so at much risk and without thought of personal gain.

The underlying teachings of the Jewish and Christian religions are based on God's teachings as recorded in the Pentateuch. All people are considered equal and entitled to share in the wealth of their community. No wonder that 'it is in countries following the social teachings of Christianity and Judaism ('Christian' countries, democracies) that people have the highest standard of living, have lives of high quality', gained as the result of past and present struggle against those who wish to exploit, against those who wish to oppress so as to exploit.

However, what happened in the past was that those who ruled, and those who wished to rule and exploit, changed patterns of belief and observance, doing so from within, being opposed by the people with varying degrees of success. This explains why there appear to be different kinds of Christian belief and practice.

And next we look at what happened to Judaism, Christianity and Islam in the past, at the conflicts and confrontations between their teachings and the ruling establishment of the day, at these interactions between church and state, religion and government.

We now look at how the Pentateuch's rules and their application were changed in the past, why they were changed and by whom, who gained and who lost, at the extent to which present belief and practice differs fundamentally from the revealed word of God. A fascinating journey which will take us through Judaism to Christianity and Islam, and then to life and living in our times.

Judaism {7}

The Monarchy (David and Solomon)

At the beginning of this period the Hebrew tribes are scattered and on their own, each more or less fighting its own battles and looking after its own interests. We see people enjoying freedom and following the Pentateuch's laws.

Then we see the tribes coming together under a single central rule with combined forces. The opposing foreign tribes were defeated. The result was a country and a people which were united and powerful. Military success went hand in hand with bringing the tribes together in one united country.

The successful military leader, King David, ruled the country. Secular and religious authority were apparently concentrated in his hands.

Then we see those who rule using their power for their own benefit and to impose their rule. We see the emergence of those who grasp power and rule and then weaken Pentateuch law so as to rule more forcefully, so as to oppress, so as to exploit the people. This led inevitably to internal confrontation and conflict which divided the country.

During the period of the monarchy, that is during the period of Saul, David and Solomon, we see central military authority being more effective in an emergency and see the military leader subsequently taking over the administration, taking over the government. This is followed by increasing centralisation of power and the formation of an establishment (secular and religious) which serves the source of power and is used to oppress the people.

What we see is increasing centralisation of power, increasing corruption and oppression, increasing enslavement of the people with consequent social stress and subsequent destruction.

The popular leader, initially supported by those who were oppressed and in need, became powerful. He started to use the people for personal gain. But David ruled for 40 years and became rich and powerful. He had properties throughout the land and took concubines and wives. He instituted a 'levy', a form of conscription.

King Solomon, greatly praised, of such wonderful wisdom, of great power, wealth and horses, having many wives. But his reign was immediately followed by the kingdom splitting into two kingdoms which fought each other, which largely disregarded Pentateuch law until both kingdoms were destroyed and the people exiled to Babylon. Much has been written about Solomon and his glorious reign, his wisdom and his riches. But Jewish scripture and other ancient sources look at his reign from the point of view of the people over whom he ruled and tell another and completely different story. {7}

Solomon continued the process David had started. Under his reign the king's power over the people increased. It is plainly told, consistent and to the point.

He ignored basic Pentateuch law and weakened its application so as to weaken resistance to oppression, so as to oppress the people.

He started to oppress the people just as soon as he was unopposed and had undisputed authority.

We are being told that he obtained his wealth by taxing the people, that this was paid as an annual tax and that this was a heavy burden on the people.

He instituted both tax collecting and a compulsory labour service.

King Solomon built the first Temple and he also built a palace for himself.

It took seven years to build the Temple and after that it took thirteen years to build Solomon's palace. Solomon's palace occupied over four times the groundspace which the Temple occupied. {7}

The king soon ignored the laws of the Pentateuch which clearly states that he should not oppress the people so as to increase his own possessions and power, that he should not put himself above the people and so enrich himself. The Pentateuch warns against him oppressing people so as to multiply his power (horses), it prohibits his taking a large number of wives and the amassing of silver and gold.

We are told that he broke the 'kingship' laws, the laws of government which protect the people.

The whole record of Solomon's reign shows a ruler who is more concerned with personal wealth and power than with leading the people towards a better life.

Solomon died after he had reigned for forty years and Rehoboam his son took over.

And Rehoboam answered the people roughly and said 'My father made your yoke heavy, I will add to your yoke; my father punished you with whips, but I will punish you with scorpions'. So he told the people he would oppress them even more than his father Solomon had done. {7}

Oppression increased during Solomon's reign and once again it was the internal conflicts which broke up the country and so destroyed it.

Israel then rebelled against the descendants of David, and installed Jeroboam king over all Israel. However, the tribe of Judah followed the descendants of David. In this way Solomon's kingdom split up into two separate kingdoms, namely Judah and Israel (Samaria).

Rehoboam (Solomon's son) ruled over Judah, and Jeroboam ruled over Israel (Samaria). Jeroboam in effect abrogated the application of the Pentateuch laws.

The application of the Pentateuch, the basic constitution which protects the people, had been abrogated and the people were worse off than before, had even less protection against the ruler and his establishment, against the misuse of his power.

It seems to me that during the period of the monarchy and of the two kingdoms there was a continuous struggle between the forces which supported God, Judaism and the people, and those forces which supported central rule, the establishment and oppression of the people. It was the rulers who generally acted contrary to Jewish law and the Jewish religion seems to have been belittled, opposed and in some ways negated by them.

It would seem that religious and secular authority were in effect centred on the king (ruler) who soon ignored the God-given benevolent social provisions of the Pentateuch. Authority for belief and practice were combined in the person of the ruler who used his authority (power) for his own personal selfish gain and disregarded the very social laws and system for the application of which the Hebrew people had been fighting for and which underlay his success.

Maccabean Dynasty (The Hasmoneans)   <8> {7}

We know little about life in Israel during the period of about 300 years between the time of the return from Babylon and the time of the taking over of the country by the Seleucids in 198 BCE. We do know that religious observance was so important that they would not even defend themselves when attacked on the Sabbath (the weekly day of rest) so as not to desecrate it.

The Seleucids robbed the Temple of its wealth and destroyed the walls of Jerusalem. They then attempted to paganise the country by brutal force. Those who observed the Jewish laws and customs were bitterly persecuted, pagan worship and practices were introduced into the Temple and they destroyed written records (scrolls) of the law whenever they could find them. The high priest Menelaus continued in office but served Jupiter.

Among the Jewish leadership were those who served the Seleucid rulers by offering greater annual taxes for the sake of obtaining personal power. They collected them from the people. At the same time they weakened and opposed the influence of the Jewish religion so as to weaken the people. It was of course the people who suffered and who became more and more discontented.

Rulers and Establishment ('state', government)   <8> {7}

Mattathias (a priest) rebelled against pagan worship. The people could stand no more and led first by Mattathias and then by his son Judah Maccabee they rebelled against the imposed vicious rule of the Seleucids.

To begin with all were united and struggled against the brutal oppression. They struggled for God (Pentateuch), freedom and the people. Against them were foreign invaders who believed in slavery and who were trying to impose their way of life through imposing their beliefs. {1}

The uprising had one central unifying purpose: to build a country in which Jewish people could live as Jews and practise their faith (in which they could apply the social laws and social system of the Pentateuch to their daily lives), and gained ground.

Mattathias, his five sons and his grandson John Hyrcanus led the uprising and supported one another. Single minded, the members of the Maccabean family were loyal to the brother who was in command at the time. What is known is that whenever the brother who was ruling at the time was either killed in battle or assassinated by the enemy, one of the other brothers simply stepped into his place, provided the required leadership and was in turn supported by the rest of the family.

Judah Maccabee was followed by Jonathan who in turn was followed by Simeon. The leadership of the three brothers covers a period of 30 years during which much of the country was freed. John Hyrcanus was able to build the country and complete the work the others had started.

Jonathan was appointed high priest about 8 years after taking over the leadership. Simeon was confirmed by the 'Great Assembly' as high priest, ethnarch (ruler) and commander of the Jewish people. Simeon's positions were to be hereditary.

Appointing Jonathan as high priest transferred religious authority and power to a secular leader. When the Great Assembly confirmed Simeon's position, a few years after he had assumed the leadership, they confirmed that religious and secular as well as military authority and power had been vested in one person and were to be hereditary.

What had happened was that able military and secular leadership absorbed religious authority and power. That this concentration of all authority and power in the hands of one person was to be permanent and later to be transferred to his descendants is an indication that the establishment of the day was already concerned with consolidating its own position.

Following the popular uprising for Judaism, for Jewish law and thus for freedom, the rulers formed a dynasty and a supporting establishment. They tasted power, meant to have it and meant to cling to it. Instead of serving God and people, the rulers battled for power with each other, allied themselves with foreign powers against each other. In so doing they divided the people and weakened all. The Jewish leadership, the Jewish establishment, disregarded the welfare of the people, disregarded Jewish law, disregarded the intent and purpose of Jewish law. <8> {7}

The religious hierarchy became subservient to the secular rulers, with the rulers presumably using the religious hierarchy to motivate and tranquillise their people. And two generations after the uprising we see increasing internal confrontation between believing (Pentateuch-observing) people on the one hand against oppressive rulers and their oppressing establishment on the other. {1}

I think that combining all power in the hands of a single ruler is against the spirit and intent of Jewish law as religious authority, which should serve God and the people, which should indicate direction and provide drive, may then too readily be misused to serve the establishment of the day instead of God and the people. {7}

The Jewish leadership, the Jewish establishment, supported centralised power, the oppressive ruling authority and its influence, since the ideas which were being imported helped them to oppress their own people. In so doing they disregarded the welfare of the people, disregarded Jewish law, disregarded the intent and purpose of Jewish law. {7}

The oppression of Jew by Jew, of the Jewish people by their own rulers and establishment, and the resulting struggle between them defeated both. It ended Maccabean rule, lost the land which had been gained, resulted in enormous hardship to the people. It resulted in the handing over of the country and its people to Herod and the subsequent introduction and popularisation by Herod of a foreign ideology based on slavery and supporting it. It was indeed this which the Maccabees had struggled against. {7}

Outstanding is that the people were unable to restrain their leaders. The result was total destruction of people and country, and the dispersion of the Jewish people. {7}

Belief and Practice ('church', religion) {8-9}

During the five generations after that of Simeon, that is during the Maccabean dynasty, the secular rulers gained control of the religious hierarchy and of what was being taught. There was discontent and opposition, but what was taught became increasingly establishment-orientated, serving an oppressing and exploiting establishment. The social laws ceased to be applied as a comprehensive system, as a way of life.

After three generations we see very clearly increasing internal confrontation, a struggle between those wishing to apply the God-given benevolent egalitarian social laws and system on the one hand against oppressive rulers and their establishment-serving religious hierarchy on the other. What had been the people's leaders had become rulers who battled for power with each other, allied themselves with foreign powers against each other, betrayed their people to a foreign power for the sake of personal power and influence. In so doing they divided the people and weakened all. This was virtually the end of independence for the country. {7}

The Jewish establishment (secular and religious) had been and were changing the application of God's benevolent social laws so that 'the law was becoming like two laws'. They argued in religious terms about social and political policies. What are recorded are the arguments, misrepresentations and falsehoods (untruths) used by establishment-orientated religious 'scholars' <9> against applying the Pentateuch's benevolent legislation, in effect misleading the population into acquiescing to changes which served the ruling establishment, which enabled the establishment to oppress and exploit the population.

It was then decided to record what was happening so that future generations would become aware of what had happened and of who had been doing what to whom. They also wanted future generations to learn from the lessons of the past. Their record of what took place is called the Talmud which covers many subjects in many volumes. To compile the whole Talmud took about 400 years in Jerusalem and about 500 years in Babylon. The Talmud was then 'frozen' ('canonised'). {8-9}

You can see how the Talmud records the bitter feelings of ordinary people about what establishment-serving scholars were doing to Pentateuch and people. And when some scholars attempted to provide their own statements with an authority they did not have, the practice was scathingly condemned in the Talmud. {9}

The Talmud describes how the God-serving religious hierarchy was replaced by an establishment-serving religious hierarchy {8}, how the people felt about this {9} and the subsequent antisocial changes to belief and practice. This is conclusively recorded in two different and separate ways which confirm each other. But Rabbinical Judaism (today's Judaism) does not teach this and so propagates the establishment's revisionist version of Jewish belief and practice. {8} <10>

Rabbinical Judaism (today's Judaism) teaches, and Jewish belief and practice follows, the Jewish establishment's version of belief and practice. This version has the essential core benevolent social laws bypassed and edited out from observance, and is followed by Jews at the present time.

We saw that the religious scholars were serving the rulers ('state', government) instead of serving God and people ('church', religion).

And saw the history of the two main confrontations, of the struggle, between the Jewish rulers ('state', government, establishment) and the people, from the recording of the Pentateuch to the birth of Christianity.

This struggle was about position, influence and control over communities, about changing God-given benevolent rules of behaviour so that people could be oppressed and exploited.

It changed Judaism, determined the fate of the Jewish people and gave rise to Christianity.

And we saw that attempts to argue against the rulers and their establishment were by themselves unable to change the course of events.

Christianity   {1}

Jesus Taught

A remnant of Jews kept alive the knowledge of the social laws of the Pentateuch. They gained motivation, numbers and strength by rallying round and following the teachings of Jesus (Teacher of Righteousness) in spite of opposition from the religious establishment. Christian beliefs were spreading largely among Jews, and Christianity was a group within Judaism. These Jews came together to follow the word of God.

Early Christians were called Jewish Christians because their membership consisted largely of Jews who had joined them and followed their beliefs and teachings. They believed Jesus was a prophet who had tried to make people more aware of the intent of the Pentateuch and had tried to intensify the application of its laws. The Pentateuch was of great importance to them and they kept its laws, keeping the sabbath and performing circumcision.

As Jews had in any case to follow and live according to the Pentateuch's laws, what were Jews and Jewish Christians arguing about?

The laws of the Pentateuch have to be followed and applied by Jews as a matter of law in their daily lives. However, it was such laws of behaviour and such social system laws which the rich simply did not want to apply and we saw above that they, the rich and powerful, had had the application of these benevolent laws bypassed {6-9}. Jesus tried to reverse this situation and to have such laws applied by people in their everyday lives.

Jesus taught that if the rich wish to be rewarded by God they need to follow all the commandments and the social laws of the Pentateuch. {1}

Jesus said that 'good deeds' by themselves are not enough to gain eternal life. Whoever keeps the commandments enters eternal life. To be a 'good person' and enter eternal life one has to keep the commandments. {1}

Matthew's gospel records Jesus making a specific point which applies in general. Those who are rich and powerful and who are not observing the important social laws, suffer and will suffer the unavoidable consequences as a result. {1}

So Jewish Christians believed in the laws of the Pentateuch and struggled for the application of these laws in daily life, struggling against an oppressive establishment which argued against and did not want to follow the social laws.

Paul's Ideology

Paul was Jewish and persecuted the Christians who were renewing their knowledge of the laws and the application of the laws in their daily lives. So he was acting on the side of, that is for, the oppressive establishment.

He was unsuccessful in this as Jewish Christianity spread and continued to spread.

He then said that he had had a 'vision' and called himself a Christian but he preached not for but against the social laws and against the social system of the Pentateuch. He preached against material independence, against social security, against freedom from oppression and exploitation.

Look again at the social laws and system of the Pentateuch <11> and you will see how the laws of the Pentateuch ensure freedom and material independence and provide a good life of high quality here and now, backed by effective social security. No one may oppress or exploit another and all are equal, as a matter of law.

It is these laws of behaviour, it is these social laws and this social system which Paul opposed and he then attempted to stop people from keeping these laws.

Paul's letters (epistles) are the oldest part of the New Testament, probably written about 50 AD, some considerable time after the death of Jesus <12>. What stands out is that no one before Paul wrote such letters and that no one did so afterwards.

Paul wrote {2} that
> 'the law brings wrath, but where there is no law there is no transgression',
saying that the God-given laws of Moses (in the Pentateuch) result in punishment for those who break the law and that a law that does not exist cannot be broken. {1}

Laws protect people when those who break them are punished. So Paul is saying that there would be no punishment if the laws were abolished, implying that antisocial activities can be allowed to take place without restraint.

Astonishingly and without good reason he states that those in authority rule by 'divine right', that whatever they do is justified because in his opinion they act on God's behalf. Whatever those in authority do or want is called 'good' by Paul and those who resist or oppose them do 'evil' and will be punished. Paul wants all to obey those in authority and to be obedient, to pay taxes and revenues, to respect and honour those in authority. {1}

He is arguing that one must fear and obey those in authority and do for them and give them all they ask, without regard to how selfish, corrupt, inhuman, vicious, murdering or evil they may be. {1}

What Paul is saying and putting forward is neither God's word nor is it what Jesus taught. Under the disguise of a religious sermon Paul is spreading political propaganda. Paul is preaching the political ideology of an oppressive establishment which wanted to be able to oppress so as to exploit without hindrance. He is preaching against observance of laws which ensure freedom, independence and equality. And he gives his opinions an authority which they would not otherwise have had by means of a self-proclaimed vision. {1}

So Paul preached against material independence, against social security, against freedom from oppression and exploitation. What he preached was the political ideology of an oppressive establishment.

This brought him into conflict with Jewish Christians and with the mostly Jewish Christian communities and he was unsuccessful in changing their beliefs and practices. He then concentrated on gaining converts from gentiles (people who are not Jewish) who presumably knew nothing or little about the laws of the Pentateuch and who would thus be more likely to follow his teachings without arguing about its content.

Paul's teachings were accepted to a considerable extent. The Gentile Christians' stories about the beginning of Christianity differ from those of the Jewish Christians and it is the versions of the Gentile Christians which were included in the Christian Canon and became official doctrine.

Paul's letters (epistles) were written about 50 AD. The Gospels were written about 70-100 AD and as a whole relate to the life and death of Jesus. Matthew's was written first, then Mark's, then Luke's. Luke also wrote The Acts.

Matthew's Record (Gospels)

Matthew's gospel was the first to be written. It appears that Matthew wrote his Gospel to counter Paul's distortions, recording what Jesus had actually been preaching. It is closest to the events and so perhaps it is not surprising that it has always been the most popular and revered of the gospels.

Matthew struggled to put the record straight, struggled to record what Jesus actually taught. Throughout the ages, Christians of goodwill chose intuitively to interpret Paul's statements about those in authority as meaning that

'the authority of those in authority only comes from God to the extent to which they themselves live according to and apply the Ten Commandments, the social laws and the social system laws' and that only those can 'love one another' who comply with all these laws. {1}

Matthew's Gospel was later followed by Mark's and this in turn was followed by Luke's gospel. The later authors were apparently aware of and knew the earlier gospels which seems confirmed by the successive changes which were made which changed the record of what Jesus taught and of the meaning of the stories and of the arguments. {1} <13>

Matthew's record was subtly changed in later gospels. Successive changes, one by one, changed meaning and intent further and further away from what is recorded in Matthew's gospel. {1}

Further and further away from Matthew's clear record and statement about what Jesus taught. Obscuring and confusing that which Jesus taught, so as to weaken arguments against Paul's distortions. {1}

So what happened was:

Jesus taught that all the laws had to be kept, that belief and practice included and had to include the Ten Commandments, the social laws and the social system of the Pentateuch.

Paul, however, acted on behalf of the rich and powerful when he tried to convince people that those in authority were God's representatives on earth and that the social laws did not have to be kept.

Paul's letter to the 'Romans' was written before the gospels. Matthew's later gospel records what Jesus actually taught and clearly makes the point that Paul was trying to subvert and turn upside down that which Jesus taught. As Matthew records what Jesus taught, this outweighs and overrides what Paul said.

Those who later favoured Paul's pro-establishment ideology could not challenge Matthew's record. Hence Matthew's gospel was subtly changed in later gospels, in an attempt to distort and hide that which Jesus had taught so as to weaken arguments against Paul's ideology.

Here also we see the establishment engaged in abrogating, in effect in annulling <14>, the benevolent social laws of the Pentateuch.

The establishment's version became accepted as official Christian doctrine and apparently it is this which tends to be taught today.

Christian Canon

Outstanding is that the contemporaneously written <15>, agreed and finalised Christian Canon and Jewish Talmud were shaped by, and independently record, the same confrontations and struggle and sequence of events. The Talmud was written contemporaneously with the gospels, starting in the first century AD. And both the Talmud and the Christian Canon were completed and agreed, canonified and frozen, at about the same time, roughly four-hundred years later. The agreement between Christian and Jewish writings is so complete that we are now reasonably certain about the main course of events. {1}

The Christian Canon continued to be compiled till it was approved by the Christian establishments and so presumably biased towards what the establishment wanted included or excluded, wanted said or unsaid. What became the Christian Canon, meaning by this the 'agreed' version of events and teachings, took about four hundred years before it was 'agreed' {5}.

It apparently took about four hundred years for written material and for people's memories to be changed, edited and modified, to conform to the establishment point of view. If it had just been a matter of recording facts, of recording the truth, the whole truth and nothing but the truth (the truth, nothing left out and nothing added), it would not have taken so long. After ten or so generations people would be regarding as factual that which they were being told was factual.

A similar if not identical process took place within Judaism during roughly the same period of time and here also the relevant social laws were side-tracked and bypassed. It does seem more than a coincidence that it took roughly the same period of time for Christianity and Judaism to contemporaneously finalise the Christian Canon and the Jewish Talmud, respectively.

Both the Talmud and the Canon tell of an outsider, of an outside establishment orientated ideology, corrupting what was being taught and undermining what people believed, corrupting and undermining what Jesus had taught.

In both religions the establishment versions became accepted as official doctrine.

Liberation Theology's 'Two Types of Christianity'

We can now understand much more clearly what Liberation Theology's teachings have been saying. As said already:

> Liberation theologians maintain that Christian belief and practice ranges along a continuous scale between two forms, one at each end. At one end of this scale is the kind which in effect serves the establishment, that is those in authority such as a government, and this kind teaches that reward will be a better life in a life to come. Liberation theologians advocate the second kind of Christianity, at the other end of the scale. They emphasise compassion and leadership in the struggle against oppressors, in the struggle for a better life here and now in this life. {5}

They (liberation theologists) are arguing that there are two kinds of Christianity. They say that there is the kind of Christianity that serves the rulers and their establishment and thus those who oppress and exploit. They say that there is also another kind of Christianity which bases its belief and practice on compassion for the poor and according to Christian texts which side with the poor against the rich, with the poor against the oppressor. {5}

Manfred Davidmann concluded that Christianity is struggling forward towards its roots in response to the social and economic problems of global humanity at the present time. Towards what Jesus taught, towards the social laws and social system of the Pentateuch. {5, 1}

Islam

Arab Life at the Time of Mohammed   {15} <16>

Arabs were mainly nomads living in the central and northern Arabian peninsula. Some of them had settled around the oases. There was no written code of laws, life was harsh and brutal.

The only restraint on an individual was the fear of vengeance. All members of a community (family, clan or tribe) were held responsible for the acts of any one of them. There was no wrong in killing someone not a member of one's tribe, but it would be unwise to do so if the victim's tribe was strong. Survival depended on the strength of one's tribe.

But no such restraints applied to communal acts of violence. The tribes were constantly at war with each other, except for four months of truce every year, with loot (material and human) apparently the key objective of intertribal skirmishes and warfare. Women and children captured in tribal warfare who were not ransomed became tribal slaves and could be bought and sold.

Mohammed is born into this kind of society of illiterate desert Arabs and teaches them (reveals to them) what God has commanded him to recite to his fellow Arabs.

Mohammed Taught

The Prophet Mohammed struggled throughout his preaching life against the powerful Meccan family which dominated Mecca, against the Quraysh. They first opposed and then persecuted him and his followers for ten years, and then he fought them for another ten years till he won. Shortly after that he died. {15}

At first Mohammed preached the word of God in this environment for roughly ten years. A small number believed, mostly of the poorer classes. The followers he drew were the rejected, the disadvantaged, the weak and the oppressed - slaves, women and minority tribes. {13-15}

His message to the Meccans was that they should abandon all forms of idolatry and devote themselves to following the directions of the one all-seeing and almighty but compassionate God, that it was necessary for people to be humble and grateful towards God and to worship Him, and the obligation of generosity and respect for the rights of the poor and the defenceless. {12}

Mohammed teaches that God's benevolent social laws and system have to be applied by people in their daily life, that those who in the past erred from God's way are in grave error {20}. The quotations from the Koran which follow speak for themselves.

The book (al-kitab, the Pentateuch) came down (tanzil) from God, the mighty, the wise-one.
> The arabic phrase for the Holy Koran is 'al-Koran'. The Pentateuch (the Five Books of Moses) is 'al-kitab', a religious book is 'mushaf'. <17>

{40:002, 45:002, 46:002}

We gave Moses guidance (al-huda)
> huda: guidance or guide.

and gave the book (al-kitab, the Pentateuch) to the Children of Israel to inherit.
A guide (huda) and a reminder (warning) to people who understand.
> To those who understand its commandments (message), it is a guide (about what is 'good', about what to do) and a warning (about what is evil, about what not to do).

{40:053-54}

We gave the Book (al-kitab, Pentateuch) to Moses, but disputes arose about it. ...
They are in serious doubt (about the belief).
{41:045}

We gave the book (al-kitab, the Pentateuch) to the Children of Israel
and gave them the knowledge and prophethood.
We provided them with good things and preferred them above (all)
people;
{45:016}

We proved the commandments (bayyinat amr) to them beyond doubt:
> Literal: We gave them clear proofs (indisputable
> evidence) of commandments.

but after the knowledge had come to them,
greed caused them to disagree among themselves.
> Greed: intense and selfish desire for wealth or power.

{45:017}

> The social laws and the social system of the Pentateuch
> have to be followed and applied by Jews as a matter of
> law in their daily lives.

> However, it was these laws of behaviour and the social
> system laws {3} which the Jewish ruling elite simply did
> not want to apply and they, the rich and powerful, had
> the application of the laws changed to suit themselves
> {8-9}.

And when Jesus came with the clear proofs (the indisputable evidence)
(al-bayyinat), he said:
I have come to you with wisdom
to clarify some of what you are differing about.
Fear God and obey (God).
God is my Lord and your Lord: therefore serve (follow) Him. That is the
right way (sirat mustakim).
But the factions among them differed.
{43:063-65}

> The social laws and the social system laws of the
> Pentateuch had been bypassed or abrogated by the
> Jewish ruling elite, by the rich and powerful.

> Jesus tried to reverse this situation and to have these
> laws again applied by people in their everyday lives. {1}

> But the ruling elite, backed by the Christian
> establishment, later modified Jesus' teachings (Christian
> beliefs) from within. {1}

(To Mohammed:) Say (to them): "I am only a mortal like you;
It has come to me (yuhi) that there is only one God.

72

So take the right way to Him, and ask His forgiveness."

> Literal: So 'you go in the right way' and ... (istakimu)

And woe to those who serve associates (mushrekin) beside Him;

> Mushrekin (associates): Guides, masters, overlords or supreme beings with whom a person associates (to which a person attributes) a god-like knowledge or authority. That which or those whom you consider to be like God, that or those whose orders you obey as if they came from God.

{41:006}

And now We have set you on the right way of our commandment (sharia amr),
so follow it, and do not follow the desires of ignorant people (those who do not have that knowledge)
for they cannot shield you from God.
{45:018}

And so Mohammed taught {20} that:

> God gave the Pentateuch to Moses but disputes arose about it (among the Jews) because of greed.

> When Jesus came clearly stating the law and asked people to follow it, again factions differed.

> Mohammed then continues, saying: 'It is revealed to me there is only one God, so take the right way to Him.'

Preaching the obligation of generosity and respect for the rights of the poor and the defenceless, soon aroused the opposition of the Meccan elite and Mohammed's followers were persecuted. {15}

Mohammed was forming a movement which all who were deprived could join. The traditional Arab tribe, and loyalty, were based on family, on blood relationships, and thus limited in size. Opposition may well have developed also from the fear that in time Mohammed's movement might unseat the ruling family, their establishment, their tribe. {15}

So here also we see the two opposed sides. On the one hand Mohammed preaching the words of benevolent and caring God (Allah), on the other side a self-serving ruling elite.

Traditions tell that during and almost immediately after the death of Mohammed his teachings of revelations from benevolent Allah who cared deeply about peoples' welfare and well-being, were collected and recorded by Zaid bin Thabit. {17-18}

Traditions also tell that about fifteen years later Caliph Uthman had an official text prepared which included Zaid bin Thabit's, that he ordered the compilers to change Zaid bin Thabit's manuscripts into reflecting 'the voice of' (the opinions of) the ruling elite, that is to make sure that their compilation stated the ruling elite's point of view. The same tradition states that Caliph Uthman then distributed copies of this ruling elite's compilation (Uthman's Koran) and ordered all other versions to be destroyed. {17-18}.

This is how Maxime Rodinson {12} describes what happened after the death of Mohammed:

> At the head of the Arab empire was the family of Quraysh which had been the most determined in its opposition to the Prophet. It was as if Mohammed had worked and preached, all for the greater glory and profit of his enemies.

It took about 300 years after the death of Mohammed before the 'reading' of the Koran was finally fixed. {17}

Throughout almost the whole of Mohammed's life as Prophet he struggled against the powerful Meccan family which dominated Mecca, against the Quraysh {15}. And after Mohammed died, the ruling elite took over and here also appears to have edited out from observance God's (Allah's) benevolent social laws and system.

Since then there has been continuous confrontation and struggle between secular and religious figureheads and hierarchies, between state (rulers, government) and religious authorities (clerics, religious hierarchy, religion). {17}:

> About what should and should not be done, about what must and must not be done, about who should be making these and similar decisions.

> About the personal role, authority, pay, standard of living and quality of life of the decision-takers.

> With each attempting to make the other serve its own ends.

It is this which shaped Muslim belief and practice to this day and it underlies the conflicts and confrontations we see today between Muslim rulers and Muslim clerics, between 'secular government' and 'rule by religious clerics'.

To me it seems that it also underlies the impoverished condition in some Muslim countries of those parts of their populations which are deprived, exploited, oppressed. {15-21}.

Findings

This work brings together Manfred Davidmann's ground-breaking discoveries from previously published separate major investigations <18> into the history of Judaism, Christianity and Islam. The complete sequence of events covering the three religions is shown here for the first time, is clear and to the point.

We saw the history of the two main confrontations between the Jewish rulers ('state', government, establishment) and their people, from the recording of the Pentateuch to the birth of Christianity. This struggle was about position, influence and control over communities, about changing God-given benevolent rules of behaviour so that people could be oppressed and exploited. It changed Judaism, determined the fate of the Jewish people and gave rise to Christianity.

We also saw that Jesus taught that all the laws had to be kept, that belief and practice included and had to include the Ten Commandments, the social laws and the social system of the Pentateuch. Paul, however, acted on behalf of the rich and powerful when he tried to convince people that those in authority were God's representatives on earth and that the social laws did not have to be kept.

Paul's letter to the 'Romans' was written before the gospels. Matthew's later gospel records what Jesus actually taught and clearly makes the point that Paul was trying to subvert that which Jesus taught. As Matthew records what Jesus taught, this outweighs and overrides what Paul said. Those who later favoured Paul's pro-establishment ideology could not challenge Matthew's record. Hence Matthew's gospel was subtly changed in later gospels.

Here also we saw the establishment engaged in abrogating, in effect in annulling <14>, the benevolent social laws of the Pentateuch. The establishment's version became accepted as official Christian doctrine and apparently it is this which tends to be taught today.

According to Liberation theologists, there are two kinds of Christianity. There is the kind of Christianity that serves the rulers and their establishment and thus those who oppress and exploit. And they say that there is also another kind of Christianity which bases its belief and practice on compassion for the poor and according to Christian texts which side with the poor against the rich, with the poor against the oppressor. {5}

Manfred Davidmann concluded that Christianity is struggling forward towards its roots in response to the social and economic problems of global humanity at the present time. Towards what Jesus taught, towards the social laws and social system of the Pentateuch. {5, 1}

Considering Islam, we saw that throughout almost the whole of Mohammed's life as Prophet he struggled against the powerful Meccan family which dominated Mecca, against the Quraysh {15}. And after Mohammed died, the ruling elite took over. We saw that hadiths (traditions) recorded that on the one hand we have the word of benevolent Allah as taught by Mohammed that people (believers) should have a good life of high quality in this life, but that on the other hand is the ruling elite's opposing viewpoint that people should be obedient and serve willingly without questioning their condition {18}. Since then there has been continuous confrontation and struggle between secular and religious figureheads and hierarchies, between state (rulers, government) and religious authorities (clerics, religious hierarchy, religion) {17} with each attempting to make the other serve its own ends.

It is this which shaped Muslim belief and practice to this day and it underlies the conflicts and confrontations we see today between Muslim rulers and Muslim clerics, between 'secular government' and 'rule by religious clerics'.

To me it seems that it also underlies the impoverished condition in some Muslim countries of those parts of their populations which are deprived, exploited, oppressed. {15-21}.

Conclusions

Underlying the Pentateuch's benevolent and egalitarian legislation are its social laws and social system, including the Ten Commandments and laws protecting the people by limiting the behaviour of their rulers.

The Jewish people undertook to live accordingly, to apply all of these in their daily lives. But their own rulers (kings, state, government, establishment) negated the application of these rules of behaviour and the people were oppressed and exploited. Rabbinical Judaism (today's Judaism) propagates the establishment's revisionist version of Jewish belief and practice. {8}

Jesus taught that all the Pentateuch's laws had to be kept, that belief and practice had to include them. Here again we saw that the establishment in effect negated the application of these benevolent rules of behaviour, that the Christian establishment's version became accepted and that the people were once again exposed to oppression and exploitation.

Mohammed knew about the events of the past and said so, calling for a return to following the ancient benevolent God-given social legislation. This knowledge may have been lost and since then there has been continuous confrontation and struggle between secular and religious figureheads and hierarchies, between state (rulers, government) and religious authorities (clerics, religious hierarchy, religion) {17}.

Notes <..>

< 1> Pentateuch, part of the Bible. Also called 'The Five Books of Moses' (namely Genesis, Exodus, Leviticus, Numbers and Deuteronomy). Also called 'Torah'.

< 2> Freedom: The right and power to act, speak, or think freely.
Liberty: The state of being free from oppression or imprisonment.
Independence: Self governing and not depending on another for livelihood or subsistence.

< 3> For a more comprehensive and more detailed listing of the social laws and social system of the Pentateuch, see {3}

< 4> For a full listing of the Ten Commandments, in biblical and plain English, see Appendix 5 of {6}. For a good discussion of its provisions see {6}.

< 5> A country's wealth includes productive assets and capital, including land, enterprise and corporation ownership, property, bank deposits and reserves.

< 6> At the time the Pentateuch was written, the sharing out of assets was to be updated after every 49 years. At present, updating at regular intervals of between three and not more than five calendar years is more appropriate.

< 7> 'Net assets' is the amount of money which would be left for distributing among the owners if everything belonging to an enterprise were sold and all its debts paid.

< 8> For a comprehensive detailed account of events, generation by generation, see {7}.

< 9> Establishment-orientated scholars, the 'experts' of the day. See {22} for a contemporary example.

<10> In {8} see 'The Five Pairs (Zugot)' which includes Figure 2 'Names of the Pairs' and Figure 3 'Laying-on of Hands'.

<11> See section on 'Pentateuch' and {3}

<12> In {1} see 'Paul'.

<13> In {1} see 'Gospels'.

<14> Abrogate: Doing away with (a law or agreement). Annul: Declaring (a law or other legal contract) invalid.

<15> Contemporaneous: At the same time, of the same period, contemporary.

<16> See {15} Section: 'Arab Life and Living at the Time of Mohammed' for sources (references) and more comprehensive information.

<17> In {18} see particularly 'Hadith 2: How Caliph Uthman Ordered the Compilation of an Official Koran Text' which clearly shows the meaning of these terms. And see the other relevant Koranic verses in {20}.

<18> See {1, 6-9, 15-21, 5}

References {..}

{ 1} 'Origin of Christianity and Judaism:
What Actually Happened, What Jesus Actually
Taught and Later Changes'
Manfred Davidmann
www.solhaam.org

{ 2} Romans **4**, 15

{ 3}　See chapter 2.1:
　　　'The God-given Human Rights, Social Laws and
　　　Social System'
　　　Manfred Davidmann

{ 4}　See chapter 3:
　　　'Family, Community, Sex and the Individual'
　　　Manfred Davidmann

{ 5}　'LIBERATION THEOLOGY:
　　　Basis - Past - Present – Future'
　　　Manfred Davidmann
　　　www.solhaam.org

{ 6}　In 'Judaism: Basis - Past - Present - Future, Part 1'
　　　Manfred Davidmann
　　　ISBN 978-0-85192-060-3
　　　see chapter 2.1: 'Struggle for Freedom:
　　　The Social Cause-and-Effect Relationship'

{ 7}　In 'Judaism: Basis - Past - Present - Future, Part 1'
　　　Manfred Davidmann
　　　ISBN 978-0-85192-060-3
　　　see chapter 2.2: 'History Speaks: Monarchy,
　　　Exile and Maccabees'

{ 8}　In 'Judaism: Basis - Past - Present - Future, Part 1'
　　　Manfred Davidmann
　　　ISBN 978-0-85192-060-3
　　　see chapter 2.3: 'At the Time of Jesus,
　　　This is What Actually Happened in Israel:
　　　The Truth about Hillel and his Times'

{ 9}　In 'Judaism: Basis - Past - Present - Future, Part 1'
　　　Manfred Davidmann
　　　ISBN 978-0-85192-060-3
　　　see chapter 2.4: 'One Law for All:
　　　Freedom Now, Freedom for Ever'

{10}　In 'Judaism: Basis - Past - Present - Future, Part 1'
　　　Manfred Davidmann
　　　ISBN 978-0-85192-060-3
　　　see chapter 5: 'The Right to the Land of Israel'

{11}　Pentateuch:
　　　Deuteronomy **17**, 14-20.

{12} Muhammad
Maxime Rodinson
Tauris Parke Paperbacks
1971, 2002

{13} Introduction to the Qur'an
Richard Bell
Edinburgh University Press, 1958

{14} Tune into the "new conscience of Islam"
Sophie Boukhari interviewing Abdou Filali-Ansari
Unesco Courier, November 2001

{15} In 'Islam: Basis - Past - Present - Future'
Manfred Davidmann
ISBN 978-0-85192-053-5
see chapter 2: 'Prophet Mohammed's Struggle
for a Better Life for All'

{16} In 'Islam: Basis - Past - Present - Future'
Manfred Davidmann
ISBN 978-0-85192-053-5
see chapter 3: 'Text, Language, Dialect and
Interpretation of the Koran'

{17} In 'Islam: Basis - Past - Present - Future'
Manfred Davidmann
ISBN 978-0-85192-053-5
see chapter 4: 'The Divine Right to Rule'

{18} In 'Islam: Basis - Past - Present - Future'
Manfred Davidmann
ISBN 978-0-85192-053-5
see chapter 5: 'Compiling the Koran:
Hadiths (Traditions) State the Underlying Reality'

{19} In 'Islam: Basis - Past - Present - Future'
Manfred Davidmann
ISBN 978-0-85192-053-5
see chapter 6: 'Uthman's Rearrangement
of the Chronological (as revealed) Koran's
Chapters'

{20} In 'Islam: Basis – Past – Present – Future'
Manfred Davidmann
ISBN 978-0-85192-053-5
see chapter 7: 'Prophet Mohammed's Word of
Allah and the Voice of the Ruling Elite'

{21} See chapter 15:
'Muslims and Jews'
Manfred Davidmann

{22} In 'The Real World in Which We Live:
The Social Rules and Social System under
Which We Suffer, Struggle, Survive and Prosper'
Manfred Davidmann
ISBN 978-0-85192-058-0
see chapter 14: 'Corrupted Economics and
Misguided (Misleading) Experts'

Press Notice

'Judaism, Christianity and Islam (Church and State, Government and Religion)': A Report by Manfred Davidmann.   (Texas Cable News)

Manfred Davidmann has shown that underlying Judaism, Christianity and Islam are the Pentateuch's benevolent and egalitarian social laws and social system which include laws protecting the people by restraining the behaviour of their rulers. Those in positions of trust, responsibility or authority must not oppress people and the laws forbid personal gain from the misuse of wealth or position.

Belief and practice were later changed covertly, but there were always those who recorded what had been done. Manfred Davidmann discovered, deciphered and collated this information, proving how beliefs and practices had been distorted or modified. In doing so, he exposed secrets to the light of day which are now fundamentally changing the teachings of the three main religions.

Manfred Davidmann's groundbreaking discoveries about Judaism, Christianity and Islam, published in nine reports over twenty-five years, the last in 2003, are acknowledged as major advances.

And in Manfred Davidmann's report "Judaism, Christianity and Islam", we see for the first time the complete sequence of consecutive events.

In Judaism, under Maccabean rule, the religious hierarchy became subservient to the secular rulers. Here Manfred Davidmann discovered the records which prove how religious scholars introduced changes which in effect enabled the ruling establishment to oppress and exploit the population. These changes gave rise to Christianity.

Today's rabbinical Judaism teaches, and Jewish belief and practice follows, the ruling establishment's version which has the essential core benevolent social laws bypassed and edited out from observance.

Jesus taught that all the Pentateuch's laws had to be kept, that belief and practice had to include the Ten Commandments, the social laws and the social system of the Pentateuch.

Manfred Davidmann shows how the establishment of the day in effect annulled the application of the Pentateuch's benevolent social laws and social system. He discovered that Matthew struggled to put the record straight and struggled to record what Jesus actually taught. But the establishment's version became accepted as official Christian doctrine and it is this which tends to be taught today.

The Koran records Prophet Mohammed repeatedly confirming the Pentateuch, referring to it both as a guide and as a warning, calling for a return to following the ancient benevolent God-given social legislation.

Validated traditions (hadith) tell that Caliph Uthman had an official text prepared of the Koran and that he instructed the compilers about its editing - also, that he then had copies of this text distributed and that he ordered all other versions to be destroyed.

Manfred Davidmann says "Humanity is once again struggling intuitively to achieve the application of these social laws and system, in response to the social and economic problems of global humanity at the present time. But struggling 'intuitively' is not enough, amounts to blindly hitting out in the dark without aim, amounts to treating symptoms instead of curing causes."

And he continues: "If we do not now observe and put into effect the social rules and social system first described in the Pentateuch, then the planet is likely to become uninhabitable for human beings in the near future."

When a scientist of Manfred Davidmann's proven track record (of achievement and objectivity) and international standing, makes such a statement, this needs to be taken seriously.

Compiled and correlated analyses and guidance can be found in the works of Manfred Davidmann.

See chapter 2.2:
'Church and State, Government and Religion:
Judaism, Christianity and Islam'
Manfred Davidmann

Chapter 2.3

Church and State, Government and Religion: Religion, Government and Education

Education or Indoctrination: Who is to Teach What to Whom

There are now Christian sects who stand up for morality and chastity against the socially corrupting promiscuity of the societies in which they live, to the extent of withdrawing their children from the state school system of their host societies, consequently suffering much stress and strain.

Another reason for withdrawing from the state educational system is to ensure that their children are taught the Bible's [1] record of how the planet and human beings were created, instead of how the planet was formed and how human beings evolved by natural selection.

The struggle is to educate, to educate our children to live good lives as human beings.

On the one hand state school systems may teach socially-corrupting politically-convenient biased information and principles {20-24} while on the other parents may believe that their religious beliefs about morality and behaviour provide a fundamentally better and more rewarding way of life and living {3, 7}.

Some countries allow children to be taught and educated while allowing for their parents' expressed humane beliefs. Other countries insist that children be educated in state schools according to the state's preferences about what has to be taught and about what must not be taught.

This brings us to the present position in Germany where some Christian groups <2> refuse to let their children be educated in state schools because of what is seen by them as socially corrupting promiscuity which is propagated under the guise of 'sex education' and because state schools teach the science of evolution by natural selection instead of the creation of the planet and human beings as told in the Bible (Pentateuch) <1>. In Germany these parents face fines and jail as a consequence of withdrawing their children from the state school system.

In the USA there is much pressure from influential, at times powerful, Christian fundamentalists insisting that state education (in some states) teach the Bible's (Pentateuch's) record of creation instead of the science of evolution by natural selection.

Religion, Government and Education

Expressed in everyday language, since about 1960 I have investigated the social organisation of life and living on this planet, the social laws and social system of the Pentateuch, and the meaning and intent of Genesis <3>, and made and published many original discoveries. Expressed in the language of religion, I revealed them.

Visiting Israel at intervals from about 1971 onwards attempting to make people aware of the key importance of applying the social laws and social system of the Pentateuch in their daily lives.

Many Christians and Jews now follow what I published <4> and some groups (cults, sects) <5> and churches in different countries have attempted to absorb some of these teachings into their beliefs {8}, selecting which of the God-given social laws and social system they feel like accepting in line with personal political ideologies.

Jewish orthodox and particularly ultra-orthodox sects, for example, still largely and blindly believe in and follow traditions which are often far-removed from the word of God as recorded in the Pentateuch. {10-13, 15}

Religious leaderships, of course, are not god-like in knowledge and understanding. That is, they are not capable of annulling or overriding God's fundamental rules and their intent, would be in error and misleading if they proclaimed themselves to be 'infallible', that is proclaimed themselves to be 'incapable of making mistakes or being wrong'. <6>

So religious leaderships do not have the right to decide which God-given fundamental rules and laws are to be believed and followed and which are not, nor may they assign their own meanings (interpretations or misinterpretations according to personal likes, dislikes or preferences) to fundamental Bible (Pentateuch) texts. In other words, religious leadership may not decide which of the social laws and social system of the Pentateuch <1> should or should not be taught, as all need to be observed and applied.

And now consider the following.

The Pentateuch is the basic constitution which safeguards the rights of the people and points the way ahead. It may not be changed in any way either by adding or by taking away. {12}

But authority for changing the application of a law comes from the Pentateuch. In matters of dispute or doubt which cannot be resolved with reference to the Pentateuch's laws, then the religious leadership and judges of the day can decide the matter. The law they will teach and the judgement which is made are binding and have to be followed. {16}

They are thus authorised to modify the application of a Pentateuch law so as to keep it effective in achieving its intent in the light of changing conditions. They may, for example, change penalties and punishments. They may not change the basic constitution, they may not change Pentateuch law. {12}

They may modify the application of a Pentateuch law and do so by man-made decisions which together form the body of common and case law.

This common law thus aims to resolve new problems (social, economic and moral) which find no answer in the Pentateuch or in existing common law, by amending existing common law or by new decisions in the spirit and intent of the Pentateuch.

We have seen that the Pentateuch is the basic constitution which safeguards the people and points the way ahead. It may not be changed in any way either by adding or by taking away. {12}

We have also seen that the Pentateuch authorises common law, that is man-made decisions modifying the application of a law so as to keep it effective in achieving its intent in the light of changing conditions.

Common law is subordinate legislation, is a collection of man-made decisions. It is these decisions which may be abrogated or amended by other man-made decisions.

What stands out is that there can be no conflict, or contradiction, between the words of a benevolent almighty all-knowing God and the reality of life and living, between God's words and the world in which we live, between God's words and science.

It is when the word of God and the reality of life and living, and of science, are seen to agree that we are close to understanding both.

And in the confrontations between religion and state concerning evolution <7> and concerning morality <8> we are closing in on the very core problems of life and living in our times, as follows.

Evolution

When the Pentateuch <1> was written, people had but little knowledge about science or evolution compared with what is known today. So concepts for which we now have precise terms were described rather than stated.

Instead of the term 'scientific law' being used, for example, we see the description that

> 'what is written applies to all people, present or absent, past or future, will happen regardless of how one feels about it, that the results of certain actions are reversed if the actions are reversed'. {10} <9>

In Genesis the then-beyond-comprehension beginning of life on earth and its evolutionary progress towards humankind is being described to people to whom terms such as 'natural selection' were completely unknown. In the Bible, evolutionary change, a new life form, is an act of creation and we are told in precise terms how mammals evolved, how homo erectus spread out, how homo sapiens spread out and replaced homo erectus, and much more. {2}

However, there were some who seemed to think that they knew all there is to be known, that they could decide what is and what is not, that what they were not aware of did not exist, that what they did not understand could not be meaningful. For example, Hebrew grammar distinguishes between proper names of persons and general nouns such as 'life form'. This distinction has been ignored by Bible translators <10>.

Manfred Davidmann's 'The Meaning of Genesis: Creation, Evolution and the Origin of Evil' {2} shows that the distinction is meaningful and needs to be made if the text is to be understood as it was intended to be understood.

We see that there is no conflict, no contradiction, no divergence, only astonishing awe-inspiring agreement, between what is stated in Genesis and what we now know about the evolution of human beings. {2}.

Genesis is about matters of enormous significance and importance to humankind at the present time. {2}

Morality   {7, 3}

We know there is no conflict or confrontation between the word of benevolent God as recorded in the Pentateuch on the one hand and social science on the other hand. We know the destructive effects on the population of promiscuity, that is of state-condoned or legalised promiscuity. These effects are known and predictable. {7}

We saw that concerning evolution, the Church has misunderstood, misinterpreted, the Bible. The state, science, is right. What is being taught at the present time agrees with what is stated in the Bible.

But concerning morality, the Church is right. The state is misinterpreting, is misapplying, scientific knowledge.

And so concerning morality the position is very different. Here it is those who struggle against state-condoned promiscuity and for morality who are struggling on God's behalf for the benefit of the oppressed and exploited population. {7, 3}

The Pentateuch contains detailed statements about what constitutes abnormal, promiscuous, adulterous sexual relations and prostitution, with associated comments.

The Pentateuch legislates in detail, stating what needs to be done and what is prohibited, by positive and negative rules of behaviour. Positive rules point the way ahead towards greater strength and liberty, negative rules (prohibitions) protect people from the antisocial behaviour of others, safeguard the people's strength and liberty. {11} <11>

The consequences of immorality and promiscuity, that is consequent weakening and breaking up of family, society and quality of life {7}, cannot be avoided {10} <12>. The Pentateuch's warnings, punishments and penalties concerning immorality are in most cases to the male {7}. Morality has to be protected by punishing immorality, by protecting people and punishing those who behave immorally. By punishing those who do not restrain their sex urges. By punishing those who spread immorality and seduce others into immoral behaviour.

In democracies or when people are struggling for their liberty, totalitarians condone and promote promiscuity so as to weaken the family and weaken the population. People are subjected to this conditioning towards immorality so as to weaken the working population to make them easier to exploit, and to weaken the society to weaken democracy. <13>

After gaining control, totalitarians of left or right or religious hierarchies then reverse the process by moving back towards greater morality, in this way enabling their people to gain strength in order to fight for and work for, their manipulating rulers. <14>

We know the predictable effects of promiscuity on the population {7}. Hence the importance of morality, of Pentateuch morality and laws of behaviour, of protecting communities and people by restraining immoral behaviour, conditioning and propaganda, by appropriately punishing the perpetrators.

Hence the importance of the stand taken by those who struggle against state-condoned teaching of promiscuity, who struggle for the teaching of morality, on God's behalf for the benefit of the oppressed and exploited population.

Education for a Better Life

Throughout history, from the writing down of the Pentateuch about 3,500 years ago, right to the present time, we have seen continuous struggle against the God-given benevolent and egalitarian social laws and social system of the Pentateuch. That the revelations by Moses, Jesus and Mohammed were followed by world-wide struggles for a better life is well-documented. This knowledge and understanding of what took place has once again been published (revealed) by Manfred Davidmann <15>.

This knowledge has been spreading since these works were first published, is being accepted within Judaism and Christianity. The works on Islam were only published recently.

But publication was followed by attempts by miscellaneous groups and movements to negate the knowledge in my writings by taking over certain parts and neglecting or misrepresenting key components.

My works show how people are confronted, manipulated or opposed by antisocial, socially irresponsible, elements. Such antisocial elements are exposed and condemned in the Pentateuch as primitive and vicious remnants of our pre-human past.

Manfred Davidmann's works are and need to be seen as an interconnected and consistent whole, which combines both religious and secular (scientific, state, social) aspects without contradiction. And they state and describe the God-given social laws and social system of the Pentateuch, their intent and relevance to life and living in our time.

Findings and Conclusions

Basic Constitution; Religious Leaderships

The Pentateuch is the basic constitution which safeguards the rights of the people and points the way ahead. It may not be changed in any way either by adding or by taking away. {12}

> Religious leaderships, of course, are not god-like in knowledge and understanding. That is, they are not capable of annulling or overriding God's fundamental rules and their intent, would be in error and misleading if they proclaimed themselves to be 'infallible', that is proclaimed themselves to be 'incapable of making mistakes or being wrong'. <6>

> So religious leaderships do not have the right to decide which God-given fundamental rules and laws are to be believed and followed and which are not, nor may they assign their own meanings (interpretations or misinterpretations according to personal likes, dislikes or preferences) to fundamental Bible (Pentateuch) texts. In other words, religious leadership may not decide which of the social laws and social system of the Pentateuch <1> should or should not be taught, as all need to be observed and applied.

The Pentateuch legislates in detail, stating what needs to be done and what is prohibited, by positive and negative rules of behaviour. Positive rules point the way ahead towards greater strength and liberty, negative rules (prohibitions) protect people from the antisocial behaviour of others, safeguard the people's strength and liberty. {11} <11>

In matters of dispute or doubt which cannot be resolved with reference to the Pentateuch's laws, then the religious leadership and judges of the day can decide the matter. The law they will teach and the judgement which is made are binding and have to be followed {16}. They are in this way authorised to modify the application of a Pentateuch law so as to keep it effective in achieving its intent in the light of changing conditions.

> They may, for example, change penalties and punishments. They may not change the basic constitution, they may not change Pentateuch law. {12}

They may modify the application of a Pentateuch law and do so by man-made decisions which together form the body of common and case law.

Religious Leadership and Judges; Common and Case Law

Common law is subordinate legislation, is a collection of man-made decisions. It is these decisions which may be abrogated or amended by other man-made decisions.

Common law aims to resolve new problems (social, economic and moral) which find no answer in the Pentateuch or in existing common law, by amending existing common law or by new decisions in the spirit and intent of the Pentateuch.

Evolution and Creationism

In Genesis the then-beyond-comprehension beginning of life on earth and its evolutionary progress towards humankind is being described to people to whom terms such as 'natural selection' were completely unknown. In the Bible, evolutionary change, a new life form, is an act of creation and we are told in precise terms how mammals evolved, how homo erectus spread out, how homo sapiens spread out and replaced homo erectus, and much more. {2}

> However, there were some who seemed to think that they knew all there is to be known, that they could decide what is and what is not, that what they were not aware of did not exist, that what they did not understand could not be meaningful. For example, Hebrew grammar distinguishes between proper names of persons and general nouns such as 'life form'. This distinction has been ignored by Bible translators <10>.

> Manfred Davidmann's 'The Meaning of Genesis: Creation, Evolution and the Origin of Evil' {2} shows that the

distinction is meaningful and needs to be made if the text is to be understood as it was intended to be understood.

We see that there is no conflict, no contradiction, no divergence, only astonishing awe-inspiring agreement, between what is stated in Genesis and what we now know about the evolution of human beings. {2}.

Morality, Life and Living

The Pentateuch contains detailed statements about what constitutes abnormal, promiscuous, adulterous sexual relations and prostitution, with associated comments.

The consequences of immorality and promiscuity, that is consequent weakening and breaking up of family, society and quality of life {7}, cannot be avoided {10} <12>. The Pentateuch's warnings, punishments and penalties concerning immorality are in most cases to the male {7}. Morality has to be protected by punishing immorality, by protecting people and punishing those who behave immorally. By punishing those who do not restrain their sex urges. By punishing those who spread immorality and seduce others into immoral behaviour.

In democracies or when people are struggling for their liberty, totalitarians condone and promote promiscuity so as to weaken the family and weaken the population. People are subjected to this conditioning towards immorality to weaken the working population to make them easier to exploit, and to weaken the society to weaken democracy. <13>

After gaining control, totalitarians of left or right or religious hierarchies then reverse the process by moving back towards greater morality, in this way enabling their people to gain strength in order to fight for and work for, their manipulating rulers. <14>

We know the predictable effects of promiscuity on the population {7}. Hence the importance of morality, of Pentateuch morality and laws of behaviour, of protecting communities and people by restraining immoral behaviour, conditioning and propaganda, by appropriately punishing the perpetrators.

Hence also the importance of the stand taken by those who struggle against state-condoned teaching of promiscuity, who struggle for the teaching of morality, on God's behalf for the benefit of the oppressed and exploited population.

Religion and Science, Church and State

It is when the word of God and the reality of life and living, and of science, are seen to agree that we are close to understanding both.

> And in the confrontations between religion and state concerning evolution <7> and concerning morality <8> we are closing in on the very core problems of life and living in our times, as follows.

We saw that concerning evolution, the Church has misunderstood, misinterpreted, the Bible. The state, science, is right. What is being taught at the present time about evolution agrees with what is stated in the Bible.

But concerning morality, the Church is right. The state is misinterpreting, is misapplying, scientific knowledge about the effects of promiscuity on the life and welfare of the population.

And so concerning morality the position is very different. Here it is those who struggle against state-condoned promiscuity and for morality who are struggling on God's behalf for the benefit of the oppressed and exploited population. {7, 3}

Manfred Davidmann's works show how people are confronted, manipulated or opposed by antisocial, socially irresponsible, elements. Such antisocial elements are exposed and condemned in the Pentateuch as primitive and vicious remnants of our pre-human past.

Manfred Davidmann's works are and need to be seen as an interconnected and consistent whole, which combines both religious and secular (scientific, state, social) aspects without contradiction. And they state and describe the God-given social laws and social system of the Pentateuch, their intent and relevance to life and living in our time.

Notes <..>

< 1>   The Pentateuch (The Five Books of Moses), part of the Bible. Also called the Torah.

< 2>   Cults, sects, small groups separated from mainstream Christianity.

< 3>   First volume of the Pentateuch

<4> See {1-6, 9-13, 15}.

<5> Sectarian: Putting the beliefs or interests of one's sect before more general interests.

<6> See {8} 'Social Concept (Policies) of the Russian Orthodox Church: Letter to the Russians'

<7> As opposed to creationism, to the Bible's (Pentateuch's) record of how the planet was formed and human beings appeared.

<8> As opposed to immorality, to promiscuity.

<9> In {10} see Appendix 4: Cause-and-effect Relationship in the Torah <1>.

<10> In {2} see Appendix 3: 'Adam' and Hebrew Grammar. Or see {5}.

<11> The information in this section has largely been reproduced from {3}: 'The Pentateuch and the Problems of Our Times'.

<12> In {10} see 'Cause-and-Effect Relationship'

<13> See {7}

<14> See {6}

<15> See chapter 2.2:
'Church and State, Government and Religion: Judaism, Christianity and Islam', which summarises findings from {1-3, 6, 8-9, 11-14, 17-19}.

References {..}

{1} 'Origin of Christianity and Judaism:
What Actually Happened, What Jesus Actually Taught and Later Changes'
Manfred Davidmann
www.solhaam.org

{ 2} In 'God and People:
      The Social Laws and Social System Underlying
      Judaism, Christianity, Islam and Democracy'
      Manfred Davidmann
      ISBN 978-0-85192-054-2
      see chapter 6.1: 'The Meaning of Genesis:
      Creation, Evolution and the Origin of Evil'

{ 3} In 'God and People:
      The Social Laws and Social System Underlying
      Judaism, Christianity, Islam and Democracy'
      Manfred Davidmann
      ISBN 978-0-85192-054-2
      see chapter 6.3: 'The Meaning of Genesis:
      Morality, Sexual Behaviour and Depravity'

{ 4} See chapter 10.1:
      'Meaning and Significance of the Names of God
      in Genesis'
      Manfred Davidmann

{ 5} See chapter 10.2:
      'Meaning and Intent of Genesis: Essential Notes on
      Hebrew Grammar'
      Manfred Davidmann

{ 6} In 'God and People:
      The Social Laws and Social System Underlying
      Judaism, Christianity, Islam and Democracy'
      Manfred Davidmann
      ISBN 978-0-85192-054-2
      see chapter 6.4: 'The Meaning of Genesis:
      Nephilim, Dominance and Liberty'

{ 7} See chapter 3:
      'Family, Community, Sex and the Individual'
      Manfred Davidmann

{ 8} 'Social Concept (Policies) of the Russian Orthodox
      Church: Letter to the Russians'
      Manfred Davidmann
      www.solhaam.org

{ 9} 'LIBERATION THEOLOGY:
Basis - Past - Present – Future'
Manfred Davidmann
www.solhaam.org

{10} In 'Judaism: Basis - Past - Present - Future, Part 1'
Manfred Davidmann
ISBN 978-0-85192-060-3
see chapter 2.1: 'Struggle for Freedom:
The Social Cause-and-Effect Relationship'

{11} In 'Judaism: Basis - Past - Present - Future, Part 1'
Manfred Davidmann
ISBN 978-0-85192-060-3
see chapter 2.2: 'History Speaks: Monarchy,
Exile and Maccabees'

{12} In 'Judaism: Basis - Past - Present - Future, Part 1'
Manfred Davidmann
ISBN 978-0-85192-060-3
see chapter 2.3: 'At the Time of Jesus,
This is What Actually Happened in Israel:
The Truth about Hillel and his Times'

{13} In 'Judaism: Basis - Past - Present - Future, Part 1'
Manfred Davidmann
ISBN 978-0-85192-060-3
see chapter 2.4: 'One Law for All:
Freedom Now, Freedom for Ever'

{14} In 'Judaism: Basis - Past - Present - Future, Part 1'
Manfred Davidmann
ISBN 978-0-85192-060-3
see chapter 3: 'Jewish Belief and Practice'

{15} In 'Judaism: Basis - Past - Present - Future, Part 1'
Manfred Davidmann
ISBN 978-0-85192-060-3
see chapter 5: 'The Right to the Land of Israel'

{16} Pentateuch
Deuteronomy 17, 8-11.

{17} In 'Islam: Basis – Past – Present – Future'
Manfred Davidmann
ISBN 978-0-85192-053-5
see chapter 5: 'Compiling the Koran: Hadiths
(Traditions) State the Underlying Reality'

{18} In 'Islam: Basis – Past – Present – Future'
Manfred Davidmann
ISBN 978-0-85192-053-5
see chapter 6: 'Uthman's Rearrangement of the
Chronological (as revealed) Koran's Chapters'

{19} In 'Islam: Basis – Past – Present – Future'
Manfred Davidmann
ISBN 978-0-85192-053-5
see chapter 7: 'Prophet Mohammed's Word of Allah
and the Voice of the Ruling Elite'

{20} In 'Management and Leadership:
Local, National, Multinational (Global),
Principles and Practice'
Manfred Davidmann
ISBN 978-0-85192-057-3
see chapter 8: 'Work and Pay'

{21} In 'The Real World in Which We Live:
The Social Rules and Social System under
Which We Suffer, Struggle, Survive and Prosper'
Manfred Davidmann
ISBN 978-0-85192-058-0
see chapter 7: 'Exporting and Importing of
Employment and Unemployment'

{22} In 'The Real World in Which We Live:
The Social Rules and Social System under
Which We Suffer, Struggle, Survive and Prosper'
Manfred Davidmann
ISBN 978-0-85192-058-0
see chapter 10: 'What People are Struggling Against:
How Society is Organised for Controlling and
Exploiting People'

{23} In 'The Real World in Which We Live:
      The Social Rules and Social System under
      Which We Suffer, Struggle, Survive and Prosper'
      Manfred Davidmann
      ISBN 978-0-85192-058-0
      see chapter 14: 'Corrupted Economics and Misguided
      (Misleading) Experts'

{24} In 'The Real World in Which We Live:
      The Social Rules and Social System under
      Which We Suffer, Struggle, Survive and Prosper'
      Manfred Davidmann
      ISBN 978-0-85192-058-0
      see chapter 17: 'Quotable Quotes about Democracy
      in the Real World'

Creationism and Intelligent Design, Evolution, Education or Indoctrination

Introduction

Manfred Davidmann has written a number of scientific books and reports that have had considerable impact. His work usually breaks new ground, opening up new areas of understanding. Outstanding is that his work and reports are generally accepted as objective, factual, proved, unbiased and independent.

When the Pentateuch <1> was written {1}, people had only little knowledge about science or evolution compared with what is known today. Hence concepts for which we now have precise terms were described rather than stated. Instead of the term 'scientific law' being used, for example, we see described that 'what is written applies to all people, present or absent, past or future, will happen regardless of how one feels about it, that the results of certain actions are reversed if the actions are reversed' <2>.

So the first step towards understanding the content of the Bible is to gain knowledge about its language, that is to understand how recorded letters and symbols were used to state the meaning of words. Such knowledge and understanding is particularly important when considering what scholars and clerics have done and are doing when they are 'interpreting' the text of the Bible.

Reading, Interpreting, Translating of Consonantal Texts

Just why there has been so much confusion about reading, interpreting and translating of consonantal texts can be seen from the following definitions {13}:

'Consonant' A letter of the alphabet other than a vowel

'Reading' Choosing between likely words which fit the written groups of consonants while allowing for the likely meaning of the sentence or verse in which they appear.

'Interpreting' Somehow deciding between, or choosing from, alternative meanings for the selected words or sentences.

Interpretation attempts to suggest or provide meaning where the text itself is unclear, ambiguous, seems to have none.

'Reading' and 'interpreting' are closely interconnected since choice of words determines the meaning of the sentence, of the text.

Translating scholars, working from a consonantal text (no vowels), had to 'read' the text. That is, they had to decide between, or choose from, alternative meanings for given groups of letters (words), considering and selecting the most likely meaning of the sentence (interpretation).

Of course, they could only 'read' and 'interpret' the text, could only select a 'most likely' meaning, within their own knowledge and understanding. That is, within the knowledge and understanding available to them at that time, in those days. {12}

When the Hebrew word "ereb" was taken to mean "evening", and the Hebrew word "boker" was taken to mean "morning", then the phrase at the end of each stage of creation in Genesis could be interpreted to mean "there was evening and there was morning, one day." A reading and interpretation which corresponded to the knowledge and understanding of those doing the translating in those times. The knowledge needed for understanding Genesis was simply not available at time of translation. <3>

But the Hebrew 'word' ereb, said Manfred Davidmann {5}, can mean "evening," or else "to mingle," or "not to distinguish between them." Likewise, the Hebrew 'word' boker can mean "morning," or "to search," "to examine," and possibly "to check carefully." The statement about evening and morning, then, can just as easily be translated as

> "there was a mingling and a uniformity and a searching for differences and an examination of differences"

- a clear statement of the process of evolutionary advance which, said Manfred Davidmann, is both valid and relevant considering our understanding of Genesis and our present scientific knowledge.

Knowledge for Understanding not Available at Time of Translation

Adam   {See 5, 11, 12}

Hebrew grammar distinguishes between proper names of persons and general nouns such as 'life form'. This distinction <4> has been ignored by Bible translators when reading and interpreting 'adam'. However, the distinction is meaningful and needs to be made if Genesis is to be understood as it was intended to be understood {5, 11}. <5>

The Bible translators were apparently not aware of knowledge such as this, and so parts of Genesis were misread, misinterpreted or mistranslated.

Manfred Davidmann clearly states and illustrates the simple, relevant and basic rules of Hebrew grammar which distinguish between individuals and life forms. These distinctions need to be made if Genesis is to be read and understood as intended, and were first made by Manfred Davidmann in 'The Meaning of Genesis: Creation, Evolution and the Origin of Evil' {5, 11}.

Politically Motivated Changes and Misinterpretations

But there are other reasons for making changes and for insisting on them!

Names of God {See 5, 10, 12}

Some 150 years ago, there were those who wondered why God was being referred to by different names in Genesis. At that time a likely explanation appeared to be that Genesis had been written by a number of people pretending it had all been written by one person but that each author naively referred to God by a different designation. This multi-author hypothesis has undertones of propaganda aimed at discrediting the Pentateuch and its benevolent social teachings, by discrediting its single-author-based religious authority.

The multi-author hypothesis was disproved some time ago {2, 3}. However, Manfred Davidmann was the first who clearly stated and explained the meaning of the different names (designations) of God in Genesis, and who illustrated their importance. {5, 10}

You can see in 'The Meaning of Genesis: Creation, Evolution and the Origin of Evil' {5} that the different designations for God are not only meaningful but also extremely important. <6>

Adam and Eve {See 5, 14, 15}

It was Manfred Davidmann who proved {5} that the allegory about Adam and Eve in the Garden of Eden describes the evolution of Homo sapiens (human beings, ourselves) from Homo erectus.

He showed, for example, that Genesis records that childbirth became more difficult as a result of the increased brain size (evolution of neocortex) which enabled Homo sapiens to know the difference between good and evil and to choose between them.

And that Genesis states the necessary division of work between the male and the female, as equals in different roles, in protecting and bringing up their children.

And much else.

Obscuring Meaning by Making Changes (Bible Versions)

There were also those who seemed to think that they knew all there is to be known, that they could decide what is and what is not, that what they were not aware of did not exist, that what they did not understand could not be meaningful.

In Genesis Chapter 5, for example, the Septuagint and the Samaritan Pentateuchs smoothed out the Masoretic chronology's listed life spans

{12}, each in a different way, and so smoothed out, obscured, clues needed for understanding the meaning of the text.

Creationism and Intelligent Design

The terms "evolution" and "natural selection" did not exist and the author of Genesis instead described the progress of evolution.

The translations (readings and interpretations) of the early translators are based on the limited knowledge and understanding available to them at the time of translation. Current translations of Genesis are in turn based on their work and we saw that conflicts have arisen because parts of Genesis have been mistranslated or misinterpreted.

Creationism apparently assumes that the resulting erroneous text correctly states God's deeds.

Following the publication of Manfred Davidmann's Genesis reports {5, 6-12}, and of the publicity they generated, the 'Creationism' hypothesis was largely abandoned in USA as untenable. But a similar hypothesis was then put forward called 'Intelligent Design'.

And it seems that 'Intelligent Design' assumes that the same erroneous text could correctly state the deeds of some other supernatural being.

Evolution, Education or Indoctrination

Manfred Davidmann shows and proves that the record of creation in the original text of Genesis corresponds in the major steps to the order in which the earth and life are known to have been formed and developed. {5}

Described is the formation of the earth and early plant life, and evolution by 'the survival of the fittest'. The evolution from reptilian to mammalian instincts, feelings and behaviour is clearly stated, as is the evolution and corresponding behaviour, feeling and thinking of human beings from humanoids (animals resembling humans) through Homo erectus (early man) to Homo sapiens (human beings, ourselves).

There is no conflict or contradiction between what is recorded in Genesis and our scientific knowledge about evolution of human beings and of our planet.

Findings and Conclusions

Conflicts have arisen because parts of Genesis have been mistranslated or misinterpreted.

The 'Creationism' hypothesis apparently assumes that the resulting erroneous text correctly states God's deeds.

And it seems that the 'Intelligent Design' hypothesis assumes that the same erroneous text could correctly state the deeds of some other supernatural being.

The source text of Genesis does not contradict the modern science of evolution.

Manfred Davidmann's research and discoveries showed and proved that the source text of Genesis, written several thousand years ago, corresponds in the major steps to the order in which the earth and life are known to have been formed and developed. {5}

Described is the formation of the earth and early plant life, and evolution by 'the survival of the fittest'. The evolution from reptilian to mammalian instincts, feelings and behaviour is clearly stated, as is the evolution and corresponding behaviour, feeling and thinking of human beings from humanoids (animals resembling humans) through Homo erectus (early man) to Homo sapiens (human beings, ourselves). {5}

There is no conflict or contradiction between what is recorded in the source text of Genesis and our scientific knowledge about evolution of human beings and of our planet.

Notes <..>

<1>   Pentateuch, part of the Bible. Also called 'The Five Books of Moses' (namely Genesis, Exodus, Leviticus, Numbers and Deuteronomy). Also called 'Torah'.

<2>   In {4} see section on 'The Social Cause-and-Effect Relationship'.
The Social Cause-and-Effect Relationship is also listed (in biblical language and in plain English) in Appendix 4 of {4}, with references to the Pentateuch text.

<3>   See {5} and {12}

<4> In {5}, see Appendix 3: 'Adam' and Hebrew Grammar

<5> I gratefully acknowledge the assistance I received from Esther Shouby without whose professional knowledge of Hebrew I might not have been able to explain the meaning of the ancient Hebrew texts.

<6> In {5}, see Appendix 1: Names of God

References {..}

{ 1} See chapter 2.1:
'The God-given Human Rights, Social Laws and Social System'
Manfred Davidmann

{ 2} Genesis, Wellhausen and the Computer
Y. T. Radday, H. Shore, M. A. Pollatschek and D. Wickmann
Zeitschrift fuer die Alttestamentliche Wissenschaft
94. Band, Heft 4, 1982
Walter de Gruyter, Berlin, New York

{ 3} A Commentary on the Book of Genesis.
Part 1: From Adam to Noah;
Part 2: From Noah to Abraham.
By U. Cassuto (1944)
Translated from the Hebrew by Israel Abrahams (1961)
The Magnes Press, The Hebrew University, Jerusalem.

{ 4} In 'Judaism: Basis - Past - Present - Future, Part 1'
Manfred Davidmann
ISBN 978-0-85192-060-3
see chapter 2.1: 'Struggle for Freedom:
The Social Cause-and-Effect Relationship'

{ 5} In 'God and People:
      The Social Laws and Social System Underlying
      Judaism, Christianity, Islam and Democracy'
      Manfred Davidmann
      ISBN 978-0-85192-054-2
      see chapter 6.1: 'The Meaning of Genesis:
      Creation, Evolution and the Origin of Evil'

{ 6} In 'God and People:
      The Social Laws and Social System Underlying
      Judaism, Christianity, Islam and Democracy'
      Manfred Davidmann
      ISBN 978-0-85192-054-2
      see chapter 6.2: 'The Meaning of Genesis:
      Pre-flood Evils and the Social Problems of Our Time'

{ 7} In 'God and People:
      The Social Laws and Social System Underlying
      Judaism, Christianity, Islam and Democracy'
      Manfred Davidmann
      ISBN 978-0-85192-054-2
      see chapter 6.5: 'The Meaning of Genesis:
      Differentiating Between Good and Evil'

{ 8} In 'God and People:
      The Social Laws and Social System Underlying
      Judaism, Christianity, Islam and Democracy'
      Manfred Davidmann
      ISBN 978-0-85192-054-2
      see chapter 6.3: 'The Meaning of Genesis:
      Morality, Sexual Behaviour and Depravity'

{ 9} In 'God and People:
      The Social Laws and Social System Underlying
      Judaism, Christianity, Islam and Democracy'
      Manfred Davidmann
      ISBN 978-0-85192-054-2
      see chapter 6.4: 'The Meaning of Genesis:
      Nephilim, Dominance and Liberty'

{10} See chapter 10.1:
      'Meaning and Significance of the Names of God
      in Genesis'
      Manfred Davidmann

{11} See chapter 10.2:
'Meaning and Intent of Genesis: Essential Notes on
Hebrew Grammar'
Manfred Davidmann

{12} See chapter 10.3:
'Bible Translations, Versions, Codes and Hidden
Information in Bible and Talmud'
Manfred Davidmann

{13} In 'Islam: Basis – Past – Present – Future'
Manfred Davidmann
ISBN 978-0-85192-053-5
see chapter 3: 'Text, Language, Dialect and
Interpretation of the Koran'

{14} 'Social Policies (Doctrine) of the Roman Catholic
Church: An Evaluation'
Manfred Davidmann
www.solhaam.org

{15} 'Social Concept (Policies) of the Russian Orthodox
Church: Letter to the Russians'
Manfred Davidmann
www.solhaam.org

Chapter 3

Family, Community, Sex and the Individual

Introduction

The work, analysis and findings reported here investigate casual sex and its effects on individuals, family and community. Also investigated is dominance and confrontation within the family and in the working environment, how men and women relate to each other, and the role of the family in bringing up children.

This report examines root causes of major social problems and shows how to resolve the problems by dealing with their basic causes. The report pulls together information from earlier reports and adds some important sections. The new material deals with how sex affects the individual, with sexual restraint and control, and with the evolution and current role of the family and of its members.

In this report are statements about effects on people, or how people respond, on how people behave, and so on. In all such cases it is understood that in every case there is a range of effects or behaviour from one end of a spectrum to the other, that what applies to one does not apply to another. So while the statements made in the report apply to a whole group or population, they cannot be said to apply to all individuals or to specific individuals.

But the effects I listed in the earlier publications now appear obvious and in the USA steps are being taken to halt and reverse the increasing corruption of their communities.

Role of the Family

How Human Beings Evolved

As far as we know the human brain evolved in three main stages {12}. Its ancient and primitive part is the innermost reptilian brain. Next evolved the mammalian brain by adding new functions and new ways of controlling the body. Then evolved the third part of the brain, the neocortex, the grey matter, the bulk of the brain in two symmetrical hemispheres, separate but communicating. To a considerable extent it is our neocortex which enables us to behave like human beings. {11}

Human emotional responses depend on neuronal pathways which link the right hemisphere to the mammalian brain which in turn is linked to the even older reptilian brain.

For human beings, primitive (reptilian) instinctive urges and behaviour are overlaid by mammalian care and affection for one's young and human care and affection for one's family and community. {11}

So the human brain includes a wide range of emotions, of feelings, of care and affection, and the capability for objective and logical thinking and evaluation.

Compared with most, if not all, other animals we also have much longer lifespans and it takes a long time before a human baby becomes an adult. Born after nine months in the mother's womb, followed by 4 to 5 years as infant, then 8 to 10 years as child being educated, and say 6 to 9 years as adolescent, about 18 to 25 years old when becoming an adult and independent member of the community.

There is a whole scale of behaviour from human to the beast-like, from behaviour based on affection for the other person to, at the other end, uncontrolled behaviour such as rape, and the seduction of the young which I see as another form of rape.

Mammalian and human parts of our brain control our reptilian ancestor's instinctive copulation urges {11}. It seems as if rapists and paedophiles do not restrain and control their bottom-level beast-like instincts, and it seems to be these which urge them on.

The instinctive sex urge aims to ensure the survival of the species. We have been able to adapt and advance by a process of natural selection and a key characteristic which distinguishes human beings from animals is that we can control the sex urge.

Role of the Family

Something like 200 million years of evolution are behind us, from reptilian beast through mammalian animal to human being. Human beings are mammals and are unique in that our children need protecting and bringing up in a humane, emotionally and mentally stimulating environment for between 18 and 21 years, to enable them to mature into socially responsible adults {11}. Men and women co-operate with each other and look after each other and their children, within the family, to do just that.

So the role of the family is

> To struggle as a family to survive.
>
> To protect and support mother and children until children become mature and independent adults capable of providing for themselves.
>
> To provide a good standard of living and a life of high quality. Which includes struggling against oppression and exploitation. And sometimes one has to fight to preserve a good way of life.
>
> To serve the interests of, and to support, each member of the family. In turn, each member of the family supports the family.

Hence human beings work primarily for their family and members of a family stand by, support and help each other in times of need. The family is the basic unit of society and it looks after the interests of all its members, as individuals as well as collectively. This gives great strength to each member of the family in the struggle for daily bread, security and happiness.

Protecting and Caring for the Next Generation

There is a genetic difference between men and women. It is women who bear the child and who need protecting and looking after while bearing the child and after childbirth. There clearly are close emotional bonds between mother and child.

It is women who generally look after people, after the welfare and well-being of the members of the family. Care, concern, affection and love, feelings and emotions, are important and matter, and women developed, and have, much skill and expertise in such matters. It is generally men who struggle outside the family to secure survival and good living for the family. A struggle for survival in a seemingly hostile environment engineered by other humans.

Primarily the family exists to protect and support its young, and this means supporting and looking after the female bearing the child within her body, through birth and while she is protecting and teaching the young how to behave. It is usually the woman whose role it is to ensure the family provides the young with the humane, emotionally and mentally stimulating environment they need to enable them to mature into socially responsible adults. She is assisted in this by her spouse, depending on her needs and depending on his own work. But it is usually the woman who copes with the personal and emotional problems of the family's members and this is challenging, demanding and difficult work demanding social ability and skills as well as care, affection, understanding and concern for people.

In the kibbutzim, that is in Israel's co-operative settlements, children were brought up communally in age groups, away from their parents. One age group would progress together from creche to nursery and then to school, living together during the week and seeing their parents, or living with their parents, only at weekends.

This may have freed both parents for work and defence in the initial struggle for survival. But the practice was continued when successful, possibly to free women for work and so increase production. But it was done at the expense of the family.

Of any group in the country, the kibbutz children consequently showed the highest incidence of mental problems. The kibbutzim have had to backtrack and now give their children a more normal and strengthening family-life experience with their parents. {13}

When women are persuaded to regard work outside of the family as more important than caring for the young or the family's members, they are in effect handing over the family's key role to outsiders such as day-care businesses and television programme makers. With disastrous results on the way the young perceive home life and adult behaviour, tending to condition the young into behaving like fictional and unreal role models, for example concerning sexual behaviour. Instead of gaining an adult understanding of the reality of living, of family values and relationships, instead of understanding and experiencing socially-responsible behaviour caring for and living with other people, instead of seeing adults (parents) behave in socially responsible way struggling in a hostile environment to do the best they can for the young and for each other.

The number of young people who run away from home and family, often becoming homeless, placing themselves at a big disadvantage right at the beginning of their lives, speaks for itself.

The family needs food and shelter and while the female looks after its young and its people, it is usually the male who struggles outside the immediate family to provide it with an income, with a standard of living, to the best of his ability {4, 5}. He is assisted in this when required by his spouse to an extent which depends on her own work within the family. He struggles outside the family to provide it with a good life against those who wish to profit from the family's needs, against those who wish to exploit, who may even wish to oppress so as to exploit.

Sexual Relations

Sex and the Individual

Sex is habit-forming and addictive but can be controlled when the will is there, when the individual is motivated to control it.

Young people are persuaded to have sex for the first time, are seduced, by those who crave for sex regardless of the cost to the young person being misused by being seduced. The cost to the young can be great. The earlier the age of seduction, the more ingrained is the habit, the greater the difficulties of later controlling it.

Having sex for the first time, first intercourse between adults, is a deeply emotional experience which binds people together in a strong bond of care and affection for each other. That is why 'men wish to sleep around but wish to marry virgins', or a succession of virgins if they are rich enough to afford the divorces.

Should the lovers separate, the emotional cost for the seduced is high indeed. Desperate feelings of isolation, loneliness, betrayal. Shock. Almost unbearable. Reluctance to commit oneself again.

With the next relationship there is still commitment, care and affection but more reserved, there is reluctance to commit oneself completely, to commit one's emotions completely, so as to avoid the pain of separation if this should occur again.

After repeated separations, there is little or no emotional commitment or care for the other person. Sex is casual, the individual sleeps around, attempting to gain the pleasure sex can bring. Looking for sex regardless of thought or feelings or care for the other person, regardless of the cost to the other person.

It appears to be well known that those who engage in sexual relations outside marriage find themselves looking in vain for the affection which is missing to an ever-greater extent from their relationships, become less and less able to commit themselves to the other person, mean ever less to each other.

So people who are aware of the likely consequences tend consciously to refrain from promiscuous relationships. When unaware of the consequences, people tend intuitively to put on the brake when tempted to behave promiscuously.

Effect on Behaviour and Community

Some men are persuaded into sleeping around, in turn attempting to persuade women to make themselves available for casual sex. When women were persuaded to make themselves sexually available they relaxed the control which had kept in check the primitive instinctive urge to copulate. Women had protected society by their chastity, had by their chastity compelled men to support and look after the mother (his wife) and their children while support was needed while the young were developing into adults, had protected and maintained the family and the community in this way.

Casual sex weakens and deadens feelings of care and affection for the other person, for partner or spouse, changing feelings of care and affection into a desire to use others for selfish pleasure regardless of the cost to the other person. So people who sleep around, who are addicted to casual sex, use other people to obtain sex, do so without concern or affection for their partners. They may then begin to behave in ways which harm other people, and may begin to pursue their own selfish interests. Apathy and neglect towards others can result.

Society corrupts itself when human care, affection and concern for one's own family, and for other people, is weakened, is bypassed by self-interest at expense of others.

There is increasing wanton antisocial behaviour such as vandalism and mugging. There is a loss of internal security, by loss of property and by attack against the person. The quality of life is lowered even further by those who pursue personal gain regardless of its cost to other people.

All this was clear in the seventies:

> In all countries where sex education has been introduced the same corruptive pattern of social change has been observed {3}: sexual experimentation starts and promiscuity increases. Promiscuity leads to increasing sexual dissatisfaction, to the weakening of family life and marriage bonds and to sexual excesses. The substitute satisfactions of smoking, drinking, and drug-taking increase and there is a lowering of the age of those involved. There is an upsurge in wanton destructive aggression in the community and a rise in aggressive juvenile delinquency. There is increasing concern over the harm done on young children by the practices and by the lack of concern and commitment of their parents, and concern has already been expressed over increasing male impotence. These effects are now obvious to any intelligent reader of the informed press.

> ... Increasing divorce rates, the resultant delinquency of children, the casual and inhuman ways some parents treat each other and their children, are almost the direct outcome of pre-marital and adulterous, that is promiscuous, sexual relations.

Destructive aggression, viciousness and brutality of people towards each other, disregard of the value of the individual and of life itself, are not normal behaviour. People who behave in such ways become isolated and divided against each other.

Women and men may then use sex as a way of getting what they want from their partner, as a way of dominating the partner. While unlikely to be stated in such simple terms between them, their actions convey the message 'do what I want and you can have sex as a reward. Obstruct me or refuse to do what I want and I will not have sex with you' which is a kind of punishment. We see assertiveness and conflict instead of affection and co-operation.

Partnerships and marriages break up when difficulties arise. People leave without regard or concern for the interests of the other members, of partner, spouse or children. They leave when they would be better off alone, when there is illness, when their present partner becomes unemployed, when a younger or wealthier 'partner' becomes available.

People who behave promiscuously (permissively) have sexual relations before marriage, or after marriage with a person other than their spouse. Promiscuity turns men against women, and women against men, and robs both of the support of their family.

> Let me put it to you in another way {2}. It is only a few years ago that you went out for the evening without bothering to lock the door. Nowadays you make sure you fasten the windows as well and in some areas keep a light on and the radio going. Just think of what has been happening to crime, delinquency, drug addiction, the younger age of those involved and the increasingly brutal way people treat each other, leaving aside dishonest business dealings. Look at the increasing number of divorces and thus of one-parent families, look at the even larger number of children being brought up in this way. ... it is happening in other democratic countries. And it is nothing new. It has happened again and again. Whenever democracy raised its head, the same knife was used to chop it off.

> History shows that free societies which allow themselves to become 'permissive' (promiscuous) weaken themselves to the point where their civilisation destroys itself, or is destroyed by outsiders. Those who wish to weaken democracy condone or encourage 'permissiveness'. On the other hand, those who restrict sex to within marriage gain creativity and increase their strength.

Sexual Restraint and Control

It is control of the sexual urge which distinguishes human beings from animals. Promiscuous unrestrained sexual behaviour indicates cold inhuman, often harsh, behaviour towards others, is characteristic of the cold unemotional behaviour of those who exploit others. Sexual self-control and restraint indicates human caring behaviour.

As permissiveness has increased so we have seen increasing the number of people using others for their own gratification and pleasure without care or concern for them, and also the number of parents behaving brutally towards each other and their children. A process driven by those who want sexual gratification, knowingly or unknowingly without regard to the costs their 'partners' have to pay.

Basic is that people behave in a way which enables them to trust and assist each other, that men and women co-operate with each other in a way which will protect and strengthen both, behaving in a way which ensures that all benefit from gains made.

So within a family, between husband and wife, it is the other person who comes first. When each spouse tries to make the other spouse happy, when each will go without something so as to make the other happy, then both can be happy.

Consider Jewish family law and traditions. When the wife has her period she is considered to be emotionally fragile. So the husband refrains from having sex from a few days before her period starts until a few days after it stops. He refrains out of care, consideration and affection for her, for his wife. She is different, has different needs, his self-denial for her sake continually renews the bonds of affection between them. As does their mutual practice of supporting each other, of putting the other person first when it comes to satisfying each other's needs. Whether or not you agree with the reasoning, sexual control is practised regularly for the sake of the other person and this strengthens the individual and cements the marriage.

Sexual restraint is an exercise in self-control, in controlling and so modifying what in the reptilian-animal part of our brain is a primitive and powerful urge aimed at the survival of the species. Sexual restraint changes it from an animal's instinctive behaviour into human behaviour based on concern and affection for the welfare of others. Not easy to do but it can be done as bereaved spouses or discarded partners can testify. Addiction to casual sex, to sleeping around, to promiscuity, is difficult to control but it can be done and the gains to the person doing so are enormous.

The United States government in 1997 set aside USD 250 million to teach children sexual abstinence, "teaching the social, psychological, and health gains to be realised by abstaining from sexual activity", teaching "abstinence from sexual activity outside marriage as the expected standard for all school-age children". {10}

Restraining and controlling sexual urges by restricting sex to within marriage gives strength to the family, to the individual and to the community, and underlies success in the struggle for a higher standard of living and higher quality of life for each and all.

Dominance

Dominance Within the Family

Within the family we should see co-operation and teamwork between equals who divide up the work which has to be done between them in a functional way so that each becomes expert and effective in his or her part of what has to be done.

But on the whole a family's income is usually earned by the male and income and money pass through his hands to the family. He then may, if he so wishes, use this controlling position to dominate the female. This applies equally well to the female who is a breadwinner, who may then use her controlling position to dominate. And applies also when the income of one is much larger than that of the other.

And both are in the position to use sex as a means of dominating the other, if they so wish. Rewarding compliance with sex, punishing disagreement by withholding sex.

Women have at times been persuaded by traditions or beliefs into accepting domination and sometimes exploitation as the norm. And women have in the past been denied education and full equality with men within the family and in the community in which they live.

The words 'assertiveness' and 'asserting' are used at times to indicate that one person is attempting to dominate the other. Dominating and 'asserting' put one person's personal gain, likes, dislikes against the other person's interests, introduces conflict and competition into what should be co-operation and teamwork.

Considering only women and children, the family protects women and children while children grow to maturity, till children become independent adults. It also protects women from disadvantages resulting from caring for and looking after the family during this period.

What keeps the family in place and gives it strength is restricting sex to within marriage. Men are then motivated to marry, to provide and care for wife and children, and themselves gain much strength from doing so.

When women are persuaded to make themselves available for sex outside marriage they help to dismantle not only their own protection and security but also that of their children.

In such circumstances the selfish instinctive behaviour of the non-feeling primitive animal is asserting itself, is attempting to dominate, overcome and control human feeling of care, affection, concern for members of one's own family and for other people in human societies.

Living in a Hostile Environment

We have seen that when one member of a family dominates others, that competition, conflict and struggle replace co-operation and teamwork. All the family's members suffer as a result.

We know that dominating does not work in normal circumstances. Authoritarian organisations are much less effective than participative ones. In authoritarian organisations morale is low, people cease to care and tend to work against each other instead of co-operating with each other for the benefit of the organisation. Which applies equally well to a family. {7, 8}

In the working environment women are just as oppressed and exploited as men are. When women receive lower wages for work of equal value then this is bad for men and women alike. When some people in a group are being underpaid, the pay of the others is being pushed down.

Outside the family a struggle is taking place. The breadwinner is competing for work and income on behalf of the family. He is also struggling against those who wish to exploit him (and thus his family) and who oppress so as to exploit.

So outside the family we see a widespread struggle against those who wish to dominate other people. Against those who want primitive power over others, against those who wish to exploit, against those who may brutally and without feeling oppress human beings so as to exploit them. And 'to exploit' includes the whole range of antisocial decisions and activities of those who put profit before people and community. {6}

We also saw that on the whole it is men who earn the family's income which then often passes through their hands to the family. And that as a result of the work men do outside the family, it is largely men who gain controlling positions in the working environment.

So on the surface it may seem as if it is men who try to dominate women within the family, that it is men who oppress and exploit women in the working environment.

Anyone who sees men and women co-operating with each other within a family, struggling side by side, back to back, and sees them co-operating with each other and helping each other in the outside working environment, for a more secure and better life for their families, knows how strong and effective they are together.

Blaming men as such, within the family and outside it, when women are oppressed and exploited, amounts to putting women against men, to separating them from each other. A 'divide so as to conquer' process which weakens both in their joint struggle for a better life. It robs men of the support of their families when they are struggling outside the family against being exploited, it robs women of the support of their families while bringing up children to adulthood, when improving their skills or knowledge when returning to work or to improve the quality of their lives.

Dominance and oppression take place within and outside the family, against men and women alike. Both men and women are exploited and oppressed in the working environment to a very considerable degree.

What we see in the working environment is a world-wide struggle to achieve a humane way of life, each person, family or community struggling to advance at their own level of development, struggling against those who wish to dominate, exploit, oppress. A struggle whose successful outcome depends on trustful co-operation, companionship and teamwork. {4, 5}

Sometimes one has to fight to preserve a good way of life, to prevent others from taking what has been achieved, or one is expected to fight on behalf of those who dominate and exploit.

The fighting is usually done by men who are conditioned to fight, maim and kill. Their training weakens and bypasses humane emotions of care, concern and affection for other people, in effect tends to brutalise them.

And we now see in some countries women joining the armed forces, police and security organisations and being trained in somewhat similar ways.

Our primitive animal ancestors behaved instinctively. Hunt for food, kill or be killed, fight or flee, copulate, care for own young for a very short and limited period. Self before others, regardless of needs of others, marking out and defending territory. Later mammals tend to have feelings, care and affection for their young. Human beings think as well as feel, and care for and look after their young for many years.

So conditioning to fight, maim and kill amounts to a throwback to primitive animal behaviour, to behaviour which puts self before others. A throwback to beast-like behaviour for those who attack, to beast-like behaviour to counter beast-like behaviour for those who defend.

But only some people behave in such corrupted ways. There are those many who put people first, who know the difference between human and inhuman behaviour, who believe in participative behaviour and in democratic government.

We saw that casual sex dehumanises, that it blocks affection and increases cold and selfish behaviour against others, that society corrupts itself when promiscuity (casual sex) spreads.

Promiscuity attacks human beings in their struggle for a better life as it:

1. Conditions people into primitive selfish uncaring behaviour which uses other people for personal gain (pleasure), creating a non-caring society, putting people against each other, at times brutalising them.

2. Weakens the family and all its members and so adversely affects the young and the way people treat each other. It weakens all the family's members by robbing them of emotional and economic support, and so makes it easier to exploit them through their needs.

Those who behave promiscuously pay a heavy price, namely lose the ability to form a satisfying emotionally deeply binding lasting and shared relationship with one other person. They also lose the emotional strength and economic backup such a shared relationship brings.

The media seem to be concentrating on portraying superstition, violence and casual-sex behaviour as acceptable, so strengthening primitive uncaring and antisocial behaviour towards others. And images penetrate deeply into the human mind.

Sexually explicit and pornographic material would seem to be taking this process even further.

So media are at present persuading and conditioning people into thinking that antisocial behaviour will not have unpleasant consequences. However, the cost to the community of the kind of negative and antisocial behaviour outlined in the sections above, of the lowering of the quality of life, is enormous. {6}

What we see is an almost intentional-seeming conditioning towards antisocial behaviour which breaks up families and so weakens individuals, and which divides people against each other and so weakens them even further.

It looks as if men are being conditioned into opting out of their responsibilities for family, wife and children. Women, on the other hand, are apparently being conditioned into giving away the real support and security they and their children could expect from husband and family, for no real gain.

To answer the question: "Who encourages antisocial behaviour?" we need to ask: "Who benefits from antisocial behaviour?" {6}

So who profits from promiscuity? At first glance it would seem that manufacturers of contraceptives and contraceptive devices have a vested interest as have organisations or associations whose income is derived from selling contraceptives and contraceptive devices. And possibly those whose income depends on advising on the use and application of contraceptives, depending on the extent to which their income depends on this.

And it is those who wish to weaken democracy and freedom who could be expected to condone and thus permit and encourage promiscuous behaviour as promiscuous behaviour separates people and turns them against each other, as it turns men against women and women against men. Indeed, they will condone and encourage any movement which turns men and women against each other so as to rob both of the strength to resist oppression and exploitation, to rob both of the strength which comes from men and women co-operating with each other.

Human rights are based on controlling primitive dominant behaviour, on concern, care and affection for our young, our families, for people, for our communities, and express themselves in co-operation and teamwork between men and women to achieve a good life of high quality.

Men and women are struggling together to achieve a better life, a humane way of living and government, and social security.

And there are ways of teaching social responsibility, of teaching the young how to take responsibility for others, how to care for, work with and look after other people. Social responsibility, the caring, giving and sharing with others, the taking on of responsibility for others including conflict management, can be and is being taught. {14}

It is in democracies that high standards of living have been achieved. In democracies people can struggle openly for a better life but we see that what has been gained has to be defended and extended.

Family's Role and Life in the Real World

The Family

The family is the basic unit of society. Its strength depends on the ability of the partners to commit themselves to each other, that is its strength depends on those who restrict sexual relations to within marriage. Men and women who do so practice a form of self-control which enables them to form a deep and lasting relationship, which in turn lays the basis for happy and contented family life for themselves and their children. The relationship between them is based on mutual trust and respect arising from the sure knowledge that they are in a vital exclusive relationship to each other, that they are working and co-operating with each other for the common good of themselves and their children.

Human beings work primarily for their family and members of a family stand by, support and help each other in times of need.

Smash the family and you undermine the strength of the people. I understand the resulting disruption was so marked in Russia that they had to back-pedal. One of the first things the Khmer Rouge did in Cambodia was to smash the family to make the people dependent on the state.

It is tough when you have to go to work to earn the money, do the shopping, look after the kids and do everything yourself. The one thing you cannot afford to be is to be ill. And you have no time for the kids either. And in a one-parent family, what the children miss is the parent's caring co-operative behaviour, is the example of responsible people looking after each other. The boy being brought up by the mother knows that both of them were left to look after themselves by the father and that is not a good example to model himself on. If you are struggling on your own so as to survive you don't have time or energy to think of freedom or to work for the community or for the betterment of humankind. {2}

Each member of the family gets strength from the others. Two heads are better than one, and work divided between two people in such a way that each can become expert in his or her own area is done much better than one person trying to do it all. The family gives people enormous emotional and economic strength to overcome life's problems. Husband and wife battle on together back-to-back and they do so successfully regardless of how tough the struggle may be. You cannot win all the battles but what cements the relationship is not just battles won but battles fought together. The depth of such a relationship between husband and wife and the wealth of strength it gives regardless of the opposition, this you know as well as I do. The children follow the example of their parents, gain the same strength and pass it on. It all depends on deep and secure emotional involvement between two people, between husband and wife. {2}

Those who understand its effects know that when sex is restrained and controlled, it performs the enormously important function of creating a special single deep emotional relationship between two people which gives them the strength to overcome life's problems, to form a strong family unit which serves and protects all its members. To be strong the relationship has to be unique and secure. It depends on the ability of the partners to commit themselves to each other. The depth of such a relationship between husband and wife can be appreciated as one sees them both battling on together successfully regardless of how tough the struggle may be.

Increasing Lifespans

Tabulating the figures already mentioned and extending the time period to the end of life, key events [1] look something like this:

Length of Period (Years)	Age (Years of Age)	Period	Event
4 - 5		Infant	
8 - 10		Child	
6 - 9		Adolescent	
	18 - 21		Becoming an adult member of family and community.
	25		Adult and independent member of family and community.
	18 - 24		Single
	20 - 26		Marriage (Children born over period of 6 years)
	41 - 47		Children become adults
	75 - 80		Death

Simplifying this a little, we have:

Age (Years of age)	Event or Period
0 - 21	Childhood and adolescence
21 - 23	Adult and single
23	Marriage
23 - 33	Children's childhood
33 - 44	Children's adolescence
44	Children now adult and largely independent
78	Life ends

123

Only about 100 years ago in the developed countries a person's lifespan was about 45 years, just long enough to bring up the next generation and help them to find their feet in the community. We now live another 35 years or so which enables us to do much more with our lives after our children have become independent. And our lives now look something like this:

Age **Event or Period**
(Years of
age)

Working outside the family (largely men)
21 - 65 At work
65 - 78 Receiving pension, freed from
         having to work

Within family (largely women)
21 - 23 At work
   23   Marriage
23 - 33 Bringing up the children during
         their childhood
33 - 44 Looking after children during
         their adolescence
44 - 65 At home or at work, as needed or
         as the individual wishes
65 - 78 Receiving pension, free from
         having to work

We saw earlier that the needs of children to be provided with caring and affectionate family life is of overriding importance <2>.

But outstanding is that those looking after people within the family, now have about 20 years of active life which can be spent as they wish, either working outside the family in paid employment, as independent professionals, or serving the community in other ways.

It is not easy to return to paid work as a professional after years of absence looking after one's family. After such a time lapse much has been forgotten and knowledge, equipment and techniques will have changed. And what is missing on returning to professional work is the years of experience which would have been gained had one stayed at work. It is then more than likely that positions of greater responsibility, and promotion to higher levels, will not be gained by those who return to work after such a long absence.

So on returning to work, women are at a disadvantage because of the time spent bringing up the children, and this disadvantage is likely to lower the level at which they can find work or work for the rest of their active life.

The family compensates women for this life-long contribution towards the upbringing of the children. It is the role of the spouse, of the husband, to continue to provide for the family. A life-long contribution from him which means she does not lose out for the rest of her life because she stayed at home to look after the children, the husband's input into the family balancing her input of bringing up the children and looking after the family's members.

As the children grow older, say 14 years old, women can usually spend increasing amounts of time updating or learning and developing skills and abilities for their future or continuing work after the children have grown up. Which is not easy to do and needs the support of her spouse.

Women, after children have grown up and backed by the family, can choose work outside the family to fulfil themselves as pay is less important for a second income.

Much professional work can now be home based. Home working may be less rewarding but is more convenient. Much can be gained by husband supporting his wife as far as he is able.

Looking at life from point of view of one's career, that is from the point of view of those who believe in profiting by compelling people through need to work for less than a fair share of the added value they produce, amounts to sacrificing the interests of one's family, and thus of oneself. The employer profits at the expense of the social and human welfare of the family's members.

What we see outside the family is a pattern of differentials which rewards service to the owners and their establishment rather than ability or service to the community. The nurse, the fire-fighter, the police officer and the teacher are at present paid comparatively little for the work they do. {1}

The community's basic needs are often not met by an uncaring social environment and the community's well-being depends on people, generally women, who use whatever time they have available, for caring for people both within and outside of family life. An employer's profit-orientated work can be well paid, community service-orientated work is not. And it is largely women who, caring for the welfare of the community, are generally the prime movers in self-help, support, protest and pressure groups, pushing forward also with other social and welfare issues.

Such work and public demonstrations and protests on such issues, are now an essential survival mechanism under beginning-of-twentyfirst-century conditions. {6}

Women's work in family and society determines individual emotional strength and well-being, the quality of life and the welfare of people as a community, and needs to be recognised and acknowledged.

Teamwork Within the Family

Teamwork implies sharing work and responsibilities in a way which ensures that all that has to be done is done well.

Success is measured by social and mental well-being as well as by standard of living and quality of life, of the family as a whole and of each member.

Key feature of the whole system is that both spouses work for the benefit of their family, of its individual members, and beyond that for the larger community of which the family is a part.

All are equal as people. What has to be done is shared out between them according to individual skill, ability, knowledge and experience. And in the end all share equally in the family's gains and losses. In other words, all are equal, contribute to the best of their ability, and stand or fall together.

The relationship between the two spouses is a functional relationship {9} and functional relationships are often misunderstood and misrepresented.

The spouses share out between themselves what needs to be done, each specialising, concentrating on, areas of work in accordance with their abilities, knowledge, understanding, likes and dislikes of each.

Equal as people, each takes the decisions falling within their own area of competence and responsibility. The husband may decide which car is to be bought or about getting a new job, the wife about which school the children should go to or where the family should live. But each discusses matters with the other family members before deciding from the point of view of what is best for the family as a whole.

They do not waste their time competing with each other but add their knowledge and experience to the decision-taking process of the other. In general, the person who decides would be the one most competent to take such decisions.

Such a functional division of work and responsibilities, of co-operation and teamwork between experts, enables us to survive and do well in the dangerous environment in which we find ourselves.

Consider shopping for food. The shopping expert takes into account the likes and dislikes of the other members of the family. And the expertise involved in shopping can be appreciated by considering what has to be thought about while shopping. How fresh is the food, how long will it have to be stored at home, how much does it cost here compared with elsewhere, has it been genetically modified and what does this mean for us. And what about nitrates in water, heavy metals, herbicides, pesticides, irradiated foods, chemical additives, more expensive organic foods, fat and sugar contents and other health risks.

It would be a waste of time for each to become expert in this field. It would be useless for each of the two people to do so and to argue continually about what is to be done. They would in this way be competing with each other by attempting to show that one is better than the other.

Conclusions

This report deals with the root causes of the major social problems. It shows how to resolve the problems by dealing with their basic causes.

Family and Children

200 million years of evolution are behind us, from reptilian beast through mammalian animal to human being. Human beings are mammals and we are unique in that our children need protecting and bringing up in a humane, emotionally and mentally stimulating environment for between 18 and 25 years, to enable them to mature into socially responsible adults. Men and women co-operate with each other and look after each other and their children, within the family, to achieve this.

Hence human beings work primarily for their family and members of a family stand by, support and help each other in times of need. The family is the basic unit of society and it looks after the interests of all its members, as individuals as well as collectively. This gives great strength to each member of the family in the struggle for daily bread, security and happiness.

Men and Women

Co-operation between men and women, within the family and as equals, would seem to be essential when bringing up their children under modern conditions of rapid change at an accelerating rate of change.

It is women who generally look after the young and other family members as people. This is the key role within the family and it occupies women full-time for some years if it is to be done well, and for more years on an at least part-time basis.

But we live much longer and the time spent full-time at home looking after the family places women at a disadvantage when returning to work outside the family after the children have been brought up. So women need to be supported when returning to work.

The family compensates women for this life-long contribution towards the upbringing of the children. It is the role of the spouse, of the husband, to continue to provide for the family. A life-long contribution from him which means she does not lose out for the rest of her life because she stayed at home to look after the children, the husband's input into the family balancing her input of bringing up the children and looking after the family's members.

Women, after children have grown up and with the family's backing, can choose work outside the family to fulfil themselves as pay is less important for a second income.

It is largely women who, caring for the welfare of the community, are generally the prime movers in self-help, support, protest and pressure groups, pushing forward also with other social and welfare issues.

Such work and public demonstrations and protests on such issues, are now an essential survival mechanism under beginning-of-twentyfirst-century conditions.

The work women do in family and society determines individual emotional strength and well-being, the quality of life and the welfare of people as a community and needs to be recognised and acknowledged.

The report discusses in some detail what is required if husband and wife are to work together as an effective team within the family.

Casual Sex

Casual sex is addictive, weakens and deadens feelings of care and affection for the other person, for partner or spouse, changing feelings of care and affection into a desire to use others for selfish pleasure regardless of the cost to the other person.

So people who sleep around, who are addicted to casual sex, use other people to obtain sex, do so without concern or affection for their partners. Apathy and neglect towards others can result.

Society corrupts itself when human care, affection and concern for one's own family, and for other people, is weakened, is bypassed by self-interest at the expense of others.

Those who sleep around pay a heavy price, namely lose the ability to form a satisfying emotionally deeply binding lasting and shared relationship with one other person. They also lose the emotional strength and economic backup such a shared relationship brings. Promiscuity turns men against women, and women against men, and robs both of the support of their family.

In such ways promiscuity breaks up families, weakens the strength of individuals and thus of the community to resist exploitation and oppression. So it would seem to be those who wish to weaken democracy and freedom who condone and thus permit and encourage promiscuous behaviour.

What keeps the family in place and gives it strength is restricting sex to within marriage. Men are then motivated to marry, to provide and care for wife and children, and themselves gain much strength from doing so. When women are persuaded to make themselves available for sex outside marriage they help to dismantle not only their own protection and security but also that of their children.

A key characteristic which distinguishes human beings from animals is that we can control the sex urge. Sex is habit-forming and addictive but can be controlled when the will is there, when the individual is motivated to control it.

In the USA steps are being taken to halt and reverse the increasing corruption of their communities by teaching the young the gains to be achieved by abstaining from sexual activity outside marriage.

There are ways of teaching social responsibility, of teaching the young how to take responsibility for others, how to care for, work with and look after other people. Social responsibility, the caring, giving and sharing with others, the taking on of responsibility for others including conflict management, can be and is being taught.

Dominance, Oppression and Exploitation

When one member of a family dominates others, then competition, conflict and struggle replace co-operation and teamwork. Dominance weakens all the family's members, robbing them of emotional and economic support, and so makes it easier to exploit them through their needs. All the family's members suffer as a result.

In the working environment we see a world-wide struggle to achieve a humane way of life, each family, person or community struggling to advance at their own level of development, struggling against those who wish to dominate, exploit, oppress. A struggle whose successful outcome depends on trustful co-operation, companionship and teamwork.

We know that dominating does not work in normal circumstances. Authoritarian organisations are much less effective than participative ones. In authoritarian organisations morale is low, people cease to care and tend to work against each other instead of co-operating with each other for the benefit of the organisation. Which applies equally well to a family.

Promiscuous behaviour and casual sexual relationships separate people and turn them against each other, turn men against women and women against men. Promiscuous behaviour and casual sexual relationships break up families, isolate people and rob people of the strength to resist exploitation and oppression.

So it appears that it is those who wish to weaken democracy and freedom who could be expected to condone and thus permit and encourage promiscuous behaviour and casual relationships.

Strength to resist oppression and exploitation comes from men and women co-operating with each other and so men and women struggle together to achieve a better life, a humane way of living and of government, and social security.

Human rights are based on controlling primitive dominating behaviour, on concern, care and affection for our young and our families, for people and for our communities. Human rights express themselves in co-operation and teamwork between men and women to achieve a good life of high quality.

It is in democracies that a high standard of living has been achieved. In democracies people can struggle openly for a better life but we see that what has been gained has to be defended and extended.

Notes and References

Notes

<1> See section on 'How Human Beings Evolved'.

For more background, see section on 'Development of Brain Functions in Humans' in reference {11}.

<2> See section 'Protecting and Caring for the Next Generation'.

The kibbutzim in Israel brought up children communally, away from their parents, and had to backtrack when they became aware of the consequences {13}.

References

{ 1} In 'Messianic Struggle:
The Worldwide Struggle for a Good and
Secure Life for All, Here and Now'
Manfred Davidmann
ISBN 978-0-85192-059-7
see chapter 3: 'Work and Pay, Incomes
and Differentials: Employer, Employee and
Community'

{ 2} If You Want a Future, Read On ...
David Baram*
Social Organisation Limited

{ 3} Sex:
Louise W. Eickoff
Consultant Psychiatrist
Guardian, 1970 Sep 12

{ 4} In 'The Human Mind and How it Works:
Group Minds in Action:
How the Human Group Mind Shapes
the Quality of Our Life and Living'
Manfred Davidmann
ISBN 978-0-85192-055-9
see chapter 9: 'The Will to Work:
What People Struggle to Achieve'

{ 5}   In 'The Human Mind and How it Works:
       Group Minds in Action:
       How the Human Group Mind Shapes
       the Quality of Our Life and Living'
       Manfred Davidmann
       ISBN 978-0-85192-055-9
       see chapter 7: 'Motivation Summary'

{ 6}   In 'Messianic Struggle:
       The Worldwide Struggle for a Good and
       Secure Life for All, Here and Now'
       Manfred Davidmann
       ISBN 978-0-85192-059-7
       see chapter 2: 'Social Responsibility, Profits
       and Social Accountability'

{ 7}   In 'Management and Leadership:
       Local, National, Multinational (Global),
       Principles and Practice'
       Manfred Davidmann
       ISBN 978-0-85192-057-3
       see chapter 3: 'Role of Managers under
       Different Styles of Management'

{ 8}   In 'Management and Leadership:
       Local, National, Multinational (Global),
       Principles and Practice'
       Manfred Davidmann
       ISBN 978-0-85192-057-3
       see chapter 2: 'Style of Management and
       Leadership'

{ 9}   In 'Management and Leadership:
       Local, National, Multinational (Global),
       Principles and Practice'
       Manfred Davidmann
       ISBN 978-0-85192-057-3
       see chapter 6: 'Organising'

{10}   Abstinence conundrum
       Tamar Lewin
       Guardian, 13/05/97

{11} In 'The Human Mind and How it Works:
      Group Minds in Action:
      How the Human Group Mind Shapes
      the Quality of Our Life and Living'
      Manfred Davidmann
      ISBN 978-0-85192-055-9
      see chapter 2: 'How the Human Brain
      Developed and How the Human Mind Works'

{12} A Triune Concept of the Brain and Behaviour
      P D MacLean
      University of Toronto Press

{13} See chapter 4:
      'Kibbutzim'
      Manfred Davidmann

{14} To Give or Not To Give
      'Everyman' TV documentary
      Editor: Jane Drabble; Producer: Angela Kaye
      Broadcast on 5/1/92 by BBC 1
      Based on book 'The Altruistic Person' by
      Professor Sam Oliner

Additions by the Editor:

David Baram*: Manfred Davidmann is the author of this work.

Press Notice

'Family, Sex and the Individual; Women's Liberation, Feminism and Community'*: a Report by Manfred Davidmann.
(KGW NewsChannel 8)

This report examines root causes of what are now major social problems and shows how to resolve the problems by dealing with their basic causes.

Human beings work primarily for their family and members of a family stand by, support and help each other in times of need. The family is the basic unit of society and it looks after the interests of all its members, as individuals as well as collectively. This gives great strength to each member of the family in the struggle for daily bread, security and happiness.

And in the report "Family, Sex and the Individual", Manfred Davidmann exposes the causes of what seems to be progressive breaking down of family life and of social strength.

This report is an unprecedented and comprehensive overview, states new insights, proves basic underlying causes.

For example, in a comprehensive review, Manfred Davidmann defines the role of the family as being:

> To struggle as a family to survive.

> To protect and support mother and children until children become mature and independent adults capable of providing for themselves.

> To provide a good standard of living and a life of high quality. Which includes struggling against oppression and exploitation - and sometimes one has to fight to preserve a good way of life.

> To serve the interests of, and to support, each member of the family. In turn, each member of the family supports the family.

The report also investigates the impact of casual sexual relations and its effects on individuals, family and community, on the social strength of individuals and communities.

Further, the report examines and relates dominance and confrontation within the family to that in the working environment and considers oppression and exploitation within and outside the family.

Manfred Davidmann was the first to clearly describe and show, eight years ago, the effects of increasing life spans on the family, on its members and on their responsibilities. He also illustrated the underlying basis of teamwork within the family, stating the various roles and responsibilities and functional relationships of its members for effective teamwork within the family.

In this report are also sections about
Protecting and caring for the next generation;
Sexual relations;
Dominance within the family;
Living in a hostile environment;
Increasing life spans;
Teamwork within the family.

See chapter 3:
'Family, Community, Sex and the Individual'
Manfred Davidmann

Additions by the Editor:

* This title was used by Manfred Davidmann on his solhaam.org website. Later the author used the title 'Family, Community, Sex and the Individual' for this work.

Chapter 4

Kibbutzim

Introduction

Kibbutzim are successful co-operative communities now experiencing both practical and ideological problems. So the study looks at what is taking place to find reasons for success and causes of problems.

This study is one of a series of eight studies of co-operatives and mutual societies* which were undertaken to determine causes of failure and reasons for success, to see how these enterprises were controlled and managed, to learn from the mistakes of others. What is taking place is fascinating and often unexpected.

The main report 'Co-operatives: Causes of Failure, Guidelines for Success'* is based on these studies. Its conclusions and recommendations are entirely relevant and cover fundamental and practical problems of co-ops and mutual societies, of members, of direction, management and control.

Kibbutzim

The kibbutz is the best known of Israel's three types of co-operative farming settlements <7>. Its members live in a single community and share the work. The word kibbutz is the Hebrew name for such a community.

Kibbutzim <1> were mainly agricultural co-operative communities. Property such as land, buildings and equipment, factories and tools, is owned by the kibbutz, is owned jointly (collectively) by the community.

There is no private wealth and members transfer all their assets (but not personal belongings) to the community when joining. The kibbutz looks after all the needs of its members and their families and usually provides communal dining, laundry and other services and facilities for its members.

Families do have private accommodation and some personal property, and what is provided depends to a considerable extent on how rich the kibbutz is, on what they can afford.

'From each according to their ability, to each according to their need' is practiced. The kibbutz looks after its members from cradle to grave and this includes education and social security. Children are largely brought up by the community.

It was only through this kind of co-operative living that a deprived people could settle successfully in a hostile environment. Aided by the community at large, the settlements successfully struggled to establish themselves and prospered.

But there are few kibbutz members who do not know that the pioneering spirit, the drive and motivation to succeed, diminished and evaporated with success. Kibbutz members are aware of the need for rejuvenating the movement, its settlements, its ideological motivation and its drive.

Children were brought up communally in age groups, away from their parents. One age group would progress from creche to nursery to school and so on, living together during the week and seeing their parents, and perhaps living with them, only at weekends.

This may have freed both parents for work and defence in the initial struggle for survival. But the practice was continued when successful, possibly to free women for work and so increase production. But it was done at the expense of the family.

Of any group in the country, the kibbutz children consequently showed the highest incidence of mental problems. The kibbutzim have had to backtrack and now give their children a more normal and strengthening family-life experience with their parents.

Kibbutzim now own and operate factories, hotels and restaurants, and much else. Degania, for example, has a factory with an annual turnover of about USD 15 million which provides roughly 75 per cent of its income. {KIB 02}

And kibbutzim are successful. Three per cent of Israel's population, about 125,000 people, live in 270 kibbutzim ranging in size from say 200 to 2,000 members. They produce something like 50 per cent of Israel's agricultural produce and about 9 per cent of its industrial goods.

Organisation and Decision-taking

All are equal regardless of the work done and all share equally in the work to be done, the available services and the democratic management of the kibbutz.

Decisions are made jointly by the General Assembly of all kibbutz members. The General Assembly decides policy and allocates responsibilities (work) to individual members by electing managers and assigning work.

One member could, for example, be given responsibility for work scheduling and for allocating work to individual members. Such work in larger kibbutzim could also be handled by committees whose members are also elected by the General Assembly, the chairperson often doing this work full time.

Members occupy their role for a limited period, say one or two years, often full time in larger kibbutzim, and jobs (roles) are rotated.

The functions covered in such ways are the usual ones found in any enterprise or community and can vary from kibbutz to kibbutz. Finance, transport, health, short-term and long-term planning, social and cultural activities, communal dining, laundry, creche facilities, and so on.

Decision-taking by the General Assembly can involve heated argument, infighting between factions and marshalling of support. Suppose money is limited, a tractor has to be bought and only one child can be sent to study at university, both fees and maintenance being required. One child out of two and your child is one of the two. Such problems can prove very divisive within such a close community.

Success and Wealth

The success of the kibbutzim became a byword in Israel. Agriculture in Israel was more capital intensive than in the USA. While urban life was tough and insecure in a taxing climate, kibbutz members had a secure and high standard of living and a good quality of life.

Life on a prosperous kibbutz includes its cultural centre or concert hall, use of swimming pool and tennis courts, film shows, lectures and concerts. <2>

As an open-air swimming pool was replaced by an even bigger one, as a new concert hall was built, as factories were started and outside labour was employed, the rest of Israel saw them as living in a 'paradise on earth', as a 'community of millionaires'. And there are many struggling Israelis who see kibbutz wealth and life-style as the result of state handouts.

How come? And what does the future hold? So let us look in a little more detail at what actually happened.

The kibbutzim were backed and supported by world-wide Jewish communities. Much if not most of the money was channelled through the Jewish Agency (Sochnut) which financed, or else provided, water supplies, electric power, roads and capital for land (when required), housing, equipment, machinery, livestock.

Here are some simple figures {KIB 04}:

> Take agriculture. Take the year 1975. In that year alone farmers received USD 130 million <3> in unlinked loans, about 83 per cent of the total investment in agriculture. 'A good part of these loans were given by the Jewish Agency, for the traditional 50 years at 2 per cent, unlinked of course, and with a grace period <4> of 20 years'.

> At Israeli inflation rates of about 40 per cent each year all the loans mentioned are practically wiped out in seven years, never mind 50 years. The loans were, for all practical purposes, free gifts to agricultural settlements <5>.

Kibbutzim received unlinked fifty-year loans with repayment starting after ten or twenty years. At interest rates far below rate of inflation, the amounts being paid back to the Sochnut were negligible compared with the loans received, in effect a free gift.

The success and wealth of kibbutzim resulted from large capital sums provided without strings by world-wide Jewish communities at considerable hardship to the communities.

No wonder the riches and success of the kibbutzim and of kibbutznicks (kibbutz members) became a byword in Israel. Living a good life in paradise on earth, that is how the rest of Israel saw them.

Agriculture, Manufacturing, Services

The underlying kibbutz ideology of shared work and shared success, of community-orientated living and social responsibility, was weakened by material success. So now socialist kibbutzim permanently employ labour from outside the kibbutz.

Year by year volunteers flocked to the kibbutzim to share in the struggle for a better and more secure life for the kibbutz and so for its members and for the community at large. Freely contributing their labour while sharing to some extent in the life of the kibbutz. But volunteers to a considerable extent ceased to be motivated by ideology. And to a considerable extent are now regarded as cheap labour by the kibbutz.

Kibbutz members had struggled hard and well and were now enjoying the fruits of their labours. Economic success, social security and wealth came in, co-operative principles went out.

Working for their own benefit, they became profit-taking owners and employers. Kfar Blum and Kfar Hanasi, for example, employ workers from outside in their factories. None of the manual workers in Kfar Hanasi's foundry is a member of the kibbutz. {KIB 01, 03}

Kibbutzim have become employers of labour. Co-operative ideology has been replaced by self-interest. To this extent is their higher standard of living and quality of life the result of profiting from the work of others.

And this outlook has began to affect life within the kibbutz.

Differential Pay – Differential Spending

Within the kibbutz all are equal, all share to the same extent. Some are more able than others, some do more than others, but all are paid the same. Earnings are pooled and divided equally. But in at least one instance are differential allowances being introduced: members are to be paid according to the market value of their work {KIB 02}.

What is the value of one person's work when compared with another? How do you assess the value to the kibbutz, to the community, of the work of a nurse, teacher, manual worker, musician or manager? Market value is a rate of pay which outside the kibbutz rewards service to directors and chief executives and not service to the community. {KIB 05}

Introducing differential pay is often the prelude to managers, directors or professionals demanding higher differentials and pay for themselves.

Demanding the higher pay which can be earned outside as a result of maximising profits regardless of its cost to the community {KIB 06-08}.

In some cases, kibbutz members and families are being enabled to do more for themselves, to have greater choice.

Ein Zivan shut its communal dining room and slashed collective expenditure, leaving more choices to individuals. {KIB 02}

Kfar Hanasi in 1995 intended to convert its large dining room into what will in effect be a restaurant. Kibbutz members will then have the choice of community dining, eating out or cooking at home. Family budgets are to be increased accordingly. {KIB 03}

The risk is that such changes can lead to greater inequality, particularly if combined with income differentials within the kibbutz. Such changes could reverse the very ideals on which community life is built by creating poor and rich kibbutz members.

It is those who expect to gain financially at the expense of others who are likely to advocate internal income differentials.

Management Takeover Attempts

Afikim, with 1,400 residents the second-largest kibbutz in Israel, has factories which are 'run on purely capitalistic lines by boards of directors, mostly outside experts appointed for their business or technical acumen.' {KIB 02}

Its industrial enterprises have been separated from the kibbutz community. Policy setting and management have been distanced from kibbutz members and it would appear that to this extent managers and directors have begun to take over control from kibbutz members.

Kibbutz members are at risk of losing control over their destiny as community-orientated decision-taking moves towards profit-maximising. And so one would like to know more about their policy setting processes, about how they hire and fire directors and managers, about how the pay of directors and managers compares with kibbutz members.

But Kfar Hanasi are now treating individual kibbutz operations as profit centres, looking at their profitability and costing labour. 'Contribution to profits' seems to be replacing 'service to community', motivation and commitment.

Borrowing had been cheap at the time kibbutzim were lent (received) donated funds from Jewish communities at next to zero interest rates compared with inflation. The prosperity of the kibbutzim had developed from the donated funds they had been lent (given) in the past. <8>

So when about ten years ago inflation in Israel reached over 200 per cent and exceeded interest rates then being charged, borrowing again seemed cheap. And kibbutzim took out large loans from banks.

But the banks were not giving money away as had the Jewish communities. Inflation dropped to 50 per cent and then to 20 per cent while interest rates stayed high at 60 per cent and then 40 per cent.

As a result many kibbutzim now have to repay what they borrowed, have to repay large debts and pay high interest charges to the banks.

In a deal completed with the government, the banks agreed to write off a quarter of the debts. The kibbutzim have to repay debts totalling something like GBP 1.5 billion. A condition is that 'kibbutzim will have to cut back on many of their non-profitable operations'. {KIB 01}

So it seems that these kibbutzim are expected to maximise profits (for the benefit of money lenders) at the expense of what may be more worth-while community-orientated activities.

Disillusion and Apathy

For some time now many able and disillusioned young have been leaving kibbutz life for more rewarding and satisfying life outside.

Kibbutzim are attempting to counter this trend by letting younger members study for professional and academic qualifications, largely of their choice. In turn the member is expected to commit himself to life on the kibbutz.

Members work to an increasing extent outside the kibbutz and their salary goes directly to the kibbutz. {KIB 03}

The system of allocating work by handing out jobs, by rotating them, is fair from the point of view of some work being more pleasant or satisfying than other kinds of work, from the point of view of members' abilities and skills, likes and dislikes. Decisions about work are made by and close to the people doing the work.

On the other hand, imposing decisions about work when these are made remotely in a managerial hierarchy, usually demotivates. In a natural reaction to the style of management, workers cease to care, lack commitment and dedicated effort. {KIB 09-12}

And now look again at what has been reported about Kfar Hanasi {KIB 03}:

1. None of the manual workers in Kfar Hanasi's foundry is a member of the kibbutz.

   Kfar Hanasi are now treating individual kibbutz operations as profit centres, looking at their profitability and costing labour.

   Differential salaries are being discussed and kibbutz members are to have the choice of community dining, eating out or cooking at home.

   Kfar Hanasi's Member Assembly has been replaced by closed circuit television apparently because it has been 'so poorly attended in recent years'.

2. Motivation is lacking, people do not seem to care any more. The young tend to leave the kibbutz, and there is a fear of people leaving.

What seems to be happening in this kibbutz is that 'contribution to profits' is coming in, pay differentials are coming in, decision-taking by members is going out, 'service to community', motivation and commitment are going out, younger members are leaving.

Conclusions

The success and wealth of kibbutzim resulted from large capital sums provided without strings by world-wide Jewish communities at considerable hardship to the communities.

But most Israelis outside the kibbutz movement were then struggling under tough conditions to make ends meet and gain a reasonable standard of living.

Although kibbutzim had the ability to give and share with others who were in need, to pass on the benefits of what they had been given, to spread the application of co-operative principles, they signally failed to do so.

Some kibbutzim have become capitalist employers of labour. Co-operative principles have been replaced by self-interest. To the extent to which this is so is their higher standard of living and quality of life the result of profiting from the work of others.

And some of these kibbutzim have separated their industrial enterprises from the kibbutz community. Policy setting and management have been distanced from kibbutz members and it would appear that to this extent managers and directors are attempting to take over control from kibbutz members. Appointing of external managers is likely to make matters worse in the end.

Kibbutz members are at risk of losing control over their destiny when community-orientated decision-taking moves towards profit-maximising.

Borrowing had been cheap at the time kibbutzim were lent (received) donated funds from Jewish communities at next to zero interest rates compared with inflation. The prosperity of the kibbutzim had developed from the donated funds they had been lent (given) in the past. <8>

So when about ten years ago inflation in Israel reached over 200 per cent and exceeded interest rates then being charged, borrowing again seemed cheap. And kibbutzim took out large loans from banks.

But the banks were not giving money away as had the Jewish communities. Inflation dropped to 50 per cent and then to 20 per cent while interest rates stayed high at 60 per cent and then 40 per cent.

As a result many kibbutzim now have to repay what they borrowed, have to repay large debts and pay high interest charges to the banks.

Within the kibbutz all are equal, all share to the same extent. Some are more able than others, some do more than others, but all are paid the same. Earnings are pooled and divided equally.

But some kibbutzim are now considering introducing income differentials. Members could then be paid according to the profit-maximising market value of their work. Together with giving members greater spending choices, there is the risk that such changes can lead to greater inequality. Such changes could reverse the very ideals on which community life is built by creating poor and rich kibbutz members.

The system of allocating work by handing out jobs, by rotating them, is fair from the point of view of some work being more pleasant or satisfying than other kinds of work, from the point of view of members' abilities and skills, likes and dislikes. Decisions about work are made by and close to the people doing the work.

On the other hand, imposing decisions about work when these are made remotely in a managerial hierarchy, usually demotivates. In a natural reaction to the style of management, workers cease to care, lack commitment and dedicated effort.

For some time now many able and disillusioned young have been leaving kibbutz life for more rewarding and satisfying life outside.

Some kibbutzim are attempting to counter this trend by letting younger members study for professional and academic qualifications, largely of their choice. In turn the member is expected to commit himself to life on the kibbutz.

And members may work to an increasing extent outside the kibbutz, their salary being paid directly to the kibbutz.

Notes and References

Notes

<1> Kibbutzim: Plural of kibbutz, more than one kibbutz, all of them.

<2> Kfar Blum {KIB 01} 1990 and Degania {KIB 02} 1993

<3> Israeli currency (Lira) converted to USD at the then current average rate of exchange.

<4> 'Grace period' means that during this period one does not have to pay back the loan or pay interest.

<5> In all fairness, while here only looking at kibbutzim, the same process was applied to industry, tourist industry and the buying of apartments. Vast sums were handed out, year by year, in effect virtually as free gifts, to those who obtained such unlinked loans <6>. But only agricultural settlements obtained loans at the negligible interest rate of 2 per cent.

<6> From {KIB 04}: The Bank of Israel's annual report for 1975 showed that at the end of 1975 the balance of loans granted on concessionary terms to agriculture, industry, households and tourism came to approximately USD 1,900 million, with the interest rate averaging less than 9 per cent. The amount of free gift, of grant in just one year, in 1975, amounted to about USD 500 million. This will continue on the unpaid part of the increasing

balance as more and more money is distributed in this way, year by year.

<7>   There are three distinct types of co-operative agricultural settlements in Israel.

KIBBUTZ (Collective Community)	Mainly an agricultural co-operative community. Land, factories, buildings and equipment are owned jointly (collectively) by the community.
MOSHAV (Farming Village)	A more or less self-contained farming village. Each farm is held and farmed independently by the settler and his family.
MOSHAV SHITTUFI (Collective Settlement)	Combines the co-operative ownership and working of land and factories (as in a kibbutz) with maintaining the strength and independence of the family (as in a moshav).

<8>   See 'Success and Wealth'

References

{KIB 01}   Israel's Kibbutz Movement Faces Changes if it is to Repay its Debts
Keith Harper,
Guardian, 13/07/90

{KIB 02}   Kibbutzim Learn to Adapt and Survive
Ian Black,
Guardian, 13/02/93

{KIB 03}   Correspondent
BBC TV, 03/06/95

{KIB 04}   Who's afraid of inflation?
Meir Mershav,
Jerusalem Post, 24/3/77

{KIB 05} In 'Cooperatives and Cooperation:
Causes of Failure, Guidelines for Success'
Manfred Davidmann
ISBN 978-0-85192-056-6
see chapter 4: 'Work and Pay'

{KIB 06} In 'Messianic Struggle:
The Worldwide Struggle for a Good and
Secure Life for All, Here and Now'
Manfred Davidmann
ISBN 978-0-85192-059-7
see chapter 2: 'Social Responsibility,
Profits and Social Accountability'

{KIB 07} In 'The Real World in Which We Live:
The Social Rules and Social System under
Which We Suffer, Struggle, Survive and Prosper'
Manfred Davidmann
ISBN 978-0-85192-058-0
see chapter 7: 'Exporting and Importing of
Employment and Unemployment'

{KIB 08} In 'The Real World in Which We Live:
The Social Rules and Social System under
Which We Suffer, Struggle, Survive and Prosper'
Manfred Davidmann
ISBN 978-0-85192-058-0
see chapter 9: 'Creating, Patenting and
Marketing of New Forms of Life'

{KIB 09} In 'Management and Leadership:
Local, National, Multinational (Global),
Principles and Practice'
Manfred Davidmann
ISBN 978-0-85192-057-3
see chapter 2: 'Style of Management and
Leadership'

{KIB 10} In 'Management and Leadership:
Local, National, Multinational (Global),
Principles and Practice'
Manfred Davidmann
ISBN 978-0-85192-057-3
see chapter 3: 'Role of Managers under
Different Styles of Management'

{KIB 11}   In 'The Human Mind and How it Works:
Group Minds in Action:
How the Human Group Mind Shapes
the Quality of Our Life and Living'
Manfred Davidmann
ISBN 978-0-85192-055-9
see chapter 7: 'Motivation Summary'

{KIB 12}   In 'The Human Mind and How it Works:
Group Minds in Action:
How the Human Group Mind Shapes
the Quality of Our Life and Living'
Manfred Davidmann
ISBN 978-0-85192-055-9
see chapter 9: 'The Will to Work:
What People Struggle to Achieve'

Additions by the Editor:

* These works are published in:

'Cooperatives and Cooperation:
Causes of Failure, Guidelines for Success'
Manfred Davidmann
ISBN 978-0-85192-056-6

Chapter 5

Quotable Quotes about Judaism

Life and Living

The works of Manfred Davidmann amount to a consistent whole which binds current knowledge together into a wide overview of life and living, in unprecedented depth.

What One Aims to Achieve   (25/12/2007)

Manfred Davidmann, in 'The God-given Human Rights, Social Laws and Social System' {1}*, states that what one aims to achieve is

to apply in our lives, and in the communities in which we live, the God-given benevolent social laws and social system of the Pentateuch,

so as to achieve a good and secure life of high quality,

by working for the benefit of the community, and

by taking part in the struggle for a better life.

We need to behave like human beings, and treat each other like human beings, and the report 'The God-given Human Rights, Social Laws and Social System' {1}* by Manfred Davidmann is a comprehensive statement of the God-given human rights which underlie all freedom, liberty and independence ... and which ... underlie and determine a good life of high quality.

He there states the basis and the need for humane behaviour, which underlie
Trustful Co-operation (Ten Commandments),
Morality (Men and Women, Family and Family Purity)
and shows what the
Unavoidable Consequences of One's Behaviour
are, in relation to the
Social and Moral Problems of Our Times
and the consequent
Planet-wide Danger
If we fail to apply these rules of behaviour.

In his 'The God-given Human Rights, Social Laws and Social System' {1}*, we also see that

We need to co-operate with each other as individuals, families and communities, supporting each other in this common struggle for a better life,

that it appears that hurt and pain, oppression and exploitation, suffering and hardship, can and should be transformed and countered by an applied sense of social responsibility, by a sense of common purpose and cooperation between people working together in teams. That is by a sense of, and by the satisfaction of, achievement in locating, countering and overcoming the source of the suffering, and

that your life is likely to be a much more rewarding life of higher quality.

From Manfred Davidmann's 'Faith' (see chapter 8)**, we see that:

When people do not act for God and people, then God withdraws his protection from them. The consequences cannot be avoided.

But God helps, protects and rewards manifold those who act for God and people.

Stand up and be counted.

This is a matter of survival, of hard work, of strain and effort, to succeed in our endeavour. And to this end we work together, all of us, human beings, proud and erect, hand in hand, irrespective of our creed or religion, the colour of our skin, the shape of our eyes, or where we happen to live, for freedom and humanity.

We think the key need at this time is to make people aware of these truths, to carry the message to the people in the name of Manfred Davidmann, to inspire them.

See 'The God-given Human Rights,
Social Laws and Social System' {1}*

Purpose of website 'solhaam.org'

The purpose of website 'solhaam.org' is to spread the knowledge of Manfred Davidmann's works and teachings, and to help people study and apply them.

Technical and scientific knowledge and its application are advancing exponentially. Absent are corresponding advances in social knowledge and their application. Political, social, scientific and medical changes which are now taking place, or being worked on, threaten the survival of humane behaviour and hence of humanity.

We believe that the survival of humane behaviour and humanity depends on learning and following these teachings, on making these works available to others, on teaching them, the aim being to gain a high quality of life.

If you like to tell us where your interest lies, and which of the works you have read, we would gladly suggest further reading and how to proceed.***

And it would help if you could recommend the site, or individual works, to others.

Quoting Out of Context

So much has been written about Christianity and Judaism that it is fairly easy to select one sentence or two from one place, and a sentence or two from a completely different place, and more from another part unrelated to the others, and so on. These can then be added together or compared to arrive at conclusions which back the personal opinion of the individual doing the selecting.

What is valid within the meaning of one record is not necessarily valid within the meaning of another. And the above process of 'quoting out of context' has been and is used to arrive at conclusions totally different from the contexts from which they were selected.

151

(Note: 'Out of context', according to the Oxford Dictionary, means 'without the surrounding words and therefore giving a false impression of the meaning')

The conclusions can be beautiful, heart warming and uplifting, but they can also be negative or destructive, subtly attempting to weaken or bypass basic precepts of the faith.

This is why I said in 'Liberation Theology' {2}* that as long as the arguments and beliefs of liberation theologians are based on feelings and emotions no matter how good and right and proper, on biblical texts quoted out of context, then their beliefs can at some time in the future once again be negated and countered and turned into dead end or self destructive directions by abstract arguments and statements about feelings and emotions, by quoting out of context.

See 'LIBERATION THEOLOGY:
Basis - Past - Present - Future' {2}*

And see 'Origin of Christianity and Judaism:
What Actually Happened, What Jesus Actually
Taught and Later Changes' {3}*

Meaning and Use of Words   (12/05/2007, in German)

Vielen Dank fuer Deine Email. In Bezug auf unser Gespraech neulich koennte Dich der Report 'Using Words to Communicate Effectively' {4}* interessieren. In klarem, einfachem und leicht verstaendlichem Englisch wird der effektive und verstaendliche Gebrauch von Worten beschrieben, der allgemein gueltig ist (auch fuer Deutsche sowie Englische Artikel).

Bedeutend sind die wenigen Saetze unter "Value Judgements or Ideology" ueber "truth" (Wahrheit).

Sowie unter "Formal and Informal Communications" die Saetze ueber anonyme Gespraeche und Geruechte.

Ich selbst finde es hilfreich und nuetzlich, die Ratschlaege unter "Traps to Avoid" beim Lesen von Quellen anzuwenden.

See 'Using Words to Communicate Effectively' {4}*

Important is what a religion or a cult stands for in real concrete terms relating to every-day life here-and-now.

Important is what a religion or a cult stands for in real concrete terms relating to every-day life here-and-now, and not just what it proclaims to be against.

The problem is that both Judaism and Christianity have in the past been moved by their hierarchies away from following and applying the social laws and social system of the Pentateuch (Five Books of Moses).

So both Judaism and Christianity as practiced today consist largely of warm traditions and practices which are in effect hollow shells of ceremonial and ritual because the social intent and teachings of the Pentateuch are not followed. And there are followers in each religion which follow without questioning the dictates of the head of their religious hierarchy.

The word 'Messiah' can have many meanings and one needs to define in clear concrete terms what it means to the person using it.

What I have done in my works is to record the word of God as written in the Pentateuch, stating that the social laws and social system of the Pentateuch need to be followed if people are to have good lives of high quality, have individual strength, independence and freedom. It is this which needs to be achieved.

Feel free to write again, if you wish. If you let me know which of my reports you have read, I may be able to suggest further reading.***

And thank you for what you say about my works, and for your honest and open letter.

The Traditional Beliefs of Judaism

There are now a number of different branches of Judaism which resulted from the negative changes made many years ago to its core social teachings and from changes based on inadequate knowledge and understanding. These branches are competing with each other for influence and power within and over the Jewish communities, each claiming to be traditional or to be establishing a more modern tradition. Those claiming to be traditional, and the other branches, teach the negatively changed version which in effect bypasses the core social teachings.

But Jewish community life within any one branch tends to be close and supportive. Much has been written which is intuitively beautiful, learned and inspiring but without clear knowledge or understanding of the core social laws and intent of the faith.

My writings describe Judaism as it was and also as it is

> See 'Struggle for Freedom:
> The Social Cause-and-Effect Relationship' {5}*
>
> and see 'History Speaks: Monarchy, Exile
> and Maccabees' {6}*

and how its core social teachings were changed and how the changes were recorded.

> See 'At the Time of Jesus,
> This is What Actually Happened in Israel:
> The Truth about Hillel and his Times' {7}*
>
> and see 'One Law for All: Freedom Now,
> Freedom for Ever' {8}*

Other relevant reports are

> 'The Meaning of Genesis:
> Creation, Evolution and the Origin of Evil' {9}*

The relevance of the Pentateuch's (Torah's) teachings at present time are described in

> 'Causes of Antisemitism' {10}*
>
> and in 'The Right to the Land of Israel' {11}*

Antisemitism

Thank you for writing. Your comments are very welcome.

The same struggle between humane and inhumane behaviour, of 'government of, by and for the people' against dictatorship, between participative behaviour, leadership, management or government, against authoritarianism and authoritarian rule, is going on all around us at all levels in all organisations.

Judaism and Christianity teach on the whole that human beings and humane behaviour are more important than unquestioning obedience to brutal dictatorship or authoritarianism.

Another determining factor underlying antisemitism is that most Jews are unaware of the social laws and social system of the Pentateuch as these are not being taught or else are being misrepresented as being irrelevant to our lives.

These matters are shown to be so (proved, shown to be fact) in my reports and you may like to let me know which of these you have read so that I can suggest further reading.***

> See 'Causes of Antisemitism' {10}*

> As regards 'human nature', have a look at the section on abstractions in 'Using Words to Communicate Effectively' {4}*.

> And then see what shapes how people behave, shapes what they do, in 'How the Human Brain Developed and How the Human Mind Works' {12}*

Pentateuch (Torah), Talmud (Mishnah and Gemara) and Halacha

Have a look at these two reports:

> See 'At the Time of Jesus,
> This is What Actually Happened in Israel:
> The Truth about Hillel and his Times' {7}*

> and see 'One Law for All: Freedom Now,
> Freedom for Ever' {8}*

There you will see much about Torah (Pentateuch), Talmud (Mishnah and Gemara) and Halacha, about talmudic arguments and stories. These two reports can show you the inner relevance and significance of the Talmud and of its statements.

Sources

{ 1}*　See chapter 2.1:
'The God-given Human Rights, Social Laws and
Social System'
Manfred Davidmann

{ 2}*   'Liberation Theology: Basis – Past – Present – Future'
         Manfred Davidmann
         www.solhaam.org

{ 3}*   'Origin of Christianity and Judaism:
         What Actually Happened, What Jesus Actually
         Taught and Later Changes'
         Manfred Davidmann
         www.solhaam.org

{ 4}*   See chapter 6:
         'Using Words to Communicate Effectively'
         Manfred Davidmann

{ 5}*   In 'Judaism: Basis - Past - Present - Future, Part 1'
         Manfred Davidmann
         ISBN 978-0-85192-060-3
         see chapter 2.1: 'Struggle for Freedom:
         The Social Cause-and-Effect Relationship'

{ 6}*   In 'Judaism: Basis - Past - Present - Future, Part 1'
         Manfred Davidmann
         ISBN 978-0-85192-060-3
         see chapter 2.2: 'History Speaks: Monarchy,
         Exile and Maccabees'

{ 7}*   In 'Judaism: Basis - Past - Present - Future, Part 1'
         Manfred Davidmann
         ISBN 978-0-85192-060-3
         see chapter 2.3: 'At the Time of Jesus,
         This is was Actually Happened in Israel:
         The Truth about Hillel and his Time'

{ 8}*   In 'Judaism: Basis - Past - Present - Future, Part 1'
         Manfred Davidmann
         ISBN 978-0-85192-060-3
         see chapter 2.4: 'One Law for All:
         Freedom Now, Freedom for Ever'

{ 9}*   In 'God and People:
         The Social Laws and Social System Underlying
         Judaism, Christianity, Islam and Democracy'
         Manfred Davidmann
         ISBN 978-0-85192-054-2
         see chapter 6.1: 'The Meaning of Genesis:
         Creation, Evolution and the Origin of Evil'

{10}* In 'Judaism: Basis - Past - Present - Future, Part 1'
       Manfred Davidmann
       ISBN 978-0-85192-060-3
       see chapter 4: 'Causes of Antisemitism'

{11}* In 'Judaism: Basis - Past - Present - Future, Part 1'
       Manfred Davidmann
       ISBN 978-0-85192-060-3
       see chapter 5: 'The Right to the Land of Israel'

{12}* In 'The Human Mind and How it Works:
       Group Minds in Action:
       How the Human Group Mind Shapes
       the Quality of Our Life and Living'
       Manfred Davidmann
       ISBN 978-0-85192-055-9
       see chapter 2: 'How the Human Brain
       Developed and How the Human Mind Works'

Additions by the Editor:

In the original text of this chapter on the solhaam.org website Manfred Davidmann referred to other reports in form of links.

Here these reports are marked { }* and the sources are stated.

** Added by the Editor

*** Go to 'www.solhaam.org' and use the 'Contact Form'

Chapter 6

Using Words to Communicate Effectively

Summary

Shows how to communicate more effectively, covering aspects of thinking, writing, speaking and listening as well as formal and informal communications.

Consists of guidelines found useful by university students and practising middle and senior managers.

Communicating with Words

Communication is the transmission of meaning to others.

Important is that 'meaning' is transferred. In other words, it is important the other persons understand what we want them to understand, that they understand the intended meaning.

More precisely, purposeful communication is the transmission of intended meaning to others.

Implied is

1. that the sender of the communication has clear knowledge and understanding of the meaning he wishes to convey, and

2. that the receiver interprets the message in such a manner that he receives the intended meaning.

Hence for effective communication the sender must determine the purpose of the communication and use words which have the same meaning for sender and receiver.

Meaning of Words

The scientific study of meaning is called Semantics.

Words and Labels

Words are labels. Labels are arbitrary.

Most common cause of misunderstanding arises from assuming that the word (a label) is the object. Two people can then be arguing about a concept, referring to it by using the same word, arguing because this word means something different to each of them.

So to be meaningful, words must establish the same thought (reference) in both the sender and receiver of a communication.

Words vary considerably as regards their value for communication. They differ in their level of abstraction. The greater the level of abstraction, the less meaning do they have.

Levels of Abstraction

1 Objects

Objects represent a relatively low level of abstraction as they can be seen and touched and their characteristics detailed accurately.

Here words are labels for objects such as table or chair.

2 Events

In addition to objects, both action and time are implied, and so these are more complex.

Examples are: Accident, sale, party.

3 Generalisations

Words are also used as labels for groups and collections of objects or events. These generalisations are more abstract and less precise.

Examples of such labels are: Furniture, machine tools, employees, parents.

Employees, for example, can be full-time, part-time, shift working, office working, home working, male, female, young, old, single, married, unskilled, skilled, professional, and more.

4 Value Judgements or Ideology

Value judgements and ideology are at the highest level of abstraction and words used as labels for them are quite useless for effective communication until the meaning of the word used is clearly defined in detail.

Examples of such labels are: Beautiful, valuable, necessary, luxury, lazy, free enterprise, truth.

Such words can be strung together and mixed with generalisations to provide good-sounding speeches and statements of the kind politicians like to use, to provide speeches and statements with no real meaning attached to the words used. Listeners or readers use their own idea of what the words mean and so their understanding of what is being said differs widely from person to person.

I listed the word 'truth' as an example of a label for a meaningless abstraction. Surely 'truth' ought to be more than a meaningless value judgement, so let us look at this in more detail.

Consider two media reports of a current event. Each reports the same event, each apparently telling the truth, each report giving its viewers different impressions of what actually happened.

How come? Can there be more than one truth?

Such reports may tell only part of what happened, may report only what seems relevant to the reporter, may then be selecting what seems to support the particular viewpoint of those who prepared the report.

Compare these 'truths' with that demanded from a witness in a court of law: 'The truth, the whole truth and nothing but the truth.'

Which means that what is required in a court of law is the truth with nothing taken away and nothing added.

If we agree on this as a definition, then the word 'truth' has become more meaningful.

Formal and Informal Communications

A distinction needs to be made between formal and informal communications. Formal communication implies that a record is kept, that what has been said or written can be attributed to its originator.

On the whole, written communications are formal. But statements may be qualified by phrases such as 'preliminary thoughts are ...'.

Oral (spoken) communication consists of direct or transmitted speech between two or more people. Oral communications are more likely to be misinterpreted than written ones, were regarded as informal but are now often recorded and treated as formal. Missing from such recordings is the body language consisting of facial expressions and gestures.

Consider an informal chat by telephone getting comments on matters of joint concern before producing a final report. Important is the possibility of a two-way flow of information, of immediate feedback, of a frank unreserved exchange of information, opinions and ideas.

The informal nature of such exploratory conversations is often ignored. People's preliminary thoughts can then be quoted against them as if they had been fully considered.

Although an answering (recording) machine ought to bleep at regular intervals while recording, conversations can be recorded in different ways by one person without the other being aware of this.

Hence one needs to make sure the other person is aware of the informal nature of the conversation. In other words, that the other person knows the conversation is not to be recorded and that the information is to be regarded as confidential until the matter has been fully considered.

There are, however, many formal oral communications, such as selection, grievance or appraisal interviews, or when negotiating. Characteristic is that a record is kept by those participating.

Rumours are hearsay. One person tells the next who tells another, and so on. But there are personal barriers as people tend to keep back, elaborate or enhance information in accordance with their likes and dislikes. Hence information tends to change in emphasis and content as it is passed from person to person. This makes rumours so unreliable a source of information.

Improving Communication

1. Clarify your own ideas before attempting to communicate them.

2. Be clear about the purpose of the communication. For example, its purpose could be to inform others, to obtain information or to initiate action.

3. See if the other person can repeat what you have said, in his or her own words.

Effective communication, however, depends also on attentive listening.

Effective Listening

Do not jump to conclusions before hearing what the other person has to say, and do not interrupt.

Interrupting prevents effective and meaningful communication, can prevent the speaker from making a valid point. Think how you would feel if you were interrupted just before making your key point.

It is up to the sender (originator) of the communication to use words which have the same meaning also for the receiver, for the listener. To ensure that you have understood the communication (message) correctly, you can repeat it in your own words to the other person.

For example, after being told how to get to a particular street one can ask "You mean, take the second street on the left?". Answers like "Yes, it is" or "Take the third on the left" confirm or improve our understanding of what we had been told.

And so, for effective listening:

1. Avoid jumping to conclusions, avoid making value judgements such as good or bad, desirable or undesirable, true or false, while the speaker is talking.

2. Listen to the full story.

3. Restate the other person's position in your own words.

Letters and Reports

1. Avoid slogans, catchwords (buzz-words), jargon.

   Use words or phrases which you could use naturally in conversation. Exception are technical terms and abbreviations which your reader will understand.

2. Use simple words and few of them.

3. Keep paragraphs and sentences short.

4. In-house e-mail is fast. Copies are readily distributed to all those interested and reach their destination almost immediately.

   Fast method for causing chaos as mistakes spread rapidly. Effects snowball as others act quickly using the mistaken information.

   Better to prepare draft replies but only post the replies after some hours, which allows considering, validating, completing and improving the draft.

Traps to Avoid

1. Avoid being blinded by words or phrases which sound good, expert, impressive, plausible or likely. Ask for a definition or explanation to be given in clear, simple, meaningful language.

2. Avoid being misled by illogical arguments, misleading publicity or propaganda.

   When propaganda is logical, and seen to be logical, it is difficult to argue against, to counter. Such propaganda is usually misleading because it is the premise, the first argument or underlying assumption, which misleads.

   In other words, a logical argument can be based on false assumptions or misleading information.

Chapter 7

The Way Ahead: Policies for a Better Future

Summary

This, Manfred Davidmann's latest work, contains findings and conclusions based on extensive research reported over a period of time in other publications.

Manfred Davidmann shows that the Torah contains a statement of scientific social laws of behaviour and of community and social organisation, such as:
    Money has to be lent by the community, free of interest.
    Outstanding loans have to be cancelled after a period of time.
    A country's wealth belongs to its inhabitants.

He proves that keeping the social laws of the Torah guarantees human rights. They apply to all people alike and have the force of law. He also explains how the application of these social laws affects not only the standard of living of all members of society, but the future of the planet as a whole.

The Law which Defines Human Rights is Clear and to the Point

Outstanding is that the Torah <1> contains a statement of scientific social laws of behaviour and of social and community organisation.

The essential social provisions of Torah law are clear and to the point. This is what the Torah lays down as a matter of law {2}:

- The community has to provide ('lend') money to those who need it, free of interest.
- All outstanding loans are to be cancelled every seventh year.

You may look at these and you may think that these are simply out of tune with modern life. One person may not charge another person interest! Cancel loans every seventh year! Why? Of course one charges interest, of course one has to repay loans! Or so it would appear.

But look at it another way. Would it not help you to find an apartment, to get married, to develop your own business if you could borrow money interest free? Would it not help you and take a great load off your mind to know that debts you have been unable to repay, are cancelled every seventh year?

And to know that debts cannot be used to oppress or exploit those in need.

Consider carefully. These laws are part of a system of social security, are aimed at preventing independent citizens from falling into need, from losing their independence, from being oppressed and exploited because of need.

A person in need has to find someone who has money to spare, has to find someone who is prepared to lend it free of interest while knowing that the debt will be cancelled within seven years if the borrower cannot repay the loan, while knowing that the borrower will then be released from the obligation to repay.

Among Jews, these laws have been common knowledge for over three thousand years, and they have the force of law.

However, Jews found it difficult to get such loans, despite the direct Torah commandment to the rich to give to those in need, to give even if the year of release from debt was close at hand. For example, about two thousand years ago, the rich preferred to ignore the law and there was much cruel hardship and oppression of Jew by Jew. <2>

Jews found other ways.

On the one hand, the community made itself responsible for helping those in need. The community collects and the community distributes, as a matter of charity.

On the other hand, vast sums donated annually by world Jewry {1} were given away not just at zero interest but at negative effective interest rates <3>. This has the effect of reducing the value of the loan each year so that loans are in effect automatically reduced to negligible amounts, that is cancelled, at the end of seven years. In this case it looks as if the laws about lending without charging interest and about cancelling debts are in fact being observed in Israel.

However, there is a big difference between the intent of the social laws of the Torah and the two ways in which we have just seen it being applied.

The social Torah laws call for the community's money to be made available to those who need it in such a way that need and indebtedness can never be used to oppress so as to exploit and enslave. The social laws of the Torah are obviously intended to help those who are falling on hard times.

In the first case above, that aid was being provided at the discretion of the giver and not as a matter of right. This means that any aid given to individuals depends on the generosity of those who give, depends on the likes and dislikes of those who distribute aid, may be totally inadequate or even unavailable to those in need.

In the second case we saw again that it is the community which collects money from people. But it is the establishment which spends it, allocating large sums which are far too often given in effect to those already well off, rich, powerful, connected.

The social laws of the Torah demand that the community's funds be used only to support those who need such support, not by charity but as a matter of rightful entitlement.

People are entitled to the social security the Torah's laws provide, but only if, and as long as, they themselves follow the Torah's social laws and apply its social system in their daily lives.

So far we have seen that loans have to be provided interest-free and debts have to be cancelled if the borrower cannot repay. But the Torah contains other laws which are just as telling, just as important, just as far-reaching in their effects.

According to the social laws of the Torah {2}

> A country's productive assets, such as land, belong to those of its inhabitants who keep the Torah's social laws.

Hence land, amenities, raw materials under the earth, fish in the sea, the atmosphere above, are all yours. This includes factories, banks and capital as well as state-owned enterprises.

> In other words, the land and its productive assets belong to, and have to be shared out among, the country's inhabitants. <14> {2}

Part of one's entitlement is also a home which is one's own. Belonging to one, under one's own control.

Getting a share of an asset does not mean you get just a piece of paper. It means that you have to be the completely independent owner of your share, in control of what is yours. The share you own, your independent control of it and the resulting income are intended to provide you with the means for independence.

You are to have control <4> over your share so as to make you independent from the boss, the government, the rich, all those who may wish to exploit your needs so as to make you serve them. There would seem to be no reason why you should not co-operate with others, joining your assets with theirs and working together with them as long as you remain in control of your assets. It is you who has to gain the advantage of the work you do.

According to Torah law

> inhabitants who keep the social laws are also entitled to have a sabbatical year every seventh year. During this sabbatical year they are entitled to be freed from work at the expense of the community.

You are entitled to your sabbatical year regardless of the work you do or the level at which you are working during the other six years. But during the sabbatical year you must not work for pay, or produce to sell. {2}

This means that during every seventh year the community has to pay you sufficient to provide you with a standard of living which corresponds to the average earnings for the country as a whole.

Everyone, regardless of what they do, is entitled to receive the same and this must be the best the community can provide for all.

Academics already enjoy regular sabbatical years. During this period their salaries are often paid by the taxpayer and to that extent their sabbaticals are in fact provided by the community.

For example, this is so in Israel when salaries are largely paid by the taxpayer and by funds contributed by world Jewry.

If heavily subsidised universities use contributed funds, or any other funds for that matter, for this purpose, then so can the community use some of its funds in the same way. If such a large and well paid section of the community regularly enjoy their sabbatical years, then there is nothing impossible about it.

Academics enjoy their sabbatical years and everyone in the community, being equally entitled to them, should have their sabbatical years as a matter of right.

Consider what sabbatical years would mean not only for you but also for those who are now in need, depressed, filled with a spirit of hopelessness and defeat, who would during such a year be free to do as they pleased.

Think of the way in which people, just like you or I, would be able to spend their time. We could travel, train for more skilled or better work, could study, gain greater understanding, could qualify.

We could have much more satisfying lives, we could do much for our own communities, could do much for those in need, for those who are underdeveloped and unable to afford our own expert skills.

If you follow the Torah's social laws then you are entitled to a regular sabbatical year. You should not have to persuade your government or establishment to grant this. It is yours by right.

Our Rights Cannot be Denied

Have another look at these four social Torah laws:

1. The community has to provide ('lend') money to those who need it, free of interest, as long as they keep the social laws.
2. All such loans, if outstanding, are to be cancelled every seventh year.
3. A country's productive assets, such as land, belong to those of its inhabitants who keep the Torah's social laws.
4. Inhabitants who keep the social laws are also entitled to have a sabbatical year every seventh year. During this sabbatical year they are entitled to be freed from work at the expense of the community.

Social security means social security for those in need, is social security for all. The basis of any insurance scheme or co-operative is to share the risk, the many providing for the few who are in need. Whichever way you look at it, social security does not mean taking from the many and giving to the privileged few, making the rich even richer. 'He is not honest who has never had the opportunity to steal' and he does not keep the social laws who in a position of responsibility misuses other people.

Our rights cannot be denied. It is only those who have not yet studied the Torah enough who would try to deny our rights.

What has been said here applies to all alike, applies to Christians, Jews, Muslims and all others. These laws are scientific laws {2}. Keeping or not keeping them has consequences which cannot be avoided. It is time that Torah law is applied in the way in which it is clearly stated, in the way in which it is intended to be applied.

Within and Between Countries

The laws and our rights apply equally well in any one country, and apply between countries.

What this means is that capital and wealth <6> belong to the community. They must not be centrally held or controlled and every family has to receive its equality-based share of capital, wealth and income, be in full control of how it uses its share and receives the resulting income.

The income <7> of those families who are well off needs to be seen for what it is, namely as the result of the community's group mind and of the community's mental as well as physical efforts. This means that there must not be any wide differentials in income between those who are well off and those who are not. Hence an increase in income needs to be shared out, say annually, in such a way that the income received by the already well-paid is increased to maintain the differential. But it is increased only after the income of the lowest paid family has increased, the maximum differential between highest and lowest being three. {15; Also 16; 13}

Just as this holds for people living in any one country so it holds for people living in different countries. Funds need to be transferred between communities (countries) in a co-ordinated way. Transferred funds have to be distributed to and within the poorer community so that here also the total income received by the wealthiest family increases. But it is increased only to maintain the differential to the poorest, doing so only after the income of the poorest has increased, the maximum permitted differential again being three.

Essential safeguards are that capital and wealth

1. may not leave the country or leave the community in other ways <8>,
2. may not be transferred from one family to another <9; 10>,
3. must not be allowed to accumulate beyond the permitted level in the hands of any family for any reason.

Capital and wealth belong to the community as a whole and have to be redistributed at regular intervals of only a few years, say every three years {15; 16; 17}. Families benefit according to size, the parents' family reducing in size as their children marry while their children qualify after marriage.

Policies for a Better Future

When talking about policies then we are talking about achieving a way of living and a quality of life which corresponds to the social laws and the social system of the Torah. We are talking about the future well-being and security of all the people and of our country. It is these which are at risk {2} and it is this which makes the policies being put forward here so important.

To have a country of one's own means both backing and security, help in time of need, a place of refuge, a source of strength. But we have much more to struggle for than just territory. To us the land is a means to an end. Being there gives us the opportunity for gaining what we have struggled to achieve over the centuries. What we are aiming at is to be a free people in our own land.

As far back as 1973 I pointed out {6} that:

- One job per family should be sufficient to provide its members with a good life. This applies equally well to the young who want to marry and set up home.
- There should be work for those who want it. There should be equal opportunity dependent only on ability.

Some progress has been made but not enough. We, the people, are still far too far from achieving these.

Consider what effect the application of the kind of laws we have talked about would have on your own well-being and on the quality of your life. Consider also what effect it would have on the commitment of people towards each other, on their willingness to support a country (community) in which people live such free and secure lives.

It is the application of these laws which we must now achieve. It is time we started this struggle for a better future.

To achieve these policies, specific objectives need to be gained and these objectives are outlined in the following section 'This is What has to be Achieved'

The more people know about these laws and understand them, the more people know just how practical they are, the quicker will we gain what is ours as a matter of right according to the social laws and social system of the Torah.

This is What has to be Achieved

Social security means social security for those in need, is social security for all. But people may not selfishly profit from benevolent social legislation, at the expense of others, at the expense of the community. For example, the community cannot give funds free of interest to those who 'need' the money for lending to the poor at high rates of interest.

Hence only those who themselves keep the social laws and live according to the social system of the Torah, may benefit from its provisions and from what we are setting out to achieve.

We have already shown that

- The community has to provide ('lend') money to those who need it, free of interest, as long as they keep the social laws.
- All such loans, if outstanding, are to be cancelled every seventh year.
- A country's productive assets, such as land, belong to those of its inhabitants who keep the Torah's social laws, and have to be shared out among them.
- Inhabitants who keep the social laws are also entitled to have a sabbatical year every seventh year. During this sabbatical year they are entitled to be freed from work at the expense of the community.

We are also setting out to achieve

- The application of the social laws of the Torah and gaining our rights, in our country, in other countries and between countries, for our communities.

- There should be work for those who want it. There should be equal opportunity dependent only on ability.
- One job per family should be sufficient to provide its members with a good life. This applies equally well to the young who want to marry and set up home.
- Four-day week, achieved by reducing the hours worked each week without loss of income and without loss of standard of living.
- All capital and all wealth belong to the community as a whole. Each family has to receive its equality-based share of capital, wealth and income, be in full control of how it uses its share and receive the resulting income.
- Any increase in income needs to be shared out in such a way that the income received by the already well-paid is increased to maintain the differential. But it is increased only after the income of the lowest paid family has increased, the maximum differential between highest and lowest being three.
- As regards those of us living in different countries, here also funds need to be transferred between the communities in a co-ordinated way. Transferred funds have to be distributed so that the total income received by the wealthiest family increases only to maintain the differential to the poorest. But it is increased only after the income of the poorest has increased, the maximum permitted differential again being three.
- Capital and wealth belong to the community as a whole and have to be redistributed at regular intervals of only a few years, say every three years. Families benefit according to size, the parents' family reducing in size as their children marry while their children qualify after marriage.
- Effective, appropriate and fair remedies are available and can be developed for putting the country's economy on a sound footing. {12-18}
- Free education and job training to be made available with grants to cover also living expenses.
- Also needed is high quality housing to acceptable standards, subsidised according to need, at prices people can afford, as a matter of right.
- The establishment, both secular and religious, of each community must be accountable to its community (and failing this then to the other communities). They are accountable not just for their successes but also for their failures, for actively supporting other communities and individuals in their need and also for failing to do so. <5>

- What are needed are properly elected and accountable secular representatives holding office for a limited non-repeating period, which serve the people and which are selected by and are accountable to the people. What is also needed is a religious leadership which serves God and people. And the income and position of secular and religious community leaders must be made to depend on their well-informed community and depend on results <12>.

The outcome has to be

- **An increasing standard of living.**
- **Satisfying work and leisure activities.**
- **Increasing quality of life.**

See ACHIEVING THESE OBJECTIVES for what can be done to change matters for the better, to improve the way in which we live and to gain these objectives.

Safeguards

One safeguard is that a family may use its share to what it considers to be its best advantage but may not sell it.

It is each family which is entitled to its share rather than each individual since the family is the basic unit of society on which the strength of the individual and of the community depends. {7}

Another provision which safeguards the people is that the sharing out of the country's assets and income has to be updated at regular intervals. The assets of the country have to be redistributed at regular intervals.

Every square foot of land, every factory matters. If the country grows richer, the people are better off, you gain automatically. Important is that all has to be looked at and redistributed at regular intervals so that no person may gain at the expense of another.

He who does not charge interest is himself not charged interest, he who provides social security for others in turn benefits from social security by the many when he is in need. He who does not oppress others is himself protected from being oppressed.

But there are those who do not follow the social laws and social system of the Torah, those who charge interest, oppress others or exploit others, those who ignore the rights of the people. Those who oppress or exploit must not be provided with resources.

Hence it is important to appreciate that rights and social security provisions are in force only between those who follow the social laws and social system of the Torah.

Another safeguard is that part of the national income is first used to provide for a free national health service and education, free to all.

Everyone is entitled to the sabbatical year but it is each family which is entitled to its sabbatical year rather than each individual.

It must be up to the individual to select and choose what he wants to do. Ranging perhaps from travel abroad and seeing the world to studying the Torah or for that matter studying for a higher qualification.

Sabbaticals are not an opportunity for the government, the state, a political party, a religious hierarchy or the management of an organisation to direct or train its employees, to condition through some kind of educational scheme, to pressurise one way or another.

The Torah states what every person is entitled to as long as that person follows its social laws.

What this means is that capital and wealth <6> belong to the community. They must not be centrally held or controlled <11> but every family has to receive its equality-based share of capital, wealth and income, be in full control of how it uses its share and receive the resulting income.

The income <7> of those families who are well off needs to be seen for what it is, namely as the result of the community's group mind and of the community's mental as well as physical efforts. This means that there must not be any wide differentials in income between those who are well off and those who are not. Hence an increase in income needs to be shared out, say annually, in such a way that the income received by the higher paid is increased to maintain the differential. But it is increased only after the income of the lowest paid has increased, the maximum differential between highest and lowest being three both in a single community and in all the communities considered together. {15; Also 16; 13}

Essential safeguards are that capital and wealth

1. may not leave the community <8>
2. may not be transferred from one family to another <9; 10>

3. must not be allowed to accumulate beyond the permitted level in the hands of any family or individual for any reason.

Capital and wealth belong to the community as a whole and have to be redistributed at regular and frequent intervals of only a few years, say about three years under present conditions. Families benefit according to size, the parents' family reducing in size as their children marry while their children qualify after marriage. <13>

In the same way power and patronage must not be allowed to accumulate in the hands of individuals or families who are wealthy and particularly not in the hands of office holders in any of the armed forces or military type organisations such as police forces and associated services, in the hands of those who held office in or controlled any of them or in the hands of those who have been in such positions.

Every establishment, both secular and religious, must be held accountable individually and collectively both now and for ever for what they did and omitted to do, for what they do and omit to do. Never again must an establishment be allowed to escape.

A community has to enforce these safeguards if it wishes to survive. And the communities will gain strength and prosper to the extent to which the application of the laws is achieved and to the extent to which they are kept.

See ACHIEVING THESE OBJECTIVES for what can be done to change matters for the better, to improve the way in which we live and to gain these objectives.

Achieving these Objectives

What can each one of us do to gain a better future for all of us through achieving these objectives.

We have to spread this knowledge about our basic human rights.

We have to come together. We have to learn how these essential Torah laws apply today to our daily lives and how they apply to community and religious leaderships.

We need to pass the information about these social laws, and about our social human rights under these laws, to other people.

If you would like more information or wish to contact other like-minded people in your area, write to us.

And if you have any comments or suggestions about what is written here, please let us know (see end of document for address).**

Role of the Establishment

(Illustrated with reference to Jewish belief and practice)

Secular and religious establishments have clearly failed to provide leadership and guidance, for reasons which are now clear {13; 17; 18}.

Power and patronage must not be allowed to accumulate in the hands of individuals or families who are wealthy. They must not accumulate in the hands of office-holders in any of the armed forces or military type organisations such as police forces and associated services. Power and patronage must not accumulate in the hands of those who control any of them or who have been in such positions.

This can be illustrated by considering Jewish belief and practice, as follows:

> Scriptures tell {3; 4} that the Jewish people twice lost their country because the Jewish establishment betrayed God and people by rejecting the laws of the Torah.

> Events now taking place clearly indicate that Israel will be lost once again because Jewish secular and religious establishments have once again rejected the social laws and system of the Torah.

> The Jewish religious establishment has continued to dance around the Golden Calf, the Golden Calf being the image which represents those who wish to oppress so as to exploit, so serving a secular establishment which only serves itself.

> At the end of the Second World War, the Allies exposed and punished the inhuman brutality of Nazi war crimes at the Nueremberg trials. The French and Russian and other people punished the quislings and collaborators who had betrayed them to the inhuman Nazis.

> The Israelis tried Eichmann in Jerusalem. But what that trial proved was that with relatively few exceptions it was the Jewish secular and religious establishment which organised for Eichmann within their own communities the deporting of their communities. The deporting of their communities to the concentration camps and thus to the gas chambers. They even misled their

communities by not telling them the truth about the deportations. {20; 6; 19}

> Now consider this: So interbred and interconnected was and still is the Jewish secular and religious establishment, and such is the tight control they exercise over the Jewish media and over the minds of their subservient communities, that as far as I know not one member of the Jewish establishment has ever been held accountable by Jews. Not one member of the Jewish establishment has been held to account for betraying their communities, for betraying God and people for the sake of Nazi-given power. Hannah Arendt {20} considers that they apparently saw themselves as first and foremost serving the Nazi rulers when they should have served and organised their people in battle against the oppressors. To my knowledge nowhere have any of them been indicted, tried, found wanting and held accountable for betraying the Jewish people.

The establishment of each community must be accountable to its community (and failing this then to the other communities). They are accountable not just for their successes but also for their failures, for actively supporting other communities and individuals in their need and also for failing to do so.

Never again must any establishment be allowed to escape to their foreign bank accounts, their tax havens, their villas and estates elsewhere, leaving behind the betrayed communities.

What is needed are properly elected and accountable secular representatives holding office for a limited non-repeating period. Representatives who serve the people and who are directly selected by, and are directly accountable to, the people. What is also needed is a religious leadership which serves God and people. And the income and position of both secular and religious community leaders must be made to depend <12> on their well-informed community and depend on results.

> Never again must communities such as the European Jewish communities be allowed to suffer,

> never again must communities in need cry out in pain for so long.

Any and every establishment, both secular and religious, must be held accountable both now and for ever for what they did and omitted to do, for what they do and omit to do.

Why should a priest, minister, rabbi, mullah, guru and others, etc., get paid more by vote of his local establishment than is earned by many in his congregation? Why should his terms of service and conditions of employment depend on the local secular establishment instead of directly on the secret vote and secret voluntary contributions of his congregation?

Communities need to make sure that the religious establishment does not teach or preach establishment-orientated beliefs and practices. In other words, the religious establishment may not teach and preach what amounts to warm consoling comforting and tranquillising beliefs and practices while leaving out the central core social laws and social system of the Torah. {21}

> Present-day rabbinical Judaism consists of a shell of comforting tranquillising beliefs and practices. It is a shell which is empty of content, as the rabbis edited out from belief and observance the Torah's central social laws and system which gave meaning to Judaism and purpose to the Jewish people.
>
> The rabbis in this way rejected, and so stopped the people from following, the essential core Torah laws, the word of God as written down by Moses. And caused the destruction of the Second Temple and of Israel and the consequent monstrous suffering of the people. {2; 3}
>
> In the same way and as matters stand today, present-day rabbinical Judaism is the fundamental cause of the weakening of Israel.
>
> God acts when the people act and holds his hand out over them. When the people do not act then God withdraws his protection from them. Hence there is an urgent need for everybody to stand up and follow the social laws and the social system of the Torah.
>
> And now stand up and be counted.

Notes

< 1>   The Torah, that is the five books of Moses (Also called Pentateuch; Part of Old Testament).

< 2>   Arab banks, for example, are prohibited by Islamic law from charging interest and do not charge interest. Their way of bypassing the apparent intent of the law is to take a part of the profits which result from the use of the money. It is like taking over a part of the assets, like becoming a partner, the borrower in effect working for the lender and it is this which the law is intended to avoid.

< 3>   Effective interest rate equals rate of interest charged minus rate of inflation.

< 4>   There are however certain safeguards which limit one's right to do as one pleases since one may not indulge in behaviour which harms other people or the community. These safeguards are essential as they ensure that assets and wealth do not accumulate in the hands of a few, that your assets and income are not controlled by a few and are not dependent on the patronage of a few. The few might otherwise use their power to oppress so as to exploit.
See also the chapter on 'Safeguards'.

< 5>   See Appendix 1: Role of the Establishment

< 6>   Such as land, buildings, factories, share holdings, farms, offices, shops, residences, accumulated wealth, machine tools, equipment, homes, and so on.

< 7>   From all sources.

< 8>   For example, on marriage.

< 9>   For example, must not be sold by one family to another.

<10>   For example, on marriage or on death.

<11>   Including communal institutions such as schools and synagogues.

<12>   Within the limits laid down for the community as a whole.

<13>   Single-parent families are recognised only if the reason for the condition is the adultery of the spouse or the death of the spouse while married. If the reason for the condition is the divorce of the spouse for any other reason, then this disqualifies. Adultery by the single parent also disqualifies.

<14>   A family (inhabitant) keeps the social laws of the Torah. The family owns a share of the assets of the community (country) they live in. But they may have a share only in one country and in one country alone, namely the country in which they live and whose assets they have created and are creating. And they may not transfer their assets directly or indirectly to another community.

References

{ 1}   The Way Ahead for Israel: Causes of Present Problems
(See 'The Money We Give is Distributed in Israel')
David Baram*

{ 2}   In 'Judaism: Basis - Past - Present - Future, Part 1'
Manfred Davidmann
ISBN 978-0-85192-060-3
see chapter 2.1: 'Struggle for Freedom:
The Social Cause-and-Effect Relationship'

{ 3}   In 'Judaism: Basis - Past - Present - Future, Part 1'
Manfred Davidmann
ISBN 978-0-85192-060-3
see chapter 2.2: 'History Speaks: Monarchy,
Exile and Maccabees'

{ 4}   In 'Judaism: Basis - Past - Present - Future, Part 1'
Manfred Davidmann
ISBN 978-0-85192-060-3
see chapter 2.3: 'At the Time of Jesus,
This is What Actually Happened in Israel:
The Truth about Hillel and his Times'

{ 5}   In 'Judaism: Basis - Past - Present - Future, Part 1'
Manfred Davidmann
ISBN 978-0-85192-060-3
see chapter 2.4: 'One Law for All:
Freedom Now, Freedom for Ever'

{ 6}   Wake Up Israel
Manfred Davidmann

{ 7}   If You Want a Future, Read On ...
(Social Effects of Promiscuity)
David Baram*

{ 8}   The Way Ahead for Israel: Causes of Present
Problems
David Baram*

{ 9}   Freedom and Bureaucracy in Israel: Protecting
the Individual's Privacy and Freedom from Misuse
of Personal Data in Computer Storage
David Baram*

{10}   The Jewish Agency Does Some Odd Things
with the Money It Gets from World Jewry
David Baram*

{11}   Jewish Law in Everyday Life Nowadays
David Baram*

{12}   In 'Management and Leadership:
Local, National, Multinational (Global),
Principles and Practice'
Manfred Davidmann
ISBN 978-0-85192-057-3
see chapter 5: 'Directing and Managing Change'
Adapting to change, deciding what needs to
be done; Planning ahead, getting results,
evaluating progress; Appraisal interviews
and target-setting meetings.

{13}   In 'Management and Leadership:
Local, National, Multinational (Global),
Principles and Practice'
Manfred Davidmann
ISBN 978-0-85192-057-3
see chapter 2: 'Style of Management and
Leadership'

{14}   In 'Management and Leadership:
Local, National, Multinational (Global),
Principles and Practice'
Manfred Davidmann
ISBN 978-0-85192-057-3
see chapter 6: 'Organising'

{15} In 'Messianic Struggle:
      The Worldwide Struggle for a Good and
      Secure Life for All, Here and Now'
      Manfred Davidmann
      ISBN 978-0-85192-059-7
      see chapter 3: 'Work and Pay, Incomes
      and Differentials: Employer, Employee and
      Community'
      Manfred Davidmann

{16} In 'Management and Leadership:
      Local, National, Multinational (Global),
      Principles and Practice'
      Manfred Davidmann
      ISBN 978-0-85192-057-3
      see chapter 9: 'Inflation, Balance of Payments
      and Currency Exchange Rates'
      (Quality of Government (national and local);
      Standard of Living and Worldwide Inequality;
      The Struggle for a Bigger Share)

{17} In 'The Real World in Which We Live:
      The Social Rules and Social System under
      Which We Suffer, Struggle, Survive and Prosper'
      Manfred Davidmann
      ISBN 978-0-85192-058-0
      see chapter 16: 'The Will to Work: What People
      Struggle to Achieve'

{18} In 'Messianic Struggle:
      The Worldwide Struggle for a Good and
      Secure Life for All, Here and Now'
      Manfred Davidmann
      ISBN 978-0-85192-059-7
      see chapter 2: 'Social Responsibility, Profits
      and Social Accountability'

{19} Lodz Ghetto.
      Television Documentary from diaries and
      monographs written in the Lodz Ghetto
      (Channel 4, UK, 6 May 1991)

{20} Eichmann in Jerusalem - A Report on the
      Banality of Evil
      Dr. Hannah Arendt
      Faber and Faber, 1963

{21} 'Origin of Christianity and Judaism:
What Actually Happened, What Jesus Actually
Taught and Later Changes'
Manfred Davidmann
www.solhaam.org

Additions by the Editor:

*   David Baram: Manfred Davidmann is the author of these works.

** Go to 'www.solhaam.org' and use the 'Contact Form'

Chapter 8

Faith and Trust in God, No Matter by What Name called

Faith and Trust in God, No Matter by What Name called

Continuously there is the race against the enemy within <1> who would separate, engulf and destroy some or all of us the human beings on this our planet and thus we listen at all times to the ticking of the clock denoting the passage of time which is either used to further our purpose or else is irretrievably lost.

This is a matter of survival, of hard work, of strain and effort, to succeed in our endeavour. And to this end we work together, all of us, human beings, proud and erect, hand in hand, irrespective of our creed or religion, the colour of our skin, the shape of our eyes, or where we happen to live, for freedom and humanity.

We climb together through mists of uncertainty, guided by our Elders <2>.

Our Elders impress upon their people the need to act, having been charged by all our people with doing this effectively.

In the history of any or all of our people:
>Whenever the guidance of the Elders has been ignored, the most terrible consequences have always followed.

We place our faith and trust in God, no matter by what name called, and in all our people all over the planet.

We are guided ably and powerfully and for this we are truly grateful.

God helps and protects those who act for God and people.

God acts when people act for God and people.

When people do not act for God and people, then God withdraws his protection from them.

Ideas, inspirations and voices are intended to guide or lead astray, to help or betray.

Beast eats beast. You cannot trust manipulating slave owners or slave drivers and cannot trust that which originates from them.

When in doubt one must do that which is right (humane, good, caring, putting people first).

God,

Beasts have continued to disown you, and they have continued to disown me,

but I have the sure knowledge that they will be weak and fall by the wayside,
while we will be strong, survive and succeed.

Their idols of wood, stone and plastic, of concrete and steel, of flesh and bones,
their golden calves,
cannot guide them or save them.

Every time they open their mouths they condemn themselves.

Whenever life has been so tough in the past then I have been very close to, almost immediately before, a major breakthrough or success.

And God has always turned tough situations into gains and advances in unexpected directions.

God

See my loneliness
See my isolation
See how my time has been wasted instead of teaching your laws in your name.

Stand by me and guide me.

Those who argue against me argue against God,
those who are against me are against God
and will suffer the inevitable consequences,
will not be listened to, will lose what influence they have, will not learn nor teach what little they will know or remember.

God

In you we trust.
Guide us in our hours of need,
show us the way to freedom.

We struggle to re-establish your law
so that all people can be freed
and gain strength and good life.

If we fail again this time, then the Covenant would be broken
completely and irredeemably.
If I were to fail then mankind would rapidly destroy itself.
Hence I cannot and will not fail.
This is a battle we simply have to and therefore will win.

If I do not succeed then this planet will be rendered uninhabitable for human beings of any shape or kind including manipulating beasts in human form.

But always there is the race against time which is either used to achieve our aims or else is irretrievably lost.

Stand Up and Be Counted

When people do not act for God and people,
then God withdraws his protection from them.
The consequences cannot be avoided.

But God helps, protects and rewards manifold those who act for God and people.

This is a matter of survival, of hard work, of strain and effort, to succeed in our endeavour. And to this end we work together, all of us, human beings, proud and erect, hand in hand, irrespective of our creed or religion, the colour of our skin, the shape of our eyes, or where we happen to live, for freedom and humanity.

Notes <..>

<1> The enemy within, that is a manipulating ruling class or slave-driving manipulators.

<2> Our Elders are known only by God and serve God and people, remain unknown to human beings.

Chapter 9

The choice is yours:
Unemployment, Charitable Social Security and Today's Religious Teachings
or
High Standard of Living, Satisfying Work and a Good Life, as God-given rights.

A covenant is an agreement in which each of the parties undertakes duties and obligations towards the other. And the Pentateuch records God's promise that human beings will have a good life of high quality as long as human beings fulfil their obligations under the covenant, as long as human beings follow God's laws, that is as long as they behave like human beings.

This is also recorded in the Pentateuch as a fundamental scientific law, the Social Cause-and-Effect Relationship. This states that the consequences of keeping or not keeping the Pentateuch's laws are inescapable, that what happens to one is in the end the inevitable result of one's own behaviour. Also clearly stated is that this is a scientific law which was defined and stated using the language of religion so that people would benefit from knowing the effects (consequences) of their behaviour.

> See 'The God-given Human Rights, Social Laws and Social
> System' {1}*, which lists detailed sources and relevant notes.

We are told that the relationship applies to all without exception and at all times, wherever one may be, regardless of type of government, form of religion or social system or country. It applies whether you like it or not, agree or disagree.

The consequences of one's behaviour are detailed both ways, clearly and powerfully illustrating intermediate stages between the two ends of the scale, and we are told that the process is reversible: Increasingly disregarding the laws (rules of behaviour) results in greater suffering and oppression, increasingly behaving according to the laws results in greater freedom, liberty, independence and a better life.

The relationship applies to all. Ignorance is no excuse, not knowing the law does not prevent consequences of one's behaviour, and the relationship is stated in a way which enables people to benefit from knowing the effects of their behaviour, even if they do not understand the underlying relationship.

The relationship is clearly stated in the Pentateuch in precise terms. History and social science confirm it, and it is confirmed by Jesus Christ and by the Prophet Mohammed. The Koran records Mohammed repeatedly confirming the Pentateuch, referring to it both as a guide and as a warning, and Arab and Muslim history illustrates the working of the cause-and-effect relationship.

> See
>
> (1) 'History Speaks: Monarchy, Exile and Maccabees' {2}*
> (2) 'Social Responsibility, Profits and Social Accountability' {3}*
> (3) 'Origin of Christianity and Judaism' {4}*
> (4) 'Prophet Mohammed's Word of Allah and the Voice of the
>   Ruling Elite' {5}*

And what we have in the Pentateuch are rules of behaviour which point to the essence of humane behaviour. We know that ignoring them results in social corruption, oppression and exploitation of the many by the few. And we know that following these rules ensures social strength and a good life for all.

If we want freedom, independence, good life of high quality, then we have to follow these laws. If we do not, then we lose freedom, independence, good life and the country in which we live. The consequences of our behaviour cannot be avoided but we can change the course of events by changing our behaviour.

Social and Economic Security

All persons have the right to be free and independent masters of their own fate and no person may oppress or exploit another. Because people can be exploited through their needs there has to be a system of social and economic security which guarantees freedom from needs and so protects people from becoming dependent on others for essential income, which protects against loss of material independence and which protects people from losing their spiritual independence.

Every community member is entitled as a matter of right to full social security. This means that community members are entitled to be supported by the community not only when they fall on hard times but also to maintain their independence as independent breadwinners for their families. For example, the community has to provide backup funds to those who need them and they have to be provided as and when required.

To prevent people being exploited through their need these funds have to be provided without charging interest. They are called 'loans' because the recipient is under moral obligation to repay them to the community if he can do so. However, such 'loans' are cancelled every seventh calendar year if the borrower has been unable to repay them.

These essential social provisions of the Pentateuch are clear and to the point. This is what is laid down as a matter of law:

The community has to provide ('lend') money to those who need it, free of interest. All such loans, if outstanding, are to be cancelled every seventh year.

And what we have in the Pentateuch are rules of behaviour which point to the essence of humane behaviour. We know that ignoring them results in social corruption, oppression and exploitation of the many by the few. And we know that following these rules ensures social strength and a good life for all.

Government and Management

The Pentateuch's laws of government relate to 'rulers', apply to all in positions of trust, responsibility or authority, no matter whether secular, religious or military, no matter what the hierarchy or organisation.

These laws control the behaviour and limit the power of government, of top executives and of the establishment, of those in positions of trust, responsibility or authority. The Pentateuch leaves little doubt about what they must not do.

Such people may not amass servants and may not oppress the people for their own benefit. They may not amass possessions and wealth, may not grasp power or behave promiscuously. In other words, they may not put themselves above others by grasping power, may not satisfy personal desires at the expense of others.

So these Pentateuch laws quoted here protect people and safeguard their strength and freedom by laying down that those in positions of trust, responsibility or authority may not grasp power, may not oppress the people, may not behave promiscuously, may not enrich themselves. Those in authority must not oppress people so as to increase their own possessions and power, must not form enforcing squads or organisations so as to multiply their own power.

Equality and Ownership

Ownership is the right to possess something and to decide what is to be done with it. If I own something it belongs to me and I decide what is to be done with it. An example would be owning a house.

Possession is having something in one's custody as distinct from owning it. If I possess something it belongs to another but I can decide how to use it. An example would be renting a house.

Another example would be deciding what to do with my money (ownership) or deciding and controlling the use of money belonging to someone else (possession).

And considering the right to ownership, two questions need to be considered. Namely where does the right come from and how is it exercised.

The right to own property varies among societies. Ownership laws which assign ownership 'rights' to owners have been devised by the owners themselves or by those who serve them.

Ownership of land and means of production, of funds and wealth, has always been accumulated at someone else's expense. All belonged to the community, belonged to all alike. And this is what Chapter 5 of Genesis appears to be saying.

A human right is a something one may legally or morally claim, is the state of being entitled to a privilege or immunity or authority to act. Human rights are those held to be claimable by any living person, apply to all living people. Every living person is entitled to them.

So ownership of land and means of production, of funds and wealth, rightfully belongs to the community, belongs to all alike, is a human right. Those who have accumulated them have only possession, which means they can use and apply them but may do so only on behalf of, and for the benefit of, the community and that they are accountable to the community for the way in which they do so.

Hence we have the use of possessions as long as we use them to provide a good living for our family, and beyond that for the benefit of the community. For the benefit of others less able or fortunate, for the benefit of the community around us and then for the benefit of communities abroad.

Role of the Biblical Prophets, and their Warnings

The sayings of the prophets show clearly that the prophets were very much aware of the consequences of what was taking place. They pointed out what was bound to happen if the rulers, their secular and religious establishments, and perhaps also the people, continued to behave as they were doing, and events proved them right.

The prophets appear to have had a clear understanding of the inevitability with which the law acts, with which events follow the Social Cause-and-Effect Relationship. And they accuse the rulers and the ruling level for what they do and hold them responsible for what their establishment does and thus for the behaviour of the people.

The prophets were not listened to, the rulers and their establishments continued to corrupt and oppress the people until both kingdoms were destroyed and the people most viciously dispersed.

The Cause-and-Effect Relationship tells us that disaster and destruction were inevitably caused by the behaviour of the rulers and their establishment, and by the resulting behaviour of the people.

So now let us look at the kind of behaviour the prophets warned against as it was that kind of behaviour which was weakening the people and thus the country.

We see that the prophets warned about the consequences of delinquency, crime, sexual permissiveness and corruption. They warned about land being concentrated in the hands of a few, of Jew exploiting and oppressing Jew, of people being oppressed and enslaved through debt and through need.

Outstanding is that the warnings of the prophets were ignored, that the establishment of the day ignored the writing on the wall. They did not act then, they did not act at other times. In so doing they did not just oppress their people, what they were doing was to destroy their people and to destroy themselves as well.

See 'History Speaks: Monarchy, Exile and Maccabees' {2}*

and see 'One Law for All: Freedom Now, Freedom for Ever' {7}*

And Now

I showed years ago, in 'Social Responsibility, Profits and Social Accountability', that we were experiencing a sequence of accidents and catastrophes which were occurring more and more frequently and were affecting more and more people.

Since then most people have become aware of this. But I also showed what could and should be done about this trend of events. However, a new factor has entered the equation. It is now possible for the first time in the history of human beings on this planet for just one or only a few socially irresponsible persons to do something or to introduce changes which could destroy us all or else make this planet uninhabitable for human beings.

So now we do not have a choice. If we do not now observe and put into effect the social laws (rules) and social system of the Pentateuch and its code of behaviour, then the planet is likely to become uninhabitable for human beings and their look-alikes.

Sources

{1}*   See chapter 2.1:
       'The God-given Human Rights, Social Laws and
       Social System'
       Manfred Davidmann

{2}*   In 'Judaism: Basis - Past - Present - Future, Part 1'
       Manfred Davidmann
       ISBN 978-0-85192-060-3
       see chapter 2.2: 'History Speaks: Monarchy,
       Exile and Maccabees'

{3}*   In 'Messianic Struggle:
       The Worldwide Struggle for a Good and
       Secure Life for All, Here and Now'
       Manfred Davidmann
       ISBN 978-0-85192-059-7
       see chapter 2: 'Social Responsibility, Profits
       and Social Accountability'

{4}*   'Origin of Christianity and Judaism:
       What Actually Happened, What Jesus Actually
       Taught and Later Changes'
       Manfred Davidmann
       www.solhaam.org

{5}*   In 'Islam: Basis – Past – Present – Future'
       Manfred Davidmann
       ISBN 978-0-85192-053-5
       see chapter: 7: 'Prophet Mohammed's Word of Allah
       and the Voice of the Ruling Elite'

{6}*   In 'Judaism: Basis - Past - Present - Future, Part 1'
       Manfred Davidmann
       ISBN 978-0-85192-060-3
       see chapter 2.1: 'Struggle for Freedom:
       The Social Cause-and-Effect Relationship'

{7}*   In 'Judaism: Basis - Past - Present - Future, Part 1'
       Manfred Davidmann
       ISBN 978-0-85192-060-3
       see chapter 2.4: 'One Law for All:
       Freedom Now, Freedom for Ever'

Additions by the Editor:

In the original text of this chapter on the solhaam.org website Manfred Davidmann referred to other reports in form of links.

Here these reports are marked { }* and the sources are stated.

The Meaning of Genesis

What Manfred Davidmann has done with his works on the Pentateuch and the Bible, on religion and church-state relations, is to expose and correct the misinterpretations and mistranslations of the past. His works are major breakthroughs, constituting essential information for understanding the meaning and significance of the Pentateuch and of the Bible.

In his "Meaning and Significance of the Names of God in Genesis" {1}*, for example, Manfred Davidmann proved the meaning and significance of the different names of God which had been lost. In "Meaning and Intent of Genesis: Essential Notes on Hebrew Grammar" {2}*, he stated the fundamental rules which were ignored at time of translation because required background knowledge was not available, with consequent mistranslations. And in "Bible Translations, Versions, Codes and Hidden Information in Bible and Talmud" {3}*, he showed how changes made in the past obscured the intended meaning.

The chapters on Genesis describe and illustrate the meaning and intent of Genesis. Each is self-contained but together they provide the knowledge needed for understanding Genesis, its allegories and their significance. These allegories illustrate and define the difference between good and evil, and the importance of behaviour on social strength, well-being and good life under modern conditions.

Manfred Davidmann's research and discoveries showed and proved that the source text of Genesis, written several thousand years ago, corresponds in the major steps to the order in which the earth and life are known to have been formed and developed.

Described is the formation of the earth and early plant life, and evolution by 'the survival of the fittest'. The evolution from reptilian to mammalian instincts, feelings and behaviour is clearly stated, as is the evolution and corresponding behaviour, feeling and thinking of human beings from humanoids (animals resembling humans) through Homo erectus (early man) to Homo sapiens (human beings, ourselves).

There is no conflict or contradiction between what is recorded in the source text of Genesis and our scientific knowledge about evolution of human beings and of our planet.

Manfred Davidmann also summarises corresponding present social problems and describe the Pentateuch's social laws and social system for overcoming them.

Creation, Evolution and the Origin of Evil {4}*

Genesis is the first volume of the Pentateuch. It begins by describing how the planet was created, in other words how it was formed, the changes which occurred as the planet aged, how plants and animals were formed, evolved and populated the planet. It describes how human beings evolved and also how the behaviour of life forms changed as human beings evolved.

When the Pentateuch (Five Books of Moses) was written, people had but little knowledge about science or evolution compared with what is known today. So concepts for which we now have precise terms were described rather than stated and were expressed in religious terms so that they could be appreciated and followed by the population.

Understanding this we see that there is no conflict, no contradiction, no divergence, only awe-inspiring agreement, between what was recorded in Genesis and what we now know about the evolution of human beings. And Genesis defines good and evil, pointing to the root of evil.

Pre-flood Evils and the Social Problems of Our Time {5}*

Genesis (in its chapters 5 and 6) describes the behaviour of human beings before the flood. There is no conscious knowledge of good and evil and of the difference between them and their behaviour is like that of their primitive ancestors. Their behaviour is stated and condemned as evil. These two chapters of Genesis outline evil behaviour.

Genesis (chapter 5) shows people amassing possessions and wealth and dominating others by brutal strength. It contains a hidden list of pre-flood evil behavior.

This chapter also summarises corresponding present social problems, and describes the Pentateuch's social laws and social system for overcoming them.

Morality, Sexual Behaviour and Depravity {6}*

Genesis chapter 6 adds unrestrained sexual behaviour. Summarises corresponding present social problems. It records what is, and is not, moral sexual behaviour and the unavoidable consequences of depravity. Clearly stated is that the consequences cannot be avoided.

Describes the Pentateuch's social laws and social system for achieving a good life of high quality.

Nephilim, Dominance and Liberty   {7}*

The Pentateuch's social laws and social system for achieving and keeping liberty and a good life of high quality are described.

Genesis chapter 6 adds and considers the gaining and misuse of power over others. Corresponding present social problems are summarised. We are told the consequences of allowing some people to misuse their abilities to manipulate, control and enslave others.

The flood follows and from here onwards Genesis shows a conscious knowledge developing of good and evil, stressing consequent reward and punishment, justice and retribution.

And the Pentateuch states and describes the social laws of behaviour and the social system which have to be kept as they enable people to gain and keep liberty and good lives of high quality.

Differentiating Between Good and Evil   {8}*

Human beings are shown to be becoming numerous and spreading out, behaving much as before the flood. Different communities developed different customs, traditions, ways of behaving.

Shows that with the life and travels of the Patriarchs, some learned to know the difference between good and evil, learned to behave humanely.

Meaning and Significance of the Names of God in Genesis   {1}*

Manfred Davidmann includes his published findings which proved the meaning and significance of the different names of God which had been lost. He describes and proves the meaning and significance of the names of God which are used in Genesis and which are of greatest importance for understanding the meaning of the text of the Bible.

Meaning and Intent of Genesis: Essential Notes on Hebrew Grammar {2}*

Here he includes his already published findings, stating the fundamental rules which were ignored at time of translation because required background knowledge was not available at that time, with consequent mistranslations. He lists and illustrates the grammatical rules which help to differentiate between references to individuals and references to groups or life forms. Essential information for understanding the meaning of Genesis.

Bible Translations, Versions, Codes and Hidden Information in Bible and Talmud {3}*

Here Manfred Davidmann includes the report he published some time ago which proved how changes made in the past obscured the original intended meaning. He also describes the ways in which hidden information has been encoded and labeled so that its original meaning could not be misunderstood or misinterpreted.

References

{1}*   See chapter 10.1:
        'Meaning and Significance of the Names of God
        in Genesis'
        Manfred Davidmann

{2}*   See chapter 10.2:
        'Meaning and Intent of Genesis: Essential Notes
        on Hebrew Grammar'
        Manfred Davidmann

{3}*   See chapter 10.3:
        'Bible Translations, Versions, Codes and
        Hidden Information in Bible and Talmud'
        Manfred Davidmann

{4}*   In 'God and People:
        The Social Laws and Social System Underlying
        Judaism, Christianity, Islam and Democracy'
        Manfred Davidmann
        ISBN 978-0-85192-054-2
        see chapter 6.1: 'The Meaning of Genesis:
        Creation, Evolution and the Origin of Evil'

{5}*   In 'God and People:
        The Social Laws and Social System Underlying
        Judaism, Christianity, Islam and Democracy'
        Manfred Davidmann
        ISBN 978-0-85192-054-2
        see chapter 6.2: 'The Meaning of Genesis:
        Pre-flood Evils and the Social Problems of Our Time'

{6}*   In 'God and People:
The Social Laws and Social System Underlying
Judaism, Christianity, Islam and Democracy'
Manfred Davidmann
ISBN 978-0-85192-054-2
see chapter 6.3: 'The Meaning of Genesis:
Morality, Sexual Behaviour and Depravity'

{7}*   In 'God and People:
The Social Laws and Social System Underlying
Judaism, Christianity, Islam and Democracy'
Manfred Davidmann
ISBN 978-0-85192-054-2
see chapter 6.4: 'The Meaning of Genesis:
Nephilim, Dominance and Liberty'

{8}*   In 'God and People:
The Social Laws and Social System Underlying
Judaism, Christianity, Islam and Democracy'
Manfred Davidmann
ISBN 978-0-85192-054-2
see chapter 6.5: 'The Meaning of Genesis:
Differentiating Between Good and Evil'

Additions by the Editor:

* Added by the editor

{1}*, {2}* and {3}* are included here in accordance with the author's notes about the content of this book.

Meaning and Significance of the Names of God in Genesis

Names of God
Meaning of the Names of God
References {..}

Names of God

Understanding the meaning and significance of the names by which God is referred to in the Bible is of the greatest importance for understanding the meaning of the text of the Bible.

Translations into English from the Hebrew text refer to God using three designations, namely God, Lord God, and Lord.

Hebrew	English
Elohim	God
Yhwh Elohim	Lord God
Yhwh	the Lord

Yhwh

This designation is generally represented by its four consonants.

It was apparently regularly pronounced with its vowels until the destruction of the First Temple. But its pronunciation was avoided from the third century BCE. From then on the Hebrew word consisting of the consonants Yhwh was pronounced 'Adonay' and translated as 'the Lord' although 'Adonay' means 'my Lords'. Hence Yhwh is being translated as 'the Lord'. {1}

The true pronunciation of Yhwh was apparently 'Yahweh', meaning 'He causes to be, He brings into existence'. In the Middle Ages vowel points were added to the consonantal form of the Bible. 'Those used for Yhwh produced the form YeHoVaH and Christian scholars then introduced the name Jehovah.' {1}.

So Yhwh, regardless of how you pronounce it, means 'He causes to be'.

Elohim

The word 'Eloha' means God, and its plural 'Elohim' means 'gods'. Elohim is usually translated as if it meant 'God'.

Yhwh Elohim

Yhwh means 'He causes to be' and also 'He brings into existence'. 'Elohim' means 'gods' but here also is usually translated as if it meant 'God'.
So 'Yhwh Elohim' means God brings into existence.

Hence the meaning and significance of the names of God is as follows:

Meaning of the Names of God

Hebrew Name	ELOHIM	YHWH ELOHIM	YHWH
Translated as	God	Lord God	the Lord
Derivation of Name	God who creates, Creating God	God who brings into existence, God who originates, Originating God	He causes to be, What took place was, What happened was, What is happening
Meaning of Name	**GOD** or **GOD (AS CREATOR).** God as creator, as creator of all that is good.	**GOD (AS ORIGINATOR)**	**GOD (AS CAUSE),** as cause of what happened. In other words, this is happening, is what happened.

Example 1: (Gen 7: 16)

And they ... went in (into the ark) ... as God (Elohim) commanded him; and the Lord (Yhwh) shut him in.

Example 2: From {3}

In (Gen 3: 17) the ground is cursed by God (Yhwh Elohim, as originator), meaning that it will be so.

(Gen 5: 29) states that God (Yhwh, as cause) has cursed, meaning that it is happening, that it is so.

For detailed comprehensive discussions, illustrations and comments

on the meaning, significance and use of the different names of God in the Bible, see reference {2}.

References

{1} Encyclopaedia Judaica
Keter Publishing House Jerusalem Ltd, 1974

{2} In 'God and People:
The Social Laws and Social System Underlying
Judaism, Christianity, Islam and Democracy'
Manfred Davidmann
ISBN 978-0-85192-054-2
see chapter 6.1: 'The Meaning of Genesis:
Creation, Evolution and the Origin of Evil'

{3} In 'God and People:
The Social Laws and Social System Underlying
Judaism, Christianity, Islam and Democracy'
Manfred Davidmann
ISBN 978-0-85192-054-2
see chapter 6.2: 'The Meaning of Genesis:
Pre-flood Evils and the Social Problems of Our Time'

Meaning and Intent of Genesis: Essential Notes on Hebrew Grammar

'Adam' and Hebrew Grammar

Eth	'Eth' is put before the object of the sentence if the object is either a definite noun (has article 'ha') or a proper noun (proper name).
	Example:
	Jim ate the bread.
	'Jim' is the subject, the doer of the action.
	'Bread' is the object of the action.
Eth adam	'Adam' is the proper name of one person, refers to the person whose name is 'Adam'.
Ha-adam	Life form(s). Example: Human beings.
	As 'Adam' stands for 'life form', one can put 'ha' in front.
	If 'Adam' is a proper name, one cannot say 'ha-adam'.
	In other words, 'ha-adam' cannot refer to a person named 'Adam'.
Eth ha-adam	The life form is the object of the sentence. The life forms are the object of the sentence.

For detailed comprehensive discussions, illustrations and comments on the meaning and significance of the different forms of 'Adam' used in Genesis, see

In 'God and People:
The Social Laws and Social System Underlying
Judaism, Christianity, Islam and Democracy'
Manfred Davidmann
ISBN 978-0-85192-054-2
see chapter 6.1: 'The Meaning of Genesis:
Creation, Evolution and the Origin of Evil'

Bible Translations, Versions, Codes and Hidden Information in Bible and Talmud

Introduction

When something does not make sense in a Bible text in the light of current knowledge, that is when we do not understand it, then it is our knowledge and understanding of the text which is inadequate.

When translators do not know or understand the intended meaning of a Bible text or think their then current knowledge or thoughts are way ahead of the Bible's, then their translations can obscure the original meaning of a text, can mislead.

And similarly misleading can be new versions which allow for or include then current popular words or phrases, views or ideologies.

The extent to which this has taken place can be judged by the examples which follow.

Knowledge for Understanding not Available at Time of Translation

Genesis describes the creation and development of the planet and of life, including the evolution of early man and modern human beings, and defines human behaviour stating what is good and what is evil. {1}

This deep knowledge has remained obscured till now because the Hebrew 'ha-adam' meaning 'life form' was ungrammatically taken to refer to an individual called 'Adam' because the term 'life form' could not be understood at that time. {5}

Similarly the meaning and significance of the names by which God is referred to in the Pentateuch (Torah, Five Books of Moses) is of great importance for understanding the text. The distinct meaning of the different names could not have been understood until recently. {1, 2}

Bible Versions (Making Changes)

In Genesis Chapter 5, the Septuagint and the Samaritan Pentateuch smoothed out the Masoretic chronology's listed life spans, each in a different way, and so smoothed out, obscured, clues needed for understanding the meaning of the text. {4}

Obscuring Meaning by Making Changes

Consider the names in Genesis Chapter 2 about rivers flowing out of Eden. Here the translators of the King James Bible apparently concluded that then current knowledge indicated that Cush and Asshur referred to Ethiopia and Assyria, even though these countries did not exist at the time of the events related in Chapter 2. By doing this they obscured the connection between chapters 2 and 10 of Genesis which confirms the meaning of the allegory of the rivers flowing out of Eden {1}, as follows:

	Name of	Hebrew	Named in Translation	
			Soncino Chumash	King James Bible
Gen 2:13	Land	Cush		Ethiopia
Gen 2:14	River	Hiddekel	Tigris	Hiddekel
	Land	Asshur		Assyria

Hidden Information in Pentateuch and Talmud

Where Pentateuch and Talmud contain hidden information, then this is pointed to, stated and confirmed, at the same time and in a number of different independent ways, to ensure the message is understood as it was intended to be understood.

In the Talmud, Jews did not openly write about Christian activists, Christian beliefs and Christians, they wrote about them in a roundabout way. A positive statement would be expressed using negatives or else turned upside down by stating its opposite. A good example is the hidden way in which the Talmud refers to Christians and early Christian beliefs in three different ways at the same time to make sure the meaning could not be misunderstood or misrepresented. {6, 8} <1>

Another example from the Talmud illustrates rather beautifully how opposites are used forcefully and convincingly to make a specific point which would have been unacceptable to the religious establishment if it had been openly stated. {7} <2>

Another example, in Genesis Chapter 5, is the hidden description of evil human behaviour before the flood. {4} <3>

And also, in Genesis Chapter 6, how verses 3 and 4 relate and confirm each other regarding the Nephilim. {9}

Use of Key Phrases for Linking Statements

A clear example of the use of key-phrases for linking statements comes from the travels of the patriarchs in Genesis. Three separate stories in different chapters form a connected statement. They are linked by the key phrase that in each case the patriarch is afraid of being killed by local men for the sake of his beautiful wife. That the linking is intentional is confirmed by a second key phrase, namely 'she is my sister'. {3} <4>

Another example, in the Gospels, connects the allegories of 'The Rich Young Man' and 'The Labourers in the Vineyard', the key phrase being 'But many that are first will be last, and the last first'. {6} <5>

And the Talmud records a key argument about whether the God-given Pentateuch or an establishment-favouring modification are to be taught and followed. Here also the statements are located in different volumes but connected by key phrases. {8} <6>

Politically Motivated Changes

Some changes have been and are politically motivated.

Take the argument in the Talmud about whether the God-given Pentateuch or an establishment-favouring modification are to be taught and followed. The argument clearly proves that it is the God-given Pentateuch which has to be followed. But Rabbinical Judaism (today's Judaism) ignores this and teaches the opposite, quoting only one statement out of context as if it were the concluding statement. {8}

A further example, from the Talmud, describes how the God-serving religious hierarchy was replaced by an establishment-serving religious hierarchy, and their antisocial changes to belief and practice. This is conclusively recorded in two different and separate ways which confirm each other. But Rabbinical Judaism (today's Judaism) does not teach this and so propagates a revisionist and antisocial version of Jewish belief and practice. {7} <7>

Another example comes from the Gospels. Matthew's gospel was the first to be written. It is closest to the events and so perhaps it is not surprising that it has always been the most popular and revered of the gospels. It was later followed by Mark's and this in turn was followed by Luke's gospel. The later authors were apparently aware of and knew the earlier gospels which seems confirmed by the successive changes which were made which changed the record of what Jesus taught and of the meaning of the stories and of the arguments. {6} <8>

Notes and References

Notes

<1> In {8} see what is recorded about R. Johanan b. Zakkai's disciple Joshua b. Hananiah.

<2> In {7}, under 'Shemaiah and Avtalyon', see '(1b) Identities and Purpose'. The verse begins with Naaman was a resident alien'.

<3> In {4} see 'Descendants of Seth (Behaviour of Human Beings'.

<4> In {3} see 'Sanctity of Marriage'

<5> See {6} about how this is recorded in different Gospels.

<6> In {8} see Figure 1 'Beth Hillel's Claims to Rule by Divine Right'

<7> In {7} see 'The Five Pairs (Zugot)' which includes Figure 2 'Names of the Pairs' and Figure 3 'Laying-on of Hands'.

<8> In {6} see 'Gospels'

References

{1}   In 'God and People:
The Social Laws and Social System Underlying Judaism, Christianity, Islam and Democracy'
Manfred Davidmann
ISBN 978-0-85192-054-2
see chapter 6.1: 'The Meaning of Genesis: Creation, Evolution and the Origin of Evil'

{2}   See chapter 10.1:
'Meaning and Significance of the Names of God in Genesis'
Manfred Davidmann

{3}   In 'God and People:
The Social Laws and Social System Underlying Judaism, Christianity, Islam and Democracy'
Manfred Davidmann
ISBN 978-0-85192-054-2
see chapter 6.3: 'The Meaning of Genesis: Morality, Sexual Behaviour and Depravity'

{4}   In 'God and People:
The Social Laws and Social System Underlying Judaism, Christianity, Islam and Democracy'
Manfred Davidmann
ISBN 978-0-85192-054-2
see chapter 6.2: 'The Meaning of Genesis: Pre-flood Evils and the Social Problems of Our Time'

{5}   See chapter 10.2:
'Meaning and Intent of Genesis: Essential Notes on Hebrew Grammar'
Manfred Davidmann

6}   'Origin of Christianity and Judaism:
What Actually Happened, What Jesus Actually
Taught and Later Changes'
Manfred Davidmann
www.solhaam.org

{7}   In 'Judaism: Basis - Past - Present - Future, Part 1'
Manfred Davidmann
ISBN 978-0-85192-060-3
see chapter 2.3: 'At the Time of Jesus,
This is What Actually Happened in Israel:
The Truth about Hillel and his Times'

{8}   In 'Judaism: Basis - Past - Present - Future, Part 1'
Manfred Davidmann
ISBN 978-0-85192-060-3
see chapter 2.4: 'One Law for All:
Freedom Now, Freedom for Ever'

{9}   In 'God and People:
The Social Laws and Social System Underlying
Judaism, Christianity, Islam and Democracy'
Manfred Davidmann
ISBN 978-0-85192-054-2
see chapter 6.4: 'The Meaning of Genesis:
Nephilim, Dominance and Liberty'

Chapter 11

The Social Laws and Social System of the Pentateuch:
(Ha Mim) The Word of Allah as Taught by Mohammed

(Ha Mim) The Word of Allah as Taught by Mohammed

    Umm al-Kitab – The Mother of the Book (Its Source)

    Guide and Warning: Be Guided (do well and prosper) or Ignore (fail, want and suffer)

Sources

Notes <..>

The right to the land in which one lives, that is the strength and success of a people, depends on how people behave towards each other. The Pentateuch <1> states which kind of behaviour gives strength, which provides a good life of high quality, which ensures independence and freedom from oppression and exploitation.

These behaviour guidelines apply to all.

In the language of religion, the land does not belong to anyone other than God. Those who live in it may use, and benefit from, the land but only as long as they follow God's laws. If they do not, then in due course the land is repossessed and transferred to someone else. Ignorance is no excuse. Those who stop following the law lose their entitlement to use it and are in due course driven out and persecuted.

In everyday language and in the language of science we know that people are affected and changed by their own behaviour and that communities stand or fall according to their actions, as a result of the behaviour of the community as a whole. Oppress and exploit and your community will get weaker and weaker and fail in the end. Follow a pattern of social behaviour and establish a social system which are based on social fairness and justice and you will gain strength and prosper and this will continue while you are doing so. People have to be told about the relevance of the social laws under present conditions.

(Ha Mim) The Word of Allah as Taught by Mohammed

Mohammed's social teachings are here stated from Koran chapters (suras) singled out by 'Abbreviated Letters', statements of revelation from compassionate and caring Allah.

The quotations from the Koran are within their context. Those recording the word of Allah as taught by Mohammed are drawn from all the suras (chapters) beginning with the abbreviated letters 'ha mim' (suras 40-41, 43-46), but not from the one sura (sura 42) which begins with the abbreviated letters 'ha mim: ain sin qaf'.

Umm al-Kitab - The Mother of the Book (Its Source)

Mohammed teaches that God's benevolent social laws and system have to be applied by people in their daily life, that those who in the past erred from God's way are in grave error.

The content of the corresponding compassionate and benevolent teachings are described as are the Koran's stated rewards for following them and the consequences of ignoring or opposing them. (See 'Prophet Mohammed's Word of Allah and the Voice of the Ruling Elite' {1}*)

The quotations from the Koran which follow speak for themselves.

The book (al-kitab, the Pentateuch) came down (tanzil) from God, the mighty, the wise-one.
> The arabic phrase for the Holy Koran is 'al-Koran'. The Pentateuch (the Five Books of Moses) is 'al-kitab', a religious book is 'mushaf'.
> <2>
{40:002, 45:002, 46:002}

We gave Moses guidance (al-huda)
> huda: guidance or guide.
and gave the book (al-kitab, the Pentateuch) to the Children of Israel to inherit.
A guide (huda) and a reminder (warning) to people who understand.
> To those who understand its commandments (message), it is a guide (about what is 'good', about what to do) and a warning (about what is evil, about what not to do).
{40:053-54}

In the name of God, the Compassionate, the Merciful,
by the book (al-kitab, the Pentateuch) that explains clearly,
We made it an arabic teaching (qur'an, koran) so that you become wiser.

The word 'koran' (Arabic: qur'an) came from the Syro-Aramaic
'qeryan' (current at the time of Mohammed) meaning teachings or
lectures.
It (the teaching) is from the mother text which we have,
'umm al-kitab': the Pentateuch referred to as mother text, as
source text.
sublime and full of wisdom.
{43:001-4}

Before (the teaching) the Book of Moses (kitab Musa)
was a standard for judging (imam) and a (source of) compassion
and this book (kitab) is confirmed in the Arabic language
to warn those who are unjust (wrongdoers) and to give good news to the
righteous.
{46:012}

We made this easy (to understand) in your own language
so that they may take heed.
Take heed: to pay (or take) careful attention; In modern Arabic:
'to remember'.
{44:058}

And now We have set you on the right way of our commandment (sharia
amr),
so follow it, and do not follow the desires of ignorant people (those who
do not have that knowledge)
for they cannot shield you from God.
{45:018}

The wrongdoers (zalamin) are supporters (awliya) of each others (help
and support, protect, each other);
Zalamin (wrongdoers): Those who transgress, wrong other people,
treat others badly, are unjust, are unfair, oppress, exploit.
but the protector (wali) of those who guard against evil (resist
temptation) is God.
{45:019}

**Guide and Warning: Be Guided (do well and prosper) or
Ignore (fail, want and suffer)**

Here Mohammed reveals the word of almighty God, stating the
Pentateuch's Cause-and-Effect Relationship in religious terms so that his
listeners can understand and be guided, can follow and prosper, are
warned about the dire consequences of not following what he is
teaching.

What happens to an individual and a community depends on present and past behaviour and not just on good intentions. The wrongdoer (unbeliever) does not understand he is drawing serious consequences (punishment) upon himself as the inevitable inescapable consequence of his own behaviour. If people reject or oppose God, if God's laws are not followed, God withdraws his protection from them. Misfortune (evil) strikes until they change their ways and return to God, that is, until they apply God's social laws and social system in their daily lives.

One has to talk to people in language they can understand and here we see how, at God's request, Mohammed revealed the Social Cause-and-Effect Relationship, referring to it in religious terms both as guide and warning.

Say (to them): "I am only a mortal like you;
It has come to me (yuhi) that there is only one God.
So take the right way to Him, and ask His forgiveness."
      Literal: So 'you go in the right way' and ... (istakimu)
And woe to those who serve associates (mushrekin) beside Him;
      Mushrekin (associates): Guides, masters, overlords or supreme
      beings with whom a person associates (to which a person
      attributes) a god-like knowledge or authority. That which or those
      whom you consider to be like God, that or those whose orders you
      obey as if they came from God.
{41:006}

(To) those who reject the warning when it is preached to them:
It is an unassailable scripture (kitab aziz).
Falsehood cannot come from it or from that which follows it,
sent down (tanzil) from one full of wisdom, worthy of praise.
{41:041-42}

Nothing is said to you that has not been said to the other messengers before you.
Your Lord is forgiving, but also punishes severely.
Say: To those who believe, it is guidance and healing;
But those who do not believe are deaf and blind.
They are like men called to from a far-off place.
{41:043-44}

He that does what is right does it for his own good;
and he that commits evil does so at his own peril.
Your Lord is never unjust to human beings (abid).
{41:046}

When We bestow favours on a human being,
and he then turns aside and withdraws himself,
evil befalls him (till) his prayer is broad.
> 'Till his prayer is broad': Till he returns to the right way by
> following God's commandments. Till he prays (follows God's way)
> on a wide front.
{41:051}

> A clear statement of the Pentateuch's 'Social Cause-and-Effect
> Relationship'. See description at beginning of this section.

> And continuing the statement of the 'Social Cause-and-Effect
> Relationship', showing how it operates, as described at the
> beginning of this section.

Those who say, God is our Master, and then continue on the right way,
shall have no fear nor shall they grieve.
> The right way is to live by following God's commandments (ayaat,
> directives, divine rules) in everyday life.
{46:013}

But those who dispute God's directives (ayaat) do not have (God's)
authority to do so.
They are driven by
the ambition to become great
> To achieve power over, to dominate, to control, others; to
> become powerful
which they will never achieve.
Therefore seek refuge in God; God hears all and observes all.
> Literal: seek protection (from or in) God.
{40:056}

Those that reject Our directives (ayaat) when they know little of them
shall have humiliating sorrow.
{45:009}

Behind them is hell,
> Hell follows them, they cannot escape.
They will not profit from their labours (earnings),
> Literal: What they earned will not make them richer.
nor will those whom they have chosen to protect them (awliya) beside
Allah.
> awliya: rulers, masters, protectors in authority
Grievous sorrow awaits them.
{45:010}

Sources

{1}*   In 'Islam: Basis – Past – Present – Future'
Manfred Davidmann
ISBN 978-0-85192-053-5
see chapter 7: 'Prophet Mohammed's Word of Allah
and the Voice of the Ruling Elite'*
from which this theme's information was extracted.

Also see
In 'Judaism: Basis - Past - Present - Future, Part 1'
Manfred Davidmann
ISBN 978-0-85192-060-3
see chapter 5: 'The Right to the Land of Israel'*

and in this book:
see chapter 2.1:
'The God-given Human Rights, Social Laws and
Social System'*
Manfred Davidmann

and
see chapter 2.2:
'Church and State, Government and Religion:
Judaism, Christianity and Islam'*
Manfred Davidmann

Notes <..>

<1> The Pentateuch, that is the five books of Moses
(Also called Torah; Part of Old Testament).

<2> In 'Islam: Basis – Past – Present – Future'
Manfred Davidmann
ISBN 978-0-85192-053-5
see chapter 5: 'Compiling the Koran: Hadiths
(Traditions) State the Underlying Reality'*
see particularly 'Hadith 2: How Caliph Uthman
Ordered the Compilation of an Official Koran Text'
which clearly shows the meaning of these terms. And
see the other relevant Koranic verses below in this
report.

Additions by the Editor:

In the original text of this chapter on the solhaam.org website Manfred Davidmann referred to other reports in form of links.

Here these reports are marked * and the sources are stated.

Creationism and Intelligent Design, Evolution, Education or Indoctrination.
And
Reading, Interpreting, Translating of Ancient Consonantal Texts like the Bible or the Koran.

Reading, Interpreting, Translating of Ancient Consonantal Texts like the Bible or the Koran.

The first step towards understanding the content of the Bible is to understand how recorded letters and symbols were used to state the meaning of words. Such knowledge and understanding is particularly important when considering what scholars and clerics have done and are doing when they are 'interpreting' the text of the Bible.

Just why there has been so much confusion about reading, interpreting and translating of consonantal texts (like the Bible) can be seen from the following definitions:

'Consonant'   A letter of the alphabet other than a vowel

'Reading'   Choosing between likely words which fit the written groups of consonants while allowing for the likely meaning of the sentence or verse in which they appear.

'Interpreting'   Somehow deciding between, or choosing from, alternative meanings for the selected words or sentences.

Interpretation attempts to suggest or provide meaning where the text itself is unclear, ambiguous, seems to have none.

216

'Reading' and 'interpreting' are closely interconnected since choice of words determines the meaning of the sentence, of the text.

Translating scholars, working from a consonantal text (no vowels), had to 'read' the text. That is, they had to decide between, or choose from, alternative meanings for given groups of letters (words), considering and selecting the most likely meaning of the sentence (interpretation).

Of course, they could only 'read' and 'interpret' the text, could only select a 'most likely' meaning, within their own knowledge and understanding. That is, within the knowledge and understanding available to them at that time, at the time of translation.

For much else, including notes and sources, see the report
'Text, Language, Dialect and Interpretation of the Koran' {1}*
by Manfred Davidmann

Creationism and Intelligent Design, Evolution, Education or Indoctrination.

When the word "ereb" was taken to mean "evening", and the word "boker" was taken to mean "morning", then the phrase at the end of each stage of creation in Genesis could be interpreted to mean "there was evening and there was morning, one day." A reading and interpretation which corresponded to the knowledge and understanding of those doing the translating in those times. The knowledge needed for understanding Genesis was simply not available at time of translation.

But the 'word' ereb, said Manfred Davidmann, can mean "evening," or else "to mingle," or "not to distinguish between them." Likewise, the 'word' boker can mean "morning," or "to search," "to examine," and possibly "to check carefully." The statement about evening and morning, then, can just as easily be translated as

"there was a mingling and a uniformity and a searching for differences and an examination of differences"

- a clear statement of the process of evolutionary advance which, said Manfred Davidmann, is both valid and relevant considering our understanding of Genesis and our present scientific knowledge.

For much else, including notes and sources, see the report
'Creationism and Intelligent Design, Evolution, Education or Indoctrination' {2}*
by Manfred Davidmann

Sources

{1}* In 'Islam: Basis – Past – Present – Future'
      Manfred Davidmann
      ISBN 978-0-85192-053-5
      see chapter 3: 'Text, Language, Dialect and Interpretation
      of the Koran'

{2}* See chapter 2.4:
      'Creationism and Intelligent Design, Evolution, Education
      or Indoctrination'
      Manfred Davidmann

Additions by the Editor:

In the original text of this chapter on the solhaam.org website Manfred Davidmann referred to other reports in form of links.

Here these reports are marked { }* and the sources are stated.

Judaism at the Crossroads, at the Final Parting of the Ways

The Social Laws and Social System which Jews have to Follow
The Talmud's Record of Changing Beliefs and Practices
Hillel
    1. Shemaiah and Avtalyon: Enemies of the Jewish People
    2. Bene Bathyra: Sons or Children of the Covenant
    3. 'Interpreting' the Pentateuch's Social Laws and Social System
Hillel's Prosbul
Sources

The Social Laws and Social System which Jews have to Follow

Jews have to follow and live according to the Pentateuch's laws. At issue are the laws of behaviour and the social system which are laid down in the Pentateuch (Torah, Five Books of Moses):

> The Pentateuch states that all are equal, that no person may oppress or exploit another, that all have the right to be free and be independent masters of their own fate.

> Every person is entitled as a matter of right to social security. This means that people are entitled to be supported by the community not only when they fall on hard times but also to maintain their independence as independent breadwinners for their families.

> For example, the community has to provide backup funds to those who need them and they have to be provided as and when required. To prevent people being exploited through their need these funds have to be provided without charging interest and such 'loans' are cancelled every seventh year if the borrower has been unable to repay them.

> Those in authority must not oppress people so as to increase their own possessions and power, are warned against oppressing people, must not be promiscuous and must not amass wealth. The role of those who are rich is seen to be that of administering their

wealth and money on behalf of and for the community and not that of enriching themselves at the expense of the community.

The Pentateuch states the Ten Commandments, the social laws and the social system laws and states in religious language the unavoidable consequences of either following or else rejecting these laws. But the Pentateuch also states that this is a scientific Cause-and-effect relationship, lists causes and effects and states that the effects are reversible dependent on how people behave.

The laws of the Pentateuch have to be followed and applied by Jews as a matter of law in their daily lives.

However, it was such laws of behaviour and such social system laws which the rich simply did not want to apply and they, the rich and powerful, had the application of the laws changed to suit themselves.

The Talmud's Record of Changing Beliefs and Practices

The Jewish establishment (secular and religious) had been and was changing the application of the laws of the Pentateuch so that 'the law was becoming like two laws'. The Talmud was then written to record what was happening so that future generations would become aware of the course of events and of who had been doing what to whom. They also wanted future generations to learn from the lessons of the past so as to be able to reverse the tragedy of the destruction of the country, of Jerusalem, of the people.

But by the time the writing of the Talmud was finished, the actual message had been buried in a mass of stories and arguments. From that time onwards the essential core legislation of the Pentateuch had been negated and bypassed and buried under arguments about many subjects.

The Talmud is part of Jewish religious teachings, is frozen (has not been changed) but its real underlying meaning and message are kept hidden, are not known, understood or taught by today's religious or secular Jewish establishments.

Hillel

The Talmud tells how Hillel gained a following and took control, how he changed Jewish belief and practice on behalf of the Jewish establishment. We are told what he did and how he did it, and that he did so

1. because he was taught by Shemaiah and Avtalyon, and
2. that he took over from the Bene Bathyra, having
3. persuaded them to hand over by using abstract rules of logic and association for interpreting the law.

1. Shemaiah and Avtalyon: Enemies of the Jewish People

This example from the Talmud illustrates rather beautifully how opposites are used forcefully and convincingly to make a specific point which would have been unacceptable to the religious establishment if it had been openly stated. We are told that

- "Naaman was a resident alien.
- Nebuzaradan was a righteous proselyte,
- the descendants of Sisera studied Torah (the Pentateuch) in Jerusalem;
- the descendants of Sennacherib taught Torah to the multitude; who were these? - Shemaiah and Avtalyon.
- The descendants of Haman studied Torah at Bene Berak."

Here we are told of great and famous people serving God, studying and teaching the Pentateuch and its laws, serving God and people. Or so it may appear at first glance.

We know next to nothing about Shemaiah and Avtalyon, but all the other people mentioned here are among the worst enemies of the Jewish people. Nebuzaradan, for example, was captain of the guard of Nebuchadnezzar, king of Babylon, and commanded the forces which burned down Jerusalem and destroyed the first Temple.

In this way the Talmud records what would have been unacceptable to the religious establishment at that time, namely that Shemaiah and Avtalyon are among the worst and most destructive enemies of the Jewish people and that Hillel followed and applied their teachings.

2. Bene Bathyra: Sons or Children of the Covenant

We saw already that the Talmud counts Shemaiah and Avtalyon among the worst and most destructive enemies of the Jewish people, representing those who wish to oppress and exploit. And Hillel told the Bene Bathyra that he ruled over them because he had served Shemaiah and Avtalyon, while they (the Bene Bathyra) had dared not to serve them.

The Bene Bathyra, the sons or children of Bathyra, of those who are doing the cutting (circumcision), who are carrying out the Brit, the sons or children of the Covenant. In other words, those who follow and apply the social laws and social system of the Pentateuch in their daily lives.

3. 'Interpreting' the Pentateuch's Social Laws and Social System

The law was apparently being decided according to the Pentateuch and in line with its intent.

But then the establishment's use of abstract rules of logic and association for interpreting the law resulted in laws which were unrelated to, perhaps even outside or opposed to, the meaning of the original text of the Pentateuch. In this way controversy increased in Israel. As the followers of Hillel increased in number, so controversy increased in Israel.

Hillel's Prosbul

Hillel's ruling 'Prosbul' was annulled in 1994.

Sources

{1}*   See chapter 2.1:
       'The God-given Human Rights, Social Laws and
       Social System'
       Manfred Davidmann

{2}* In 'Judaism: Basis - Past - Present - Future, Part 1'
Manfred Davidmann
ISBN 978-0-85192-060-3
see chapter 2.3: 'At the Time of Jesus,
This is What Actually Happened in Israel:
The Truth about Hillel and his Times'

{3}* In 'Judaism: Basis - Past - Present - Future, Part 1'
Manfred Davidmann
ISBN 978-0-85192-060-3
see chapter 2.4: 'One Law for All:
Freedom Now, Freedom for Ever'

{4}* In 'Judaism: Basis - Past - Present - Future, Part 1'
Manfred Davidmann
ISBN 978-0-85192-060-3
see chapter 2.1: 'Struggle for Freedom:
The Social Cause-and-Effect Relationship'

{5}* In 'Judaism: Basis - Past - Present - Future, Part 1'
Manfred Davidmann
ISBN 978-0-85192-060-3
see chapter 2.2: 'History Speaks: Monarchy,
Exile and Maccabees'

{6}* 'Origin of Christianity and Judaism:
What Actually Happened, What Jesus Actually
Taught and Later Changes'
Manfred Davidmann
www.solhaam.org

{7}* In 'Judaism: Basis - Past - Present - Future, Part 1'
Manfred Davidmann
ISBN 978-0-85192-060-3
see chapter 3: 'Jewish Belief and Practice'

Additions by the Editor:

In the original text of this chapter on the solhaam.org website Manfred Davidmann referred to other reports in form of links.

Here these reports are marked { }* and the sources are stated.

Chapter 14

Israel and The Social Laws and Social System of the Pentateuch

The right to the land in which one lives, that is the strength and success of a people, depends on how people behave towards each other. The Pentateuch <1> states which kind of behaviour gives strength, which provides a good life of high quality, which ensures independence and freedom from oppression and exploitation.

These behavioural guidelines apply to all, and Jewish history proves the matter.

Israel

To the Jewish people, Israel is the promised land, the land which was promised to Jews by God and that it is thus their land.

It is perhaps because this property, this land in which milk and honey flows, has been singled out in such a special way by God, that so many try to benefit from the good life surely granted to all its inhabitants, that so many have struggled and are struggling to own and control this most desirable of all properties.

Persians, Babylonians, Seleucids and Egyptians all had a go as did Macedonians, Romans, Ottomans and Arabs. Christianity and Islam struggled to possess it for many years. Last but not least the Hebrews, the Jews of today, twice gained the country God had promised them only to be driven out later. Returning each time, they have now returned once again and re-established for the third time their rule over the country.

One can understand that such a wonderful gift from God should be in such demand - but how come the land changed hands so frequently, how come the bailiffs came so often and so regularly?

Perhaps it is simplistic to consider that God would enter into a one-sided and unconditional commitment, saying "There it is. It is yours to do with as you please" and then turn his back on subsequent proceedings.

There is the matter of the 'Covenant'. It is this which makes Jews the 'chosen' people. At Mount Sinai, Jews in effect agreed the Covenant, that contract between God and the Jewish people by which Jews agreed to accept and observe the Pentateuch's rules of behaviour and to be held accountable for the extent to which they did so. If they observed these rules of behaviour, then they and their descendants would live secure lives of high quality in the promised land.

So Jews are entitled to stay and use the land but only to the extent to which the Pentateuch's rules of behaviour are followed and observed. The bailiffs have come in so often in the past to expel the land's occupants because these did not observe these essential rules of behavior.

In the language of religion, the land of Israel does not belong to anyone other than God. Those who live in it may use and benefit from the land but only as long as they follow God's laws. If they do not, then in due course the land is repossessed and transferred to someone else. Ignorance is no excuse. Those who stop following the law lose their entitlement to use it and are in due course driven out and persecuted. (See 'The Right to the Land of Israel' {1}*)

The Social Laws and Social System of the Pentateuch

The contract document, namely the Pentateuch, was written down at the time, has not been changed, is public knowledge.

It lays down in precise terms a comprehensive social system and rules of behaviour which form the basis of, and ensure, a quality of life and a standard of living which have still not been achieved. It also states clearly the rewards for observing and the dire consequences of ignoring or breaking its rules of behaviour.

We are told that the consequences of one's behaviour are inevitable since they are determined by a scientific and inescapable Cause-and-Effect Relationship (See 'The Right to the Land of Israel' {1}*). Hence the right to the land of Israel and the future prosperity of its inhabitants depend on following the social laws and the social system of the Pentateuch. Ignorance is no excuse. What is outstandingly important is that the Cause-and-Effect Relationship applies to all people and at all times, and history clearly and convincingly illustrates the working of the relationship.

The Pentateuch teaches that all are equal and that one may neither exploit nor be exploited, and sets out a social system for ensuring that these laws are applied, for ensuring that rulers and establishments serve their people.

The social system guarantees everyone's personal and material independence with the community supporting those who are in need, supporting those whose independence is threatened or those who wish to establish their own material independence, say by setting up their own enterprise.

The role of the establishment (your leadership, rulers, managers, bureaucracy) is to lead you in the struggle for a better and more secure life of better quality, struggling by your side and for you, living as you do and at your standard of living.

The laws of government in the Pentateuch in effect lay down that it is the establishment which should serve the people and not the other way about.

The establishment may not enrich themselves, may not form enforcing organisations or systems, may not have a better quality of life than that of the community.

However, it is much easier to tell the rich to share their wealth than actually convince them to do so. But history has proved beyond doubt that the consequences of one's behaviour are as stated. The reason some of our lives resemble hell rather than heaven is because we have been unable to ensure that all are equal, because we have allowed some of us to oppress and exploit the others.

In everyday language and in the language of science we know that people are affected and changed by their own behaviour and that communities stand or fall according to their actions, as a result of the behaviour of the community as a whole. Oppress and exploit and your community will get weaker and weaker and fail in the end. Follow a pattern of social behaviour and establish a social system which are based on social fairness and justice and you will gain strength and prosper and this will continue while you are doing so. The people have to be told about the relevance of the social laws and under present conditions.

Sources

{1}*   In 'Judaism: Basis - Past - Present - Future, Part 1'
        Manfred Davidmann
        ISBN 978-0-85192-060-3
        see chapter 5: 'The Right to the Land of Israel'*

from which this theme's information was extracted.

Also in this book:
        see chapter 2.1:
        'The God-given Human Rights, Social Laws and
        Social System'*
        Manfred Davidmann

and
        see chapter 2.2:
        'Church and State, Government and Religion:
        Judaism, Christianity and Islam'*
        Manfred Davidmann

Notes <..>

<1> The Pentateuch, that is the five books of Moses
    (Also called Torah; Part of Old Testament).

Additions by the Editor:

In the original text of this chapter on the solhaam.org website Manfred Davidmann referred to other reports in form of links.

Here these reports are marked * and the sources are stated.

Chapter 15

Muslims and Jews

Introduction

A key part of this work is a comprehensive summary of the struggles of the Muslims (the followers of Mohammed) against the Meccan ruling elite of the Quraysh while Mohammed was alive, and of their conflicts with the Jewish Medinan clans.

The sequence of events listed here has largely been taken from chapter 2 {5}, which relates primarily to Mohammed's struggle for recognition of his mission and message. Added here is the information about the small Jewish clans of Medina.

It is a factual record of what took place, from the work of well-known scholars and academics such as Richard Bell, Peter Mansfield and Maxime Rodinson, which confirm and complement each other. Meaning by this that it is a record of what actually happened.

And this factual record leads to unexpected but convincing conclusions.

Arab Life at the Time of Mohammed

We saw in chapter 2 {5} that there were no restraints to communal acts of violence, that might was right.

> According to Peter Mansfield there were raids and reprisals aimed at driving off the opponents' camels. Women and children captured in tribal warfare who were not ransomed became tribal slaves and could be bought and sold. {2}

Warlike raids were frequent, and Richard Bell records:

> These for the most part aimed at capture of booty rather than at bloodshed. But it was a rough game, in which the attempt to drive off cattle and other booty often led to fighting and bloodshed. The law of retaliation prevailed. {1}

A defeated tribe's males could be slaughtered even after surrendering, their women and children enslaved, their possessions distributed among the victors, when there was no fear of retaliation. With loot (material and human) apparently being the key objective of intertribal skirmishes and warfare.

The tribes were constantly at war with each other, except for four months of truce every year. {4}

Apart from those who were full members of the tribe by descent, there would be others attached to it such as slaves. There were also 'clients' of the tribe who had asked for the sheikh's temporary protection, for example while pasturing their flocks on his land. {2}

Mohammed is born into this kind of society of illiterate desert Arabs. Life was harsh and a continuous struggle for survival.

And how Mohammed lived, and what he did or did not do, are the direct consequence of having to struggle, survive and succeed against great odds in that kind of society.

Sequence of Events

The information in the table which follows is arranged thus:

Date   **Meccan Elite** (History of Mohammed's struggle against the Meccan elite)

          Jewish Clans (Information about the Medinan Jewish clans, and history of the confrontations between Mohammed's followers and these clans. Set in as shown.)

                  Outcome (Listing of outcomes of these confrontations. Set in as shown.)

613-622	Mohammed taught that people should follow the edicts of the one all-seeing and almighty but compassionate God, and the obligation of generosity and respect for the rights of the poor and the defenceless. {3}

Preaching the obligation of generosity and respect for the rights of the poor and the defenceless, soon aroused the opposition of the Meccan elite.

Attacks upon the Meccan gods at length drew down persecution upon Mohammed's followers {1}. Mockery and insults turned into persecution and in 615 Mohammed advised some of his followers to take refuge in the Christian country of Abyssinia {3}. A number of his followers emigrated to Abyssinia.

Mohammed had now struggled to preach the word of God in this environment for roughly ten years. A small number believed, mostly of the poorer classes. The followers he drew were the rejected, the disadvantaged, the weak and the oppressed - slaves, women and minority tribes. {1, 5}

620-622	Negotiations with parties from Yathrib (Medina) led to agreement. Mohammed gave the signal for his Meccan followers to slip quietly away to Medina. On September 622 Mohammed and his companions made their way to Medina and joined them. {1}

In Medina, Mohammed was the religious leader, the acknowledged head of the community (umma) of emigrants (muhajirun) which had federated with the eight major Medinan tribes called the supporters (ansar). {1, 2}

> Medina was also the home of some clans which professed Judaism. The Aws and the Khazraj (two of these eight tribes) each had clients from nomadic clans and from the Jewish clans, and the Jewish clans were included in the arrangement as allies of one of the eight clans (ansar).

622-623	The needs of the Muhajirun (the emigrants who had left Mecca and come to Medina) were pressing. Needed were booty and supplies to sustain the impoverished Muslim community. {1, 2}
	Small expeditions began to molest the Meccan caravans.
	Many of Mohammed's followers disliked this new attitude.
	Further difficulty was caused by an attack on a small caravan at Nakhlah at the beginning of Rajab II as it raised the question of fighting in the sacred months.
624 Feb	An attempt to intercept one of the chief Meccan caravans returning from Syria led to a battle at the wells of Badr. The Quraysh army was defeated.
	But the booty had not been so great as had been expected, and difficulties arose as to the division of it. {1}
624 Apr	This was followed by the expulsion of one of the Jewish clans, the 'Bani Qainuqa', from Medina {1}
	The Qaynuqa, who were traders and goldsmiths of Medina, retired to their strongholds where they were besieged. They surrendered to the Muslims after 15 days, and were given three days to leave the city, without their arms and probably without their goldsmiths' tools as well.
	The Jewish clan had to hand over their arms, their homes and properties, and apparently also the working tools on which their living depended.

625 Mar A large Meccan force appeared before Medina.

The Muslims decided to accept this Quraysh challenge, marched out and positioned themselves at Uhud, a hill to the north of the town. On the way, however, a portion of their army broke off and returned to Medina. The Muslims were defeated. {1}

The Quraysh, having no quarrel with Medina, withdrew. Some of the Muslim forces followed, and claimed a victory. {1}

Muslim raiding was resumed. {1}

A main drive was the search for booty and supplies to sustain the impoverished Muslim community. {2}

625 Aug Morale among the Muslims was low after the unsuccessful battle with the Meccans. {1}

> The Muslims sent an ultimatum to the 'Bani Nadir', another Jewish clan {1}, demanding that if they did not leave Medina within ten days they would be put to death. If they left, however, they would continue to own their palm groves and receive part of the produce.
>
> The Nadir held out 15 days before surrendering to the Muslims.
>
>> They were allowed to leave but had to abandon their weapons and were not entitled to take their date harvest.
>>
>> So the Jewish clan had to hand over their weapons, their homes, land and harvest.

627 The Meccans, finding their trade still being interfered with, formed a great coalition against Medina, which brought together a large force outside the town. As they lay inactive, the unity of their coalition began to wear out, and a storm of wind and rain finally dispersed it. {1}

When the Meccans unsuccessfully besieged Medina, the Qurayza, the last major clan of Jews in Medina, were neutral.

After the Meccans departed, the Muslims attacked the strongholds of the Qurayza. After 25 days the Qurayza asked to surrender on the same terms as the Nadir.

The Muslims demanded an unconditional surrender, which the Qurayza accepted.

All the men of Qurayza (about 600) were put to death, were ruthlessly slaughtered, the women and children sold as slaves {1} and the Muslims took all that had belonged to the Qurayza.

The decision to kill the male Qurayza and to enslave and sell their women and children, was not taken by the Prophet Mohammed.

A ruthless episode which it is difficult to reconcile with Mohammed's teachings 'that people should follow the edicts of the one all-seeing and almighty but compassionate God, and the obligation of generosity and respect for the rights of the poor and the defenceless. {3}'

627/8   The Muslims thought they were strong enough to force their way into Mecca. Their Beduin allies, however, failed them. {1}

Professing peaceable intentions they set out, ostensibly to perform the pilgrimage. They found their way blocked by Meccan forces, and halting at the borders of the 'haram', at 'Hudaibiyah', entered into negotiations. The treaty they made was a disappointment to the Muslims. {1}

233

628 May	This was followed in May 628 by an attack on the last independent Jewish clan of Khaibar. {1}
	In May-June the Muslims conquered the oasis.
	The settlement with the Jewish clan stipulated that they would continue to live there, but pay a tax on half of their produce.
629 Sep	A Muslim expedition northwards unexpectedly met strong Byzantine resistance and was defeated at Mutah. {1}
629 Dec	An expedition was got together to overwhelm Mecca. Negotiations meanwhile took place, and Mecca was entered almost without fighting. {1, 2}
	The conditions were the acceptance of Islam and the payment of the 'zakat' or tax for the support of the Muslim community. {1}

Findings

We saw that at the time of Mohammed there were no restraints to communal acts of violence (See section 'Arab Life at the Time of Mohammed'). Warlike raids were frequent and aimed at capture of booty. The possessions of the defeated were distributed among the victors, with loot (material and human) apparently being the key objective of intertribal warfare. Women and children captured in tribal warfare who were not ransomed became tribal slaves and could be bought and sold.

Small and thus in practice virtually defenceless, the Jewish clans were allied to ('clients' of) large Medinan Arab tribes and the record shows that the Jewish clans never attacked the Muslims.

When attacked by the emigrants (muhajirun), these small Jewish clans were apparently left unprotected by their Arab Muslim allies who were of the ansar.

We also saw that

> Mohammed taught that people should follow the edicts of the one all-seeing and almighty but compassionate God, and the obligation of generosity and respect for the rights of the poor and the defenceless. {3}

The attacks on the Jewish clans were simply not motivated or caused by religion. In accordance with the then current Arab way of living, these attacks were driven by the search for booty and supplies to sustain the impoverished emigrants, the Muslim community. The record shows without doubt that whenever the Muhajirun (emigrants) suffered a setback, they next attacked one of the small Jewish clans to take over their arms, homes, properties, working tools, palm groves and harvest. To obtain booty and supplies in accordance with the then current ways of struggling for survival.

References

{1}   Introduction to the Qur'an
       Richard Bell
       Edinburgh University Press
       1958

{2}   The Arabs
       Peter Mansfield
       Penguin Books
       Third edition, 1992

{3}   Muhammad
       Maxime Rodinson
       Tauris Parke Paperbacks
       1971, 2002
       ISBN 1 86064 827 4

{4}   Tune into the "new conscience of Islam"
       Sophie Boukhari interviewing Abdou Filali-Ansari
       Unesco Courier
       November 2001

{5}   In 'Islam: Basis – Past – Present – Future'
       Manfred Davidmann
       ISBN 978-0-85192-053-5
       see chapter 2: 'Prophet Mohammed's Struggle
       for a Better Life for All'

Additions by the Editor:

The author's fundamental works about Islam are published in:
'Islam: Basis – Past – Present – Future'
Manfred Davidmann
ISBN 978-0-85192-053-5

The Global (Worldwide) Struggle for a Better Life and
The Root of all Evil, the Source of All Good, and the Messianic Struggle

Hidden Causes of Struggle; What People are Struggling Against

**The Global (Worldwide) Struggle for Social Decision-making.
In all Organisations and Communities, at all Levels**

Antisocial Telepathic Manipulations

Church and State; Religion, Government and People

Judaism, Christianity and Islam: The Messianic Struggle for a Better Life

**Freedom, Liberty, Independence, Good Secure Life.
Now and for Ever**

The Messianic Struggle in Our Time: Extracts from my Diary and Press Notices.

Introduction
Human and Inhuman Behaviour
The Human Mind, Mental Health and Mental Illness
Conflict Within the Mind
Conflict between Church and State
Government, Management and Leadership
    Organisation
    Authoritarian Organisation
    Participative Organisation
    Style of Government, Management and Leadership
The Struggle for Social Decision-making
    The Meaning of 'Democracy' (Participative Organisation)
    Personal Power and Control (Authoritarian Organisation)
    Top-level Leaderships (Global Operations and Agreements)
Global (Worldwide) Struggle
    Worldwide Struggle
    The Hidden Factor

Introduction

In this report, Manfred Davidmann exposes humanity's innermost secrets to the light of day.

As you read the report, you are brought ever closer to humanity's hidden core confrontations and the reality of the struggle for a better life. That is, you will see what humankind is struggling against; you will see the fundamental cause. You will see the core and source of evil, corruption, brutality, perversion, oppression and enslavement.

This report is about past and present struggles, achievements and defeats, about whole communities betrayed and misled, about religious teachings distorted and even turned upside down. And it is about how to achieve our own well-being, about our ensuring that we as individuals have good and satisfying lives.

And you will see how that which is good arises from the selfless and unstinting efforts of human beings cooperating for the common good.

And if the facts are unexpected or if you do not like the facts then don't blame me. I am merely recording them.

Human and Inhuman Behaviour   {16}

The human brain evolved in three main stages. Its ancient and primitive part is the innermost core reptilian brain. Next evolved the mammalian brain by adding new functions and new ways of controlling the body. Then evolved the third part of the brain, the neocortex, the grey matter, the bulk of the brain in two symmetrical hemispheres, separate but communicating. To a considerable extent, it is our neocortex which enables us to behave like human beings. {1} <1>

So the human brain consists of these three different but interconnected brains and the way in which these three brains interact with each other underlies human behaviour. {1} <1>

Our primitive animal ancestors behaved instinctively. Hunt for food, kill or be killed, fight or flee, copulate, care for own young for a very short and limited period. Self before others, regardless of needs of others, marking out and defending territory.

Later mammals tend to have feelings, care and affection for their young.

Human beings think as well as feel, and care for and look after their young for many years.

So conditioning to fight, injure and kill amounts to a throwback to primitive animal behaviour, to behaviour which puts self before others. A throwback to beast-like behaviour for those who attack, and also a throwback to beast-like behaviour for those who have to defend themselves.

Similarly, society corrupts itself when human care, affection and concern for one's own family, and for other people, are weakened by self-interest, by selfishness, by personal gain at expense of others. {16}

In such circumstances the instinctive behaviour of the non-feeling primitive animal is asserting itself, is attempting to override human feelings of care, affection, concern for members of one's own family and for other people in human societies.

And there is increasing antisocial behaviour such as vandalism and mugging. There is a loss of internal security, by loss of property and by attack against the person. The quality of life is lowered even further by those who pursue personal gain regardless of its cost to other people.

But only some people behave in such corrupted ways. There are those many who put people first, who know the difference between human and inhuman (instinctive beast-like) behaviour, who believe in cooperative behaviour and in democratic government.

And there are ways of teaching social responsibility, of teaching the young how to take responsibility for others, how to care for, work with and look after other people. Social responsibility, the caring, giving and sharing with others, the taking on of responsibility for others including conflict management, can be and is being taught. {6}

The Human Mind, Mental Health and Mental Illness {22}

Here we see how conflict arises within the mind, look at mental health and illness, look at dominance. We are here looking at what motivates and drives human beings, seeing how the human mind shapes the way in which we live, suffer, struggle and achieve.

But when it comes to how the human mind functions and operates, or to what happens within the mind under stress or at times of conflict, we talk about an 'unconscious' part of the mind, accepting that there is much which is taking place without our being aware of it. {1}

Psychology has been defined as 'the scientific study of the human mind and its functions, especially those affecting behaviour in a given context'. And Stevens considers that
> '... all psychological phenomena, from slips of the tongue to the most elaborate psychiatric symptoms (are) determined by events proceeding beneath the threshold of consciousness ... ' {5}

That is, we are not aware of where they come from and how they originate.

Psychologists and psychiatrists have for some time looked at how people behave and why, at how internal stress originates, at what causes mental breakdown. Mental tension is said to result from unresolved conflict and they have been attempting to identify the opposing forces which are in conflict.

Sigmund Freud (Psychoanalysis) saw the conflict in his patients, explained it as a conflict between love and hate, concluding that sexuality was all-important.

The unconscious is a part of the mind which is said to be inaccessible to the conscious mind but which affects behaviour and emotions. Mental disorders can be caused by conflict between the unconscious and conscious parts of the mind and Freud considered that such conflicts can be resolved by bringing repressed fears and conflicts into the conscious mind.

I think that by bringing hidden conflict into the open he came close to seeing that a key problem was that of controlling sexuality, of controlling primitive urges and behaviour.

Carl Jung (Analytical Psychology) called the unconscious part of the human mind the 'Personal Unconscious' and, like Freud, considered it to be the cause of complexes. Jung apparently concluded that
     'the personal unconscious is composed of complexes {5} and these' he considered to be independently capable of influencing consciousness without our being aware of them. <2>

What Jung called 'personal unconscious' appears to consist of component entities with independent feelings or thoughts which behave as if they were personalities.

Jung also suggested that there existed something else which he called 'Collective Unconscious' which he supposed to be made up of what he called 'archetypes'. He considered archetypes to be some kind of primitive mental images inherited from our earliest ancestors, examples being predator, sexual and enemy archetypes. Later he had to elaborate this model by including also archetypes of archetypes.

When Jung refers to a 'collective unconscious', he is referring to what could be primitive urges and behaviour which human beings subdue and control, and which human beings need to subdue and control.

Conflict Within the Mind {22}

Psychotherapy considers that the conscious mind reasons and evaluates and the unconscious mind is said to underlie action based on intuition and emotion. When there is conflict between the conscious and the unconscious minds, between reason and emotion, then this conflict can produce mental tension.

The question which has remained unresolved so far is just what the 'opposing forces' are which produce the tension.

Manfred Davidmann considers that there is no conflict when reason and emotions both aim to achieve humane behaviour and existence (human, normal).

Similarly, there is no conflict when reason and emotions both aim at inhumane behaviour and existence (inhuman, abnormal).

So conflict arises when feelings and emotions which insist on humane behaviour are opposed by verbal skills and reasoning insisting on behaviour contrary to human rights and welfare.

And conflict also arises if a person's feelings and emotions insist on behaviour contrary to human rights and welfare, but are opposed by reason, knowledge and understanding which insist on humane behaviour.

Hence conflict within the mind can arise when people are being misinformed or misled into inhumane behaviour, and also when they are being manipulated through their emotions into behaving inhumanly without knowing why they are doing so (such as blindly doing as told or as directed by the top).

And thus conflict can be seen as arising from the clash between opposing social ideologies. These conflicts arise within the human mind and shape our minds, mental well-being and also behaviour. As can be seen below, they are similar to the conflicts which arise between church and state.

Conflict between Church and State {27, 34-35}

Here Manfred Davidmann was the first to define and explain in clear meaningful language the meaning of what was simply being referred to as 'church' and 'state', defining also 'government' and 'religion' to lay bare the real causes of conflict and confrontation between them.

So before we consider their aims and purpose, and the conflicts and confrontations between them, we begin by looking at what people mean and imply when they use words such as 'church' and 'state' {27}, as follows:

Church
> Refers to the religion's clergy, or to its hierarchy. It can also refer to the religion's organisation, its decision-making processes, the doctrine it follows and the policies it applies.

State
> Somewhat vague term which refers to the combination of government and the community (country, population) being governed. Its use ignores important distinctions between people, government and the government's style of management, and their often conflicting interests. For example it does not distinguish between a government which serves its people and one which serves a country's rulers.

So 'church' and 'state' are vague terms which mean and imply different things to different people. They are vague because their meanings are imprecise and roundabout.

Such terms are often used to avoid bluntly stating harsh realities, or used instead of a term one considers improper. And they are often used dishonestly when they are used to conceal and deceive. <18>

More precise and useful are the words {35}:

Government
> The group or organisation ruling a country or conducting its affairs. It can also refer to the government's style of management (authoritarian or participative, that is dictatorial or democratic).

Religion
> A system of faith and worship, based on belief in the existence of a God (mostly benevolent), usually expressed by believers living according to its doctrine (principles, rules of behaviour, customs).

So that there are different kinds of states and different kinds of churches {34}:

> Some states consist of governments which serve the rulers by oppressing the people so that they can be exploited and such states stifle opposition and protest. Here those at the top and their experts tell people what they should do and have to do.

> Other states consist of governments where those who govern serve the people and are accountable to them, where decisions are made at the lowest possible level by referendum with experts

explaining the consequences both ways when a decision has to be made.

Similarly some churches teach a version of religion which serves the rulers and so in effect condition their people into gladly serving the rulers, into gladly allowing themselves to be exploited, the general approach then being 'gladly accept the tough life you are leading, the reward will come in a next life'.

And other churches preach that it is the will of God that all people are equal, that no person may exploit another, that it is the role of the government, of the establishment, to serve the people.

So we see that there is no conflict when both the government and the church believe in authoritarian rule, that is when

states consist of governments which serve the rulers by oppressing the people so that they can be exploited, stifling opposition and protest, those at the top and their experts telling people what they should do and have to do.

And when churches serve rulers by in effect conditioning their people into gladly serving the rulers, into gladly allowing themselves to be exploited, their general approach then being 'gladly accept the tough life you are leading, your reward will come in a next life'.

And similarly there is no conflict when both the government and the church believe in participative government, that is

When states consist of governments where those who govern serve the people and are accountable to them, where decisions are made at the lowest possible level by referendum with experts explaining to the people the consequences both ways when a decision has to be made.

And when churches preach that it is the will of God that all people are equal, that no person may exploit another, that it is the role of those who rule, of the government, of the establishment, to serve the people.

But there is conflict and confrontation

when 'religion' and 'government' ('church' and 'state') preach, teach and practice opposing 'ideologies' (authoritarian rule opposing participative government), or when their hierarchies compete with each other for power.

So Manfred Davidmann concludes {27, 34-35} that

> What is clear is that differences of opinion, conflicts and confrontations between a 'church' and a 'state' arise only when church and state believe in and practice opposing ideologies, and to the extent to which they do so.

What matters regarding agreement, conflict or confrontation between a 'state' and a 'church' is the social ideology which each of them believes in, teaches and practices. Conflict and confrontation are about the right to social decision-making, and social decision-making depends on the kind of social ideology those in power believe in, teach and practice. <3>

Government, Management and Leadership   {15}

Participation, meaning by this 'participation in decision-making', was first coined, and defined, by Manfred Davidmann when he published his analysis and recommendations about the style of management, in 1981. He defined, described and illustrated his scale of 'style of management and government' from 'fully participative' at one end of the scale, to 'fully authoritarian' at the other end.

Manfred Davidmann's concept of participative government and management, of participation in decision-making, has become a household word, in daily use when referring to government and management styles, worldwide. His concepts are applied all the way from village government and community projects to national policies and elections, are applied by cooperatives, companies and global corporations alike.

What Manfred Davidmann has done in his work on the general management of enterprises and communities is to lay the foundation for, and develop, what is now called 'management science'.

His works on style of management and on participation in decision-making in management, leadership and government, are widely known, studied and applied, sprouted a whole literature ranging from the scientific on the one hand to, on the other hand, misleading politically motivated misrepresentations.

Organisation   {15}

The whole pattern of different ways of organising is a sequence from one extreme to the other, is a kind of scale. At one end of the scale is the completely authoritarian organisation, at the other end the fully participative organisation. Governments, corporations (companies) and other organisations fall somewhere along the scale.

Authoritarian Organisation   {15}

Kings ruled by 'divine' right and they enforced obedience through, in the end, the death penalty. Under private ownership, authority is derived from ownership of the means of production and the penalty for disobedience is dismissal. In each case authority is centred at the top. It is the owners who delegate authority to the chief executive, and it is immaterial whether the owners are shareholders as in some countries, or the state in countries such as Russia.

In authoritarian organisations, it is orders which are passed down from above and the manager's role is to pass orders down the 'chain of command'. He is usually not expected to make decisions and so carries little responsibility. He does order and may compel the worker to carry out the tasks demanded from him, to produce.

Those who run society on such lines find that the working population does not willingly work for the benefit of only its rulers and then they attempt to compel the working population to work. The stick is unemployment and the compelling force is the fear of the economic consequences of unemployment, is the threat of need.

Hence it is those who believe in an authoritarian kind of organisation who advocate that the level of unemployment should be kept above a certain minimum level or that it should be increased, and who want to reduce social security spending.

Or they attempt to persuade and condition the working population into willingly serving and working for the rulers and their establishment regardless of the working population's hardships, suffering and need.

Which applies to community organisation and government in the same way.

Participative Organisation   {15}

Employees participate when they agree to allow themselves to be organised by an employer, and organisation which is based on consent of those being organised is participative. In a participative organisation people accept responsibility for work to be done, accept that it is their job to carry out a part of the organisation's activities and that they will be held accountable for the quality of their work. The manager's job is to back his subordinate by removing obstacles from the subordinate's path, the subordinate asking for such assistance as the need arises. The manager coordinates the work of the group which he manages with that of the higher group in which he is a subordinate.

The shop steward is elected so that his authority stems from those who elected him and who work in factory and office. The source of his authority is the consent of the managed to be managed. The method of power is the withdrawal of that consent which is in effect the withdrawal of one's labour, for example by going on strike.

And similarly a representative or delegate is elected so that his authority stems from those who elected him and who are members of the community, who are citizens. The source of his authority is the consent of the governed to be governed. The method of power is the withdrawal of that consent which is in effect the withdrawal of one's cooperation, of delegated authority, for example by demonstrating.

An organisation built on this basis is participative, and this means that participation through decision-making, including setting of targets, takes place at all levels of the organisation {15}, and this applies equally well to government, management and leadership.

Style of Government, Management and Leadership {15}

We have described here in outline the two systems of organisation which can be regarded as forming either end of the scale. The position of any organisation on this scale depends in each case on the balance between the two kinds of authority, that is depends on the degree of participation in decision-making which is practised.

One can place on this scale any system of running a company or of governing a country, by considering, for example,

> whether and to what extent decisions are being made at the various levels or whether people merely follow orders, or whether and to what extent people are free to withdraw their labour, are free to strike.

In other words, by considering to what extent authority is centred at the top, or where the balance of power lies between management and worker, or between government and citizen.

The position where an organisation is placed thus depends on the balance of authority between ruler and ruled, between owner and worker, between the establishment and the population.

The way in which countries are managed, that is their style of management, of government, of course varies from country to country and changes as time passes {15}. Authoritarian attitudes result in confrontation, leadership and cooperation result in economic success.

And we now know that the real struggle is not between political left and right but is a struggle for democracy against dictatorship (authoritarian style of management) in all community organisations and at all levels, is for participating in social decision-making in all organisations and at all levels.

The Struggle for Social Decision-making <4> {19}

The Meaning of 'Democracy' (Participative Organisation) <5> {20}

Manfred Davidmann outlined and defined the role of representatives and the decision-making process:

> Participative (democratic) organisation rests on the population electing representatives, on the basis of each person having one vote. Representatives are responsible to, and accountable to, the population for putting into effect policies decided by the population. What underlies participative organisation (democracy) is decision-making by the people at the level of the people. And representatives, governments or government officials do not have the authority or right to reduce or sign away the participative (democratic) rights of the electors, of the population.

> What needs to be stressed is that in a participative (democratic) organisation policies are decided by a well-informed population at the level of the population and that policies then become binding on management or government. <6>

In an authoritarian organisation, the policy decisions are taken at the top or near the top by the hierarchy (establishment) and are binding on the organisation's members. Decision-making at the top is sometimes referred to as 'deciding centrally'. Authoritarian organisation is the opposite of democracy and underlies dictatorship.

And what we see is conflict between authoritarian minds wishing to dominate, control and exploit on the one hand and, on the other hand, citizens wishing to maintain and improve the standard of living and quality of life for the population as a whole by democratic (grass-roots level) decision-making. {20}

So the real struggle is not between political left and right, but is a struggle for participation (the right to make decisions).

And there is the fundamental problem that ill-informed or misguided voters may be persuaded or conditioned into taking harmful or socially destructive decisions.

Personal Power and Control (Authoritarian Organisation) {19}

Authoritarian minds attempt to take over and place democratically controlled organisations under authoritarian control. They do so by struggling to take over the decision-making in the management and control of companies, enterprises and all types of community organisations.

The confrontation between on the one hand elected policy-making bodies, and on the other hand those who are supposed to put their policies into effect, can be seen in many areas.

We can see the struggle in all organisations and at all levels. It is a struggle against authoritarian management or government for the right to make decisions. And in all democratic organisations it is a struggle against the authoritarian mind taking over the decision-making.

A continuous battle is taking place between on the one hand policy-deciding by the many through elected assemblies, and on the other hand policy-deciding at the top, by a few. This is clearly shown by the way in which full-time officials and executives attempt to take power away from their policy-setting assemblies, after which they attempt to impose their will on the membership or population.

These attempts to take over and control decision-making processes are far more one-sided than would be the case if we were looking at unrelated chance events, at unrelated local struggles. At times the pattern seems progressive as if it were planned.

Top-level Leaderships (Global Operations and Agreements) {19}

Recently negotiated top-level trading agreements (GATT and the proposed MAI) appear to be taking away the control over key aspects of the internal affairs of participating countries. Taking control away from their elected governments, giving the control to multinational corporations. {19}

MAI stands for 'Multilateral Agreement on Investment'. But its name does not reflect those aspects which are of deep concern.

Disturbing are not only the provisions of this proposed treaty but also that the provisions were debated in complete secrecy till a leaked copy became available on the Internet in 1997. Apparently it was adverse publicity relating to its restrictive provisions which delayed completion as concerned groups of citizens publicised their concerns. And some governments have now withdrawn their support.

It appears that under MAI the national governments would have handed over control, that is authority to act, over much of the economic and social welfare of their citizens to multinational corporations (that is to those who own and direct these corporations), if they had agreed to this treaty.

In other words, multinationals would have been given overriding authority over democratically elected governments.

Global (Worldwide) Struggle

Worldwide Struggle

In 'The Will to Work: What People Struggle to Achieve' {3}, Manfred Davidmann clearly defines and describes motivation, its basis, and 'motivating'. Starting by considering motivation from the point of view of the employer (productivity, remuneration, job satisfaction), this leads to considering what people want and what they struggle to achieve. A key part of the report is community orientated, including a detailed step-by-step listing of what people are struggling to achieve, their needs and wants, their achievements and objectives. This progression shows underdeveloped and developed people as they are, human beings at different stages of an identical struggle for a better life against those who wish to profit from their condition. <7>

We see a worldwide struggle to achieve a humane way of life. Each person, family or community is struggling to advance at their own level of development, struggling against those who wish to dominate, exploit, oppress. {16, 3}

The struggle is against those who wish to dominate other people. Against those who wish to exploit, against those who may brutally and without feeling oppress human beings so as to exploit them. {2, 3}

And 'to exploit' includes the whole range of antisocial decisions and activities of those who put profit before people and community. {4, 19}

In 'Liberation Theology' {26}, Manfred Davidmann explores why life is a struggle, why life is so tough for so many human beings on this planet. Exploring why thousands of years of struggle, why the enormous technological powers we command, why the vast human manpower, abilities and skills which are now at our disposal, are not providing us with secure lives of high quality.

And so 'Liberation Theology' starts by finding answers to some basic questions, such as:
Why do we have to struggle?
What are we struggling against?
What are we struggling for?
Why do we not have good lives of high quality?

Quoting from the report:

> Where there is struggle there must be resistance, there is opposition. We have to struggle because our attempts to achieve good lives for ourselves and our children are being resisted, are opposed.

> We have to struggle to protect earlier gains as well as to improve our lives. Hence we are struggling to defend our present standard of living and we are struggling to better it. Which means that the opposition is attacking us to lower our standard of living and to prevent us from improving it.

> We as thinking feeling human beings ought to be able to do very much better. So now more questions present themselves:

>> Who or what is doing all this to us, is attacking us? Who or what is attempting to reduce the quality of our lives, is attempting to prevent us from improving it? Who or what is attempting to increase the toughness of life itself, is attempting to increase our need?

>> Why this intense, brutal and hidden struggle when there is enough for all of us, when all can have good secure lives of high quality.

>> Why is it done in such a hidden way, why the secrecy?

In secular terms, what is it that would wish to prevent us from increasing our standard of living, that would wish to reduce our standard of living and our social security?

Here also the answer appears to be that we are struggling against those who wish to exploit others, who wish to oppress so as to exploit, who see their wealth and power increasing whenever they lower our pay relative to their own so as to increase their own profits and wealth and power over us.

It is they who wish to reduce, and so struggle to reduce, our social security since higher unemployment, greater personal need, and physical as well as emotional weakness, reduce our bargaining strength and make us more dependent on them for survival. They are enabled in this way to exploit us through our need and to push down our pay even further when compared with their own much greater gains. And this is why they are operating so furtively behind their masks.

And so we see a worldwide (global) struggle to achieve a humane way of life and living.

We know that dominating does not work in normal circumstances. Authoritarian organisations are much less effective than participative ones. In authoritarian organisations morale is low, people cease to care and tend to work against each other instead of cooperating with each other for the benefit of the organisation. {15}

It is in democracies that a high standard of living has been achieved. In democracies people can struggle openly for a better life but we see that what has been gained has to be defended and extended. {16, 15}

So why does this struggle take place in all organisations, at all levels, in all communities and countries? Why do we have to struggle? Why are all of our communities and countries being managed more or less on behalf of their rulers or ruling level? Why are not at least half of our communities and countries being managed completely by, on behalf of, and for, their people?

There is simply no way in which
>   this lack of balance between the authoritarian and the participative,
>   this authoritarian rule and government in so many countries worldwide,
>   this widespread struggle in democratic countries for a better life,
can be due to chance alone.

Quite clearly an additional unknown factor is operating and determining how people live together, causing people to have to struggle at all levels, organisations, communities and countries, for a better life.

The Hidden Factor

We have already covered much ground, reviewed the results of decades of published research by Manfred Davidmann. And what we have seen can be summarised as follows:

> We saw that society corrupts itself when human care, affection and concern for one's own family, and for other people, are weakened by self-interest, by selfishness, by personal gain at expense of others.

In such circumstances the instinctive behaviour of the non-feeling primitive animal is asserting itself, is attempting to override human feelings of care, affection and concern for members of one's own family and for other people in human societies.

When society allows itself to be corrupted, there is increasing antisocial behaviour such as vandalism and mugging. There is a loss of internal security, by loss of property and by attack against the person. The quality of life is lowered even further by those who pursue personal gain regardless of its cost to other people.

So in our societies there is conflict between human care, affection and social responsibility on the one hand and primitive animal urges towards selfish gain regardless of the cost to others.

And the conflict was seen to arise from the clash between opposing social ideologies which advocate affection and concern for people, family and community on the one hand, and on the other hand selfishness and the urge for personal gain at expense of others.

These conflicts which arise within the human mind and shape our minds, mental well-being and also behaviour, are similar, and indeed appear identical, to those which arise between church and state.

We saw that there is conflict and confrontation between church and state
>when 'religion' and 'government' ('church' and 'state') preach, teach and practice opposing 'ideologies' (authoritarian rule opposing participative government), or when their hierarchies compete with each other for power.

So what matters regarding agreement, conflict or confrontation between a 'state' and a 'church' is the social ideology which each of them believes in, teaches and practices.

So conflict and confrontation are about the right to social decision-making, and social decision-making depends on the kind of social ideology those in power believe in, teach and practice.

We saw that how any country or organisation is ruled or managed depends on, and can be seen from, the balance between the two kinds of authority (authoritarian or participative), thus depends on the balance of authority between ruler and ruled, between owner and worker, between the establishment and the population. And so it can be observed from, can be seen by, the degree of participation in decision-making which is practised.

Authoritarian organisation is the opposite of democracy and underlies dictatorship. Authoritarian attitudes result in confrontation. Democratic leadership and cooperation result in economic success.

And we now know that the real struggle is not between political left and right but is a struggle for democracy against dictatorship (authoritarian style of management) in all community organisations and at all levels, is for participating in social decision-making in all organisations and at all levels, is a struggle for participation (the right to make decisions).

And what we see is conflict between authoritarian minds wishing to dominate, control and exploit on the one hand and, on the other hand, citizens wishing to maintain and improve the standard of living and quality of life for the population as a whole by democratic (grass-roots level) decision-making.

A continuous struggle is taking place between on the one hand policy-deciding by the many through elected assemblies, and on the other hand policy-deciding at the top, by a few. We can see the struggle in all organisations and at all levels. It is a struggle against authoritarian management or government for the right to make decisions. And in all democratic organisations it is a struggle against the authoritarian mind taking over the decision-making.

These attempts to take over and control decision-making processes are far more one-sided than would be the case if we were looking at unrelated chance events, at unrelated local struggles. At times the pattern seems progressive as if it were planned.

Recently negotiated top-level trading agreements (GATT and the proposed MAI) appear to be taking away the control over key aspects of the internal affairs of participating countries. Taking control away from their elected governments, giving the control to multinational corporations. In other words, multinationals appear to be aiming at getting overriding authority over democratically elected governments.

We saw underdeveloped and developed people as they are, human beings at different stages of an identical struggle for a better life against those who wish to profit from their condition, we saw a worldwide struggle to achieve a humane way of life. Each person, family or community is struggling to advance at their own level of development, struggling against those who wish to dominate, exploit, oppress.

The struggle is against those who wish to dominate other people. Against those who wish to exploit, against those who may brutally and without feeling oppress human beings so as to exploit them.

It is in democracies that a high standard of living has been achieved. In democracies people can struggle openly for a better life but we saw that what has been gained has to be defended and extended.

So why does this struggle take place in all organisations, at all levels, in all communities and countries? Why do we have to struggle? Why are all of our communities and countries being managed more or less on behalf of their rulers or ruling level? Why are not at least half of our communities and countries being managed completely by, on behalf of, and for, their people?

There is simply no way in which
> this lack of balance between the authoritarian and the participative,
> this authoritarian rule and government in so many countries worldwide,
> this widespread struggle in democratic countries for a better life,

can be due to chance alone.

Hence quite clearly an additional unknown factor is operating and determining how people live together, causing people to have to struggle at all levels, organisations, communities and countries, for a better life.

So now we go on to explore some of the darker, more hidden, parts of the human mind, so as to locate and describe what people have to struggle against, what has been so continuously attacking people, to locate and describe this hidden unknown factor.

Human Group Minds {21}

When Manfred Davidmann first announced his Group Mind Theory in 1973, this theory and his concepts and terms such as 'group minds', were completely new and unheard of. The second edition was published in 1998 and made available on the internet in 1999.

Manfred Davidmann's Group Mind Science is objective, demonstrating enormous beneficial and healing powers. Following the work of Freud and Jung, it is regarded as scientifically proved, as meaningful, objective and practical, as applying worldwide to all human beings in all societies and cultures and at all stages of development.

His human group minds and how they function, that is the Group Mind Science he originated, are now widely quoted and discussed, have sprouted a whole literature about group minds ranging from publications of scientific institutions and in reference books, to unscientific misleading look-alikes about human minds.

Manfred Davidmann's report 'The Human Mind' {21} on how human minds work and operate, on human group minds, reviews the mind theories of Freud and of Jung and outlines Manfred Davidmann's Group Mind Theory. Included in the report are comprehensive but concise reviews of mental health and mental illness, of why people are struggling and what they are struggling against, how conflict arises within the mind, of the way in which society is organised, of dominance, conflict and cooperation.

The subconscious existence and workings of group minds become apparent by the extraordinary way in which they affect and determine what individuals and communities do. The sections of this report which deal with how we live and struggle, describe how our minds shape our lives, communities and society.

The workings of group minds is shown to explain how human communities and society are organised and the consequent confrontations and struggles from dictatorship to democracy. The Group Mind Theory was proved by the way in which it explains and predicts human activities and organisation as well as mental problems of individuals and society's social problems. The insights of Manfred Davidmann's Group Mind Science enable us to solve such problems effectively.

It is a mind science which allows for telepathic contacts between people and the available evidence has been detailed on the basis that if there are telepaths using their abilities then such activities can be observed by their effects. Previously reported work by others shows that telepathic activity is well known and documented. A considerable amount of telepathic activity is taking place and known to be taking place.

Here also we see a hidden struggle between opposite factions which, for example, accounts for the feeling of resistance and mental struggle so strongly felt by those who are creating, for the compulsions experienced by authors and artists, and for the mental problems of voice hearers. <8, 25>

Manfred Davidmann concluded that it is this which is causing people to have to struggle for a better life, which is opposing them and holding them down, that the observed unknown factor consists of hidden antisocial telepathic manipulations. <25> {21}

Nephilim and Globalisation   {10}

Nephilim   {10}

The immense knowledge and understanding which underlies the Pentateuch (of which Genesis is a part) could not have been understood or comprehended by those living when the Pentateuch <17> {17} was recorded. And what is there has been overlaid with the dust of millennia, with accumulated interpretations and comments limited by the then current knowledge, understanding and misconceptions. It was Manfred Davidmann who proved that what is stated in Genesis <16> is thus much more meaningful than is generally appreciated. {7} <10>

And people have always wondered just who the nephilim were (or are) who are stated in Genesis to be well-known and powerful.

The Pentateuch states {10} that there are among us people with extraordinary abilities who are likely to be powerful or influential and well known. They are called 'nephilim' and their abilities apparently enable them to influence, organise, manipulate, control and dominate other human beings.

We are told that these 'nephilim' are without distinguishing physical characteristics, that they intermarry with other human beings and that their extraordinary abilities and skills are hereditary <11>.

Genesis is associating nephilim with evil, possibly as a hidden cause. They are misusing their abilities for personal gain, are corrupting, are dominating, are the 'fallen' ones.

We are told that Nimrod was one of the nephilim, and that the beginning of his kingdom was Babel in the land of Shinar. In this way is Nimrod linked with the events told in the allegory <12> of The Tower of Babel.

'Tower of Babel'   {10}

Here Manfred Davidmann showed that this allegory consists of two intertwined, interwoven and interconnected, stories. The first is about building the tower, the second is about the scattering of people and their developing different languages.

We are told that their aim was to reach heaven and become god-like, to set themselves up in opposition to God. Which means that Nimrod who is referred to as their king is attempting to gain, to assign to himself, god-like authority and power. <13>

So they are apparently driven by Nimrod who, being one of the nephilim, is using his extraordinary abilities for setting himself up as all-powerful supremo in opposition to God, that is in opposition to humane behaviour, equality, independence, liberty, shared wealth and good life for all. <13>

The people were scattered because they were building the tower. We are told that they then stopped building the city but pointedly are not told that they stopped building the tower.

Common explanation for it not being stated that they stopped building the tower is that it follows that they had to stop building the tower when they were dispersed. But 'building the tower' is the primary cause of the scattering and so it seems that there is another reason why it is not mentioned.

The most likely reason is that they kept on building 'towers' wherever they lived, that they kept on doing what 'building towers' stands for wherever they built their smaller settlements and communities. And that 'tower' stands for organisation, command structure, chain of command of kings, of rulers, of those with authority, of leaderships.

So it appears that they stopped building this city and consequently the tower they had been building. And, having been dispersed, they continued to build cities, smaller cities, elsewhere, each presumably with its own smaller 'tower'.

Thus the allegory states that if any become too powerful, a threat to that which is humane and good, then they need to be, and are to be, dispersed. In other words, their tower (power, organisation, country, empire, corporation, monopoly, government, rulers, multinational, global corporation) needs to be dispersed.

What follows in Genesis is the direct line of descendants {10} to Abram, that is to Abraham the Patriarch. So the point is being made that 'Good' developed, prospered and gained strength following the scattering of the power-seekers and the development of separate and distinct languages, customs and traditions. {11}

And here, so far, we have seen:

> Human beings are capable of distinguishing between good and evil and of choosing good while rejecting evil. But the nephilim among them are corruptly and evilly misusing their extraordinary and hereditary abilities to dominate, corrupt, control and manipulate other human beings.

> They are with us here and now just as before, within our communities at the present time. That they are referred to as 'fallen' indicates that their abilities are being used for selfish ends, that their behaviour is 'evil'. Their descendants are 'mighty' (powerful) and 'of renown' (well-known, prominent, in the public eye).

> In other words, there are among us people with extraordinary abilities which are hereditary and who are using these abilities for their own selfish corrupt ends, and who are likely to be powerful or influential and well known.

> Nimrod, for example, being one of the nephilim, is using his extraordinary abilities for setting himself up as all-powerful supremo in opposition to God, that is in opposition to humane behaviour, equality, independence, liberty, shared wealth and good life for all. <13>

> And the allegory of the Tower of Babel states that if any become too powerful, a threat to that which is humane and good, then they need to be, and are to be, dispersed. In other words, their tower (power, organisation, country, empire, corporation, monopoly, government, rulers, multinational, global corporation) needs to be dispersed.

> Power corrupts, absolute power corrupts absolutely. Hence the great need, and the importance of the need, for scattering and dispersal, for multiplicity and variety.

> Power corrupts, absolute power corrupts absolutely. Humanity and human behaviour depend on diversity, on opposition and balance, on democracy. <14>

The Root of all Evil (Nephilim)

Following Manfred Davidmann's report 'The Meaning of Genesis: Creation, Evolution and the Origin of Evil', we now know Genesis to be an accurate description in religious language of the way the planet was created (formed), of the evolution and of the behaviour of early man and of human beings as they evolved {7}. When Genesis was recorded, people had no knowledge of concepts such as evolution or life form, telepathy or telepaths. Concepts like these had simply not been formulated or defined. Instead of being stated using well-defined words, such concepts were described in language people could understand at that time.

Instead of the term 'scientific law' being used, for example, we see described that 'what is written applies to all people, present or absent, past or future, will happen regardless of how one feels about it, that the results of certain actions are reversed if the actions are reversed'. {7}

And Genesis' description of the abilities of the nephilim, and of the behaviour of those among them who are misusing their abilities for exploiting and oppressing ordinary people {10}, namely that

> there are among us people with extraordinary abilities which are hereditary and who are using these abilities for their own selfish corrupt ends, and who are likely to be powerful or influential and well known,

corresponds to and parallels what has been said here about telepathic organisation, manipulation and exploitation of ordinary people.

So we may take it that 'nephilim' means 'telepaths' and that Genesis refers to those who are using their extraordinary abilities for selfish and corrupt ends.

In this way Genesis confirms what Manfred Davidmann proved about telepaths and about telepathic organisation, manipulation and exploitation of ordinary people. We now know that Nephilim (telepaths) are among us and are competing with each other in a race for local and global power over people and resources, for god-like power, authority, riches and a life of luxury. And Genesis states that if any nephil <15> becomes too powerful, a threat to that which is humane and good, then the nephil's organisation needs to be, and has to be, dispersed. {10}

In other words, there are among us individuals with extraordinary abilities for influencing, organising, manipulating, controlling and dominating other human beings. Their abilities being hereditary, they are with us here and now just as before, within our communities at the present time. Some of these individuals are likely to be using their abilities for selfish corrupt ends, and they are likely to be powerful or influential and well known. Power corrupts, absolute power corrupts absolutely, and Genesis states that their power and influence needs to be split into many small parts and scattered (dispersed).

In other words, the 'Unknown Factor' which is the cause of our having to struggle all our lives wherever we may be, is the telepathic manipulation and exploitation of ordinary people.

This can now be taken as fully proved, as established fact.

Conflict between Church and State, between Religion, Government and People

The opposing forces which are in conflict between church and state have been identified {27} as opposing social ideologies, as follows:

There is no conflict when both the government and the church believe in authoritarian rule, that is when

> states consist of governments which serve the rulers by oppressing the people so that they can be exploited, stifling opposition and protest, those at the top and their experts telling people what they should do and have to do.

> And when churches serve rulers by in effect conditioning their people into gladly serving the rulers, into gladly allowing themselves to be exploited, their general approach then being 'gladly accept the tough life you are leading, your reward will come in a next life'.

And similarly there is no conflict when both the government and the church believe in participative government, that is

> When states consist of governments where those who govern serve the people and are accountable to them, where decisions are made at the lowest possible level by referendum with experts explaining to the people the consequences both ways when a decision has to be made.

> And when churches preach that it is the will of God that all people are equal, that no person may exploit another, that it is the role of those who rule, of the establishment, to serve the people.

But there is conflict and confrontation

> when 'religion' and 'government' ('church' and 'state') preach, teach and practice opposing 'ideologies' (authoritarian rule opposing participative government), or when their hierarchies compete with each other for power.

What is clear is that differences of opinion, conflicts and confrontations between a 'church' and a 'state' arise only when church and state believe in and practice opposing ideologies, and to the extent to which they do so.

So what matters regarding agreement, conflict or confrontation between a 'state' and a 'church' is the social ideology which each of them believes in, teaches and practices. Conflict and confrontation are about the right to social decision-making, and social decision-making depends on the kind of social ideology those in power believe in, teach and practice. <3>

Social Laws and Social System of the Pentateuch in Judaism, Christianity and Islam

Underlying the three main religions of Judaism, Christianity and Islam is the Pentateuch <17>. Its benevolent social laws and social system underlie all human rights, freedom, independence and liberty, underlie a good life of high quality for all {17} <9>.

For example, the laws of the Pentateuch restrain the behaviour and limit the power of 'rulers', that is of government, of top executives and of the establishment, of those in positions of trust, responsibility or authority, no matter whether secular, religious or military, no matter what the hierarchy or organisation. {29, 30}. The Pentateuch {37} states clearly what they must not do.

They may not amass servants and may not oppress the people. They may not amass possessions and wealth, may not grasp power or behave promiscuously. In other words, they may not put themselves above others by grasping power, may not satisfy personal desires at the expense of others. And a ruler (person in position of trust, responsibility or authority) has to follow these laws and abide by them every day if he wishes 'to prolong his days in his kingdom, he and his children'. For 'kingdom' read 'position' and include 'influence'.

So these Pentateuch laws lay down that those in positions of trust, responsibility or authority must not oppress people so as to increase their own possessions and power. These laws forbid personal gain from the misuse of authority, wealth or position. Those in positions of trust, responsibility or authority may not grasp power, may not oppress the people, may not behave promiscuously, may not gain wives or wealth. {17}

And now we see that struggle between church and state, religion and government, is about the application in our everyday lives of the social provisions of the Pentateuch. Its benevolent and egalitarian legislation, its social laws and social system, include the Ten Commandments and laws protecting the people by limiting the behaviour of their rulers. The struggle is between those who wish to oppress so as to exploit and those who wish to live good lives of high quality which would be theirs if the social laws and social system of the Pentateuch were followed. <4>

The history of the struggle is a fascinating story in which those in authority struggled in the past and are struggling in our time to delete the social and 'good government' laws of the Pentateuch from observance, that is to prevent them being observed, applied and enforced, to prevent people from even finding out about the existence of these benevolent revelations, to change religious belief and practice so that believers would gladly serve oppressive rulers and slave drivers instead of serving benevolent God and people. A horrendous story of human suffering imposed and being imposed in the name of private profit for the benefit those in authority.

So the Pentateuch underlies the three main religions of Judaism, Christianity and Islam. Its benevolent social laws and social system underlie all human rights, freedom, independence and liberty, underlie a good life of high quality for all. And we now see and understand

> the basic struggle and confrontation all over the planet in all aspects and levels of life and living

> between those who wish to oppress so as to exploit and

> those who wish to live good lives of high quality which would be theirs if the social laws and social system of the Pentateuch were followed. {27}

THE MESSIANIC STRUGGLE FOR A BETTER LIFE

History of the Messianic Struggle

What has been uncovered by Manfred Davidmann during the last twenty years by biblical archaeology tells us what took place. In outline, what actually happened was as follows:

Moses

Following Moses, the Jewish people undertook to live according to the Pentateuch's provisions, to apply all of them in their daily lives. But

Judaism was then corrupted from within, by its rulers and by its ruler-serving religious establishment who edited out from observance the 'Good Government' (Kingship) laws and the benevolent social laws and social system laws, and who obscured the 'Social Cause-and-Effect Relationship' as this stated that the punishing consequences of ignoring the Pentateuch's laws were inevitable. And the people were oppressed and exploited. {29-32, 27}

From the recording of the Pentateuch to the birth of Christianity, there were two main confrontations between the Jewish rulers ('state', government, establishment) and their people. This struggle was about position, influence and control over communities, about changing God-given benevolent rules of behaviour so that people could be oppressed and exploited. It changed Judaism, determined the fate of the Jewish people and gave rise to Christianity. {30, 27}

Jesus

The rulers had corrupted Judaism. Jesus then taught that all the laws had to be kept, that belief and practice included and had to include the Ten Commandments, the social laws and the social system of the Pentateuch which include the Good Government (Kingship) laws. The beliefs of Christianity thus include the social laws and social system of the Pentateuch. {33, 17, 27}

Paul, however, acted on behalf of the rich and powerful when he tried to convince people that those in authority were God's representatives on earth and had to be obeyed, and that the social laws did not have to be kept. Paul's letter to the 'Romans' was written before the gospels. Matthew's later gospel records what Jesus actually taught and clearly makes the point that Paul was trying to subvert that which Jesus taught. As Matthew records what Jesus taught, this outweighs and overrides what Paul said. Those who later favoured Paul's pro-establishment ideology could not challenge Matthew's record. Hence Matthew's gospel was subtly changed in later gospels. {33, 27}

Jesus taught that all the Pentateuch's laws had to be kept, that belief and practice had to include them. The Christian establishment later abrogated, in effect annulled <5>, the benevolent social laws of the Pentateuch and in this way corrupted Christianity from within. The Christian establishment's version became accepted as official Christian doctrine and the people were once again exposed to oppression and exploitation. {33, 27, 35, 36}

Mohammed

About two-hundred years later, Mohammed pointed out what had happened to Jews and Christians and to the inevitable outcome of not following the Pentateuch's teachings, and that all the laws of the Pentateuch had to be kept. {44}

Throughout almost the whole of Mohammed's life as Prophet he struggled against the powerful Meccan family which dominated Mecca {39}. And after Mohammed died, the ruling elite took over {41}. Hadiths (traditions) record that on the one hand we have the word of benevolent Allah as taught by Mohammed that people (believers) should have a good life of high quality in this life {42, 44}, but that on the other hand is the ruling elite's opposing viewpoint that people should be obedient and serve willingly without questioning their condition {43, 44}.

Mohammed knew about the events of the past and said so, calling for a return to following the ancient benevolent God-given social legislation. This is not taught and also not taught as such are Mohammed's teachings that the consequences of not following the benevolent social laws and social system of the Pentateuch in this life are grim and inevitable, that to follow them results in believers having good and secure lives of high quality {44}.

After Mohammed's death, Caliph Uthman had an official manuscript of the Koran compiled, edited and distributed. We are told that he ordered the compilers always to prefer the ruling-elite's version of Islam and that he then ordered all other Koranic materials to be destroyed. {42-44}

Since then there has been continuous confrontation and struggle between secular and religious figureheads and hierarchies, between state (rulers, government) and religious authorities (clerics, religious hierarchy, religion) {41} with each attempting to make the other serve its own ends. {27}

To this Point of Time

What these religions have in common is that in each case a ruling elite succeeded in bypassing or overturning humanity's essential God-given benevolent Pentateuch-recorded social provisions and human rights, in this way exposing their communities and whole populations to oppression and exploitation. {17}

And among the consequences we see around us at the present time are that

> Rabbinical Judaism (today's Judaism) propagates the establishment's revisionist version of Jewish belief and practice. {31}

> Many Christians are now taught a tranquillising ruler-serving ideology and to blame themselves for the punishing inevitable consequences of following their church's teachings {35, 36}.

>> But Manfred Davidmann concluded that with Liberation Theology we see Christianity struggling forward towards its roots in response to the social and economic problems of global humanity at the present time. Towards what Jesus taught, towards the social laws and social system of the Pentateuch. {27}

> Within Islam we see confrontation and struggle between secular and religious figureheads and hierarchies, between state (rulers, government) and religious authorities (clerics, religious hierarchy, religion) {41} with each attempting to make the other serve its own ends. The poverty-stricken and uneducated condition of so many Muslims in Islamic countries speaks for itself. {39-45, 27}.

And there are religions which teach, as a matter of policy:
That the poor are poor and evermore shall be so!
That reward for obedient suffering in the service of the rich and powerful comes in some other life!
Or after death in some imaginary other existence!

The Messianic Struggle

Religion and Reality

So far I have defined religion as

> A system of faith and worship, based on belief in the existence of a God (mostly benevolent), usually expressed by believers living according to its doctrine (principles, rules of behaviour, customs).

And shown that

> what matters regarding agreement, conflict or confrontation between a 'state' and a 'church' is the social ideology which each of them believes in, teaches and practices. Conflict and confrontation are about the right to social decision-making, and

266

social decision-making depends on the kind of social ideology those in power believe in, teach and practice. <3>

We saw that

some churches (religions) serve rulers by in effect conditioning their people into gladly serving the rulers, conditioning their people into gladly allowing themselves to be exploited, the church's general approach then being 'gladly accept the tough life you are leading, your reward will come in some kind of other life'.

and that

struggle between church and state, religion and government, is about the application in our everyday lives of the social provisions of the Pentateuch.

Its benevolent and egalitarian legislation, its social laws and social system, include the Ten Commandments and laws protecting the people by limiting the behavior of their rulers.

The struggle is between those who wish to oppress so as to exploit and those who wish to live good lives of high quality which would be theirs if the social laws and social system of the Pentateuch were followed. <19>

So the word 'religion' is also used as a euphemism <18> for a movement (organisation, hierarchy) which serves the rich and powerful by brainwashing (conditioning, indoctrinating) the population, particularly their young when impressionable, into willingly and gladly serving the rulers, conditioning its believers into gladly allowing themselves to be exploited. Into gladly accepting the tough life they are leading, their reward given to them in some kind of other life. Conditioning them into willingly accepting that the rich and powerful live in heaven on earth in this life while they, the people, suffer and live harsh lives being merely promised fantastic rewards in some other life after death.

Faith and belief are part of 'religion'. The individual believer can be convinced, can be made to feel certain, that his religious beliefs are true, that they correspond to reality. Regardless of evidence, regardless of proofs to the contrary.

But following Manfred Davidmann's publications, we now know that, one after the other, the Jewish, Christian and Muslim ruling establishments modified the religious beliefs of their people so as to bypass, abrogate, in effect annul, the 'God-given' social laws and social system of the Pentateuch, so as to tranquillise their people into obedience. {17}

I have already said

> The Pentateuch underlies the three main religions of Judaism,
> Christianity and Islam.
>
> Its benevolent and egalitarian social laws and social system
> include the Ten Commandments and laws protecting the people
> by limiting the behaviour of their rulers. Those in positions of
> trust, responsibility or authority may not grasp power, may not
> oppress the people, may not behave promiscuously, may not gain
> wives or wealth.
>
> The Pentateuch's social laws and social system underlie all human
> rights, freedom, independence and liberty, underlie a good life of
> high quality for all.
>
> And struggle between church and state, religion and government,
> is about the application in our everyday lives of the social
> provisions of the Pentateuch. {17}

Why the Pentateuch is so Special

The Pentateuch was collated and written down about 3400 years ago,
has been handed down and preserved unaltered to this day as a
consonantal text without vowels.

When the Pentateuch was written, people had but little knowledge
about science or evolution compared with what is known today. So
concepts for which we now have precise terms were described rather
than stated. Instead of 'this is a scientific law', for example, we see
'what is written applies to all people, present or absent, past or future,
will happen regardless of how one feels about it, that the results of
certain actions are reversed if the actions are reversed'. <7> {10}

Genesis can now be understood as it was intended to be understood,
following the publication of "The Meaning of Genesis: Creation,
Evolution and the Origin of Evil" by Manfred Davidmann. {7}

There is no conflict or contradiction between evolution by natural
selection and what is written in Genesis. Conflicts have arisen because
parts of Genesis were misunderstood and misinterpreted as the
necessary scientific knowledge was not known at time of translation,
and parts were consequently mistranslated in spite of best intentions.

The later chapters and verses in Genesis describe the formation of the
earth and early plant life, the survival of the fittest, the evolution from
reptilian to mammalian instincts and behaviour, and the evolution of
human beings from humanoid to Homo erectus to Homo sapiens and
their corresponding changes of behaviour, feeling and thinking. It

defines human behaviour by stating what is good and what is evil. {7, 17}

The Pentateuch records how human beings learned to distinguish and overcome the brutal inhuman behaviour of their primitive past and learned the behaviour of human beings. It does so by clearly defining what is known as good and evil, the difference between them and the root cause of evil.

Trustful Cooperation (Ten Commandments)   {17}

The Ten Commandments <22> are so important and are so well known because behaviour in accordance with these rules is the basis for people trusting each other and so for people cooperating and working well with each other. The Ten Commandments underlie freedom, independence and strength to oppose and resist oppression. Wherever there is any independence of the mind and material freedom today it exists because people followed these rules of behaviour and it exists to the extent to which they do so. {29}

The Pentateuch's laws are just and it warns against preferring the rich or favouring the poor {38} and much trust and community friendliness is gained when people follow these principles.

But consider that these laws apply equally to the rich and powerful. It is also the rich and powerful who must not steal from the poor even the little which the poor have. It is the rich and powerful who must not cast longing glances at what little the rest of us possess, it is the rich and powerful who must not aim to gain at our expense.

The Social Cause-and-Effect Relationship

We saw <23> how determining and far-seeing the Pentateuch's rules are by the way in which rulers (those in authority) are restrained in a few sentences which protect the people from being oppressed and exploited by their rulers.

And Manfred Davidmann revealed that the Pentateuch also states {29, 17} the Social Cause-and-Effect Relationship as a scientific law which applies to all without exception and at all times, and that the law is listed in detail so that people would benefit from knowing the effects (consequences) of their behaviour.

This law states that the consequences of keeping or not keeping the Pentateuch's laws are inescapable, that what happens to one is in the end the inevitable result of one's own behaviour.

We are told that the process is reversible: Increasingly disregarding the laws (rules of behaviour) results in greater suffering and oppression, increasingly behaving according to the laws results in greater freedom, liberty, independence and a better life. {29}

We are also told that the relationship applies wherever one may be, regardless of type of government, form of religion or social system or country. It applies whether you like it or not, agree or disagree. {29}

The relationship is stated in precise terms, stated both in religious terms and described in plain language {29}. History and social science confirm it. {17} <21>

So what happens to one is in the end the inevitable result of one's own behaviour. And we can change the course of events by changing our behaviour, but only to the point of no-return.

The prophets knew and understood this relationship, and predicted accordingly, just as we now know and understand it.

The Pentateuch not only outlines that those in responsible positions need to practice restraint or be restrained but also states in clear language the scientific law that the consequences of not restraining the powerful and the opinion-formers are unavoidable, detailing the consequences both ways. The pattern of events confirms the Pentateuch's statements, both in history and in our time.

If we want freedom, independence, good life of high quality, then we have to follow these laws. If we do not, then we lose freedom, independence, good life and the country in which we live. The consequences of our behaviour cannot be avoided but we can change the course of events by changing our behaviour, but only to the point of no-return. {29}

The Messianic Struggle in Our Time <24>

> For Freedom, Independence and Liberty,
> For a Secure and Good Life of High Quality,
> **My Knowledge Must be Taught to the People,**
> **By Me and In My Name**

Extracts from my Diary and from Press Notices   {52} <24>

1977
The people have to know, have to learn, understand and follow the word of God if God's anger is to be turned away.

Jerusalem 1980
The knowledge which I have must be taught by me and in my name to the people.

April 1990
I have to lead the people to freedom. The knowledge which I have must be taught by me and in my name to the people, must reach the people and spread among them.

To 1992 Apr
I have worked hard to spread God's word but the people and their establishment do not wish to listen, have left me almost completely isolated, without the support and means required for getting the kind of publicity which is so necessary. I have been prevented from making my voice heard, worldwide.

To 1994 Jul
It also seems that the planet will destroy itself, meaning by this that it would become uninhabitable for human beings of any shape or kind.

To 2000 Dec
But for me these have been years of hard work and achievement. I have written and published much which had to be told.

2001 {35}
At the present time, the fate and future of humankind, of all human beings, is balanced on a razors edge between oppression, exploitation and enslavement on the one side, and liberty, equality and a good life for all on the other side.

2003 {17}
So now we do not have a choice. If we do not now observe and put into effect the social laws (rules) and social system of the Pentateuch and its code of behaviour then the planet will become uninhabitable for human beings.

To 2004 Sep
The quality of life has continued to deteriorate from bad to worse for the human beings on this planet.

To 2006 Apr
The quality of life has continued to deteriorate.
But I have published more of what I know.

To 2007 Apr

I feel strongly that time has almost run out for humanity and its look-alikes, that the planet may soon become uninhabitable for them all.

2007 Apr

He (Manfred Davidmann) states "A new factor has entered the equation. It is now possible for the first time in the history of human beings on this planet for just one or only a few socially irresponsible persons to do something or to introduce changes which could destroy us all or else make this planet uninhabitable for human beings."

> (Los Angeles Times)
> About 'The God-given Human Rights, Social Laws and Social System' {17}

2007 May

Manfred Davidmann says "Humanity is once again struggling intuitively to achieve the application of these social laws and system, in response to the social and economic problems of global humanity at the present time. But struggling 'intuitively' is not enough, amounts to blindly hitting out in the dark without aim, amounts to treating symptoms instead of curing causes."

And he continues: "If we do not now observe and put into effect the social rules and social system first described in the Pentateuch, then the planet is likely to become uninhabitable for human beings in the near future."

When a scientist of Manfred Davidmann's proven track record (of achievement and objectivity) and international standing, makes such a statement, this needs to be taken seriously.

Compiled and correlated analyses and guidance can be found in the works of Manfred Davidmann.

> (Texas Cable News)
> About 'Judaism, Christianity and Islam   (Church and State, Government and Religion)' {27}

In My Name

My published works are fundamental and original. Together they make up a single comprehensive and self-contained body of knowledge consisting of all the publications at present available on the solhaam website*.

These works not only clearly describe and outline what human beings are thinking and doing, and how they treat each other, but also what has to be done, and how human beings need to behave, if human beings are to survive. The future of humankind depends on these works and on the knowledge they contain.

My teachings and my knowledge are spreading, being used worldwide to an ever increasing extent and are changing what people think and believe and how they live.

However, my works have sprouted whole literatures based on their contents and about their subject areas, ranging from publications of scientific institutions and in reference books, to unscientific and misleading look-alikes.

Much has been used only partially or used out of context, selected to suit the personal likes, dislikes, preferences or purposes of those apparently using my published works for their own personal or hidden political ends or for self-glorification. Much has been rephrased, misinterpreted and misrepresented, has been quoted or used without giving credit to the author.

These seem to attempt to obscure, negate or bypass the key core fundamental content of my works, of my teachings.

So my works have to be taught, and need to spread, as a whole and as they are, without change. Which means that they have to be taught and spread in my name, with nothing added and nothing taken away.

If this were not done, then my core teachings about what humane behaviour is, about the benevolent social laws and the social system of the Pentateuch, and about the behaviour which needs to be followed if human beings are to survive, would have been negated by the root of all evil.

And thus the source and intellectual ownership of my teachings, their knowledge, discoveries, achievements, insights, revelations and advances in human knowledge and understanding, need to be clearly attributed, that is stated, giving credit to me as the author, without exception.

The benevolent social laws and the social system of the Pentateuch were negated and turned upside down, three times in the history of human beings. If this were allowed to happen a fourth time, the result would be the end of humanity on this planet.

And so we have come to the final parting of the ways, to the final moment of decision. The future and survival of human beings and of their look-alikes is now balanced on a razor's edge, depends on my teachings as a whole being acknowledged and taught in my name and accepted and followed worldwide.

Stand Up and Be Counted   (Diary Extract <24>)

"If we fail again this time, then the Covenant would be broken completely and irredeemably. If I were to fail then mankind would rapidly destroy itself. Hence we cannot and will not fail. This is a battle we simply have to and therefore will win.

If we do not succeed then this planet will be rendered uninhabitable for human beings of any shape or kind including manipulating beasts in human form.

But always there is the race against time which is either used to achieve our aims or else is irretrievably lost.

When people do not act for God and people, then God withdraws his protection from them. The consequences cannot be avoided.

But he rewards manifold those who act for him.

God helps and protects those who act for God and people.

Stand up and be counted.

This is a matter of survival, of hard work, of strain and effort, to succeed in our endeavour. And to this end we work together, all of us, human beings, proud and erect, hand in hand, irrespective of our creed or religion, the colour of our skin, the shape of our eyes, or where we happen to live, for freedom and humanity."

Notes <..>

< 1>   {1} quoting 'A Triune Concept of the Brain and Behaviour'; P D MacLean; University of Toronto Press, 1973.

For comprehensive information on how the human mind evolved and works, see {1}.

< 2>   {5} quoting from 'The Collected Works of C J Jung, CW8, paras. 200-203'

< 3>   For background information and underlying knowledge and understanding, see section

'Relevant Current and Associated Works' **
which lists titles (as links) as well as short
descriptions.

< 4> The information in this section comes from the
comprehensive report 'What People are Struggling
Against: How Society is Organised for Controlling
and Exploiting People'. See {19}.

< 5> Extracted from {20} which discusses the meaning of
democracy, and its necessary requirements, in
more detail.

< 6> See also {18} for a more comprehensive discussion
of the electing, appointing and appraisal of
managers, directors and elected representatives,
the right to know, the right to be heard, and of
work, pay and differentials.

< 7> Using {3} you can assess how far the
country/community you are living in has advanced
in the struggle for independence and a good life for
all, or where you yourself are on this scale.

< 8> In {22} see 'Creativity' and 'Hearing Voices'.

< 9> Where to be free means to be independent, which
means not being dependent on, and not being
controlled by, another person, group, organisation,
or thing.

And where liberty means freedom from captivity,
slavery, imprisonment or despotic control by
others, means freedom from social, economic,
political, mental or physical control by others, that
is freedom from antisocial control or manipulation
by others.

And antisocial is understood as being contrary to
the benevolent rules of behaviour and organisation
brought together in Part 4 {25}.

<10> The information in reports {7-11, also 12-14}
enables us to understand Genesis to a much greater
extent, gives us a better understanding of the
Pentateuch's contents.

<11> 'Heredity' is the inheritance of mental or physical characteristics from parents or ancestors. So 'hereditary' does not imply 'to all sons' nor does it imply 'in every generation'.

<12> An allegory is a story or description in which the characters and events symbolise some deeper underlying meaning {28}

<13> For detailed analysis, references, proofs and derivations, see {10}.

<14> See {4, 19, 15, 18}

<15> nephil: One of the nephilim.
nephilim: The plural form of 'nephil'; More than one nephil

<16> Genesis. First volume of the Pentateuch. See <17>.

<17> Pentateuch. Also known as 'The Five Books of Moses' (namely Genesis, Exodus, Leviticus, Numbers and Deuteronomy). Also called 'Torah'. Part of 'Old Testament'.

<18> A vague, mild or inoffensive word or phrase used instead of one considered improper or too harsh or blunt, is called a 'euphemism'. Euphemisms are dishonest when they are used to avoid facing unpleasant activities or to conceal and deceive. Dishonest uses are frequent in political and military language. {28}

EXAMPLES

Meaning	Term(s) Used (Euphemism)	Source
Toilet room	Washroom, bathroom, restroom, men's room or women's room	{49}

Mass firing of employees	Layoffs, downsizing, rightsizing	{49}
Death	'Passed away' or 'departed'	{50}
Obscene language	Adult language	{50}
Strikes	Industrial action	{51}
Manfred Davidmann's terms 'Exporting employment' and 'Importing unemployment'	Outsourcing	{47}
Multinational corporation	Global corporation	{48}
'Multinational operations' or 'Corporate multinational operations'	Globalisation	{46, 48}
Oppressive absolute rule	Rule by 'divine right'	{15}

<19>   For a more comprehensive and more detailed listing of the social laws and social system of the Pentateuch, see {17}

<20>   Abrogate: Doing away with (a law or agreement). Annul: Declaring (a law or other legal contract) invalid.

<21>   In {17} see section on 'Unavoidable Consequences of One's Behaviour'.

The Social Cause-and-Effect Relationship is also listed (in biblical language and in plain English) in Appendix 4 of {29}, with references to the Pentateuch text.

<22> For a full listing of the Ten Commandments, in biblical and plain English, see Appendix 1 of {33}. For a good discussion of its provisions see {29}.

<23> In this report, see the first four paragraphs in 'Social Laws and Social System of the Pentateuch in Judaism, Christianity and Islam'

<24> Copyright © Manfred Davidmann 1977, 1980, 1990, 1992, 1994, 1996, 2000, 2004, 2006, 2007 All rights reserved

<25> When individuals, communities and populations are manipulated, then behaviour is all-important. This report (Part 4) {25} shows how we can overcome corrupt manipulations, how behaviour determines our standard of living and the quality of our lives, and describes the kind of behaviour and social organisation on which depend liberty, freedom and a good and secure life for all. <9>

References {..}

{ 1} In 'The Human Mind and How it Works: Group Minds in Action: How the Human Group Mind Shapes the Quality of Our Life and Living' Manfred Davidmann ISBN 978-0-85192-055-9 see chapter 2: 'How the Human Brain Developed and How the Human Mind Works'

{ 2} In 'The Human Mind and How it Works: Group Minds in Action: How the Human Group Mind Shapes the Quality of Our Life and Living' Manfred Davidmann ISBN 978-0-85192-055-9 see chapter 7: 'Motivation Summary'

{ 3} In 'The Human Mind and How it Works:
Group Minds in Action:
How the Human Group Mind Shapes
the Quality of Our Life and Living'
Manfred Davidmann
ISBN 978-0-85192-055-9
see chapter 9: 'The Will to Work:
What People Struggle to Achieve'

{ 4} In 'Messianic Struggle:
The Worldwide Struggle for a Good and
Secure Life for All, Here and Now'
Manfred Davidmann
ISBN 978-0-85192-059-7
see chapter 7: 'Social Responsibility and
Accountability: Summary'

{ 5} Private Myths: Dreams and Dreaming
Anthony Stevens
Penguin Books, 1996

{ 6} To Give or Not To Give
'Everyman' TV documentary
Editor: Jane Drabble; Producer: Angela Kaye
Broadcast on 5/1/92 by BBC 1
Based on book 'The Altruistic Person' by
Professor Sam Oliner

{ 7} In 'God and People:
The Social Laws and Social System Underlying
Judaism, Christianity, Islam and Democracy'
Manfred Davidmann
ISBN 978-0-85192-054-2
see chapter 6.1: 'The Meaning of Genesis:
Creation, Evolution and the Origin of Evil'

{ 8} In 'God and People:
The Social Laws and Social System Underlying
Judaism, Christianity, Islam and Democracy'
Manfred Davidmann
ISBN 978-0-85192-054-2
see chapter 6.2: 'The Meaning of Genesis:
Pre-flood Evils and the Social Problems of Our Time'

{ 9} In 'God and People:
The Social Laws and Social System Underlying
Judaism, Christianity, Islam and Democracy'
Manfred Davidmann
ISBN 978-0-85192-054-2
see chapter 6.3: 'The Meaning of Genesis:
Morality, Sexual Behaviour and Depravity'

{10} In 'God and People:
The Social Laws and Social System Underlying
Judaism, Christianity, Islam and Democracy'
Manfred Davidmann
ISBN 978-0-85192-054-2
see chapter 6.4: 'The Meaning of Genesis:
Nephilim, Dominance and Liberty'

{11} In 'God and People:
The Social Laws and Social System Underlying
Judaism, Christianity, Islam and Democracy'
Manfred Davidmann
ISBN 978-0-85192-054-2
see chapter 6.5: 'The Meaning of Genesis:
Differentiating Between Good and Evil'

{12} See chapter 10.1:
'Meaning and Significance of the Names of God
in Genesis'
Manfred Davidmann

{13} See chapter 10.2:
'Meaning and Intent of Genesis: Essential Notes on
Hebrew Grammar'
Manfred Davidmann

{14} See chapter 10.3:
'Bible Translations, Versions, Codes and Hidden
Information in Bible and Talmud'
Manfred Davidmann

{15} In 'Management and Leadership:
Local, National, Multinational (Global),
Principles and Practice'
Manfred Davidmann
ISBN 978-0-85192-057-3
see chapter 2: 'Style of Management and
Leadership'

{16} See chapter 3:
'Family, Community, Sex and the Individual'
Manfred Davidmann

{17} See chapter 2.1:
'The God-given Human Rights, Social Laws
and Social System'
Manfred Davidmann

{18} In 'Cooperatives and Cooperation:
Causes of Failure, Guidelines for Success'
Manfred Davidmann
ISBN 978-0-85192-056-6
see chapter 2: 'Cooperatives and Cooperation'
and chapter 3: 'Causes of Failure, Guidelines for
Success'

{19} In 'The Real World in Which We Live:
The Social Rules and Social System under
Which We Suffer, Struggle, Survive and Prosper'
Manfred Davidmann
ISBN 978-0-85192-058-0
see chapter 10: 'What People are Struggling Against:
How Society is Organised for Controlling and
Exploiting People'

{20} In 'The Real World in Which We Live:
The Social Rules and Social System under
Which We Suffer, Struggle, Survive and Prosper'
Manfred Davidmann
ISBN 978-0-85192-058-0
see chapter 11: 'Democracy Under Attack:
Top-level Leadership and Decision-making'

{21} In 'The Human Mind and How it Works:
Group Minds in Action:
How the Human Group Mind Shapes
the Quality of Our Life and Living'
Manfred Davidmann
ISBN 978-0-85192-055-9
see chapter 3: 'The Human Group Mind
and How It Works'
see chapter 4: 'Manipulated Communities
and Populations'

see chapter 5: 'Manipulated Individuals'
see chapter 6: 'Freedom, Liberty and Good Life:
Overcoming Corrupt Manipulations'

{22} In 'The Human Mind and How it Works:
Group Minds in Action:
How the Human Group Mind Shapes
the Quality of Our Life and Living'
Manfred Davidmann
ISBN 978-0-85192-055-9
see chapter 3: 'The Human Group Mind
and How It Works'

{23} In 'The Human Mind and How it Works:
Group Minds in Action:
How the Human Group Mind Shapes
the Quality of Our Life and Living'
Manfred Davidmann
ISBN 978-0-85192-055-9
see chapter 4: 'Manipulated Communities
and Populations'

{24} In 'The Human Mind and How it Works:
Group Minds in Action:
How the Human Group Mind Shapes
the Quality of Our Life and Living'
Manfred Davidmann
ISBN 978-0-85192-055-9
see chapter 5: 'Manipulated Individuals'

{25} In 'The Human Mind and How it Works:
Group Minds in Action:
How the Human Group Mind Shapes
the Quality of Our Life and Living'
Manfred Davidmann
ISBN 978-0-85192-055-9
see chapter 6: 'Freedom, Liberty and Good Life:
Overcoming Corrupt Manipulations'

{26} 'Liberation Theology: Basis - Past - Present – Future'
Manfred Davidmann
www.solhaam.org

{27} See chapter 2.2:
'Church and State, Government and Religion:
Judaism, Christianity and Islam'
Manfred Davidmann

{28} Oxford Dictionary

{29} In 'Judaism: Basis - Past - Present - Future, Part 1'
Manfred Davidmann
ISBN 978-0-85192-060-3
see chapter 2.1: 'Struggle for Freedom:
The Social Cause-and-Effect Relationship'

{30} In 'Judaism: Basis - Past - Present - Future, Part 1'
Manfred Davidmann
ISBN 978-0-85192-060-3
see chapter 2.2: 'History Speaks: Monarchy,
Exile and Maccabees'

{31} In 'Judaism: Basis - Past - Present - Future, Part 1'
Manfred Davidmann
ISBN 978-0-85192-060-3
see chapter 2.3: 'At the Time of Jesus,
This is What Actually Happened in Israel:
The Truth about Hillel and his Times'

{32} In 'Judaism: Basis - Past - Present - Future, Part 1'
Manfred Davidmann
ISBN 978-0-85192-060-3
see chapter 2.4: 'One Law for All:
Freedom Now, Freedom for Ever'

{33} 'Origin of Christianity and Judaism:
What Actually Happened, What Jesus Actually
Taught and Later Changes'
Manfred Davidmann
www.solhaam.org

{34} In 'Judaism: Basis - Past - Present - Future, Part 1'
Manfred Davidmann
ISBN 978-0-85192-060-3
see chapter 5: 'The Right to the Land of Israel'

{35} 'Social Policies (Doctrine) of the Roman Catholic
Church: An Evaluation'
Manfred Davidmann
www.solhaam.org

{36} 'Social Concept (Policies) of the Russian Orthodox
Church: Letter to the Russians'
Manfred Davidmann
www.solhaam.org

{37} Pentateuch: Deuteronomy 17, 14-20

{38} Pentateuch: Leviticus 19: 15

{39} In 'Islam: Basis – Past – Present – Future'
Manfred Davidmann
ISBN 978-0-85192-053-5
see chapter 2: 'Prophet Mohammed's Struggle
for a Better Life for All'

{40} In 'Islam: Basis – Past – Present – Future'
Manfred Davidmann
ISBN 978-0-85192-053-5
see chapter 3: 'Text, Language, Dialect and
Interpretation of the Koran'

{41} In 'Islam: Basis – Past – Present – Future'
Manfred Davidmann
ISBN 978-0-85192-053-5
see chapter 4: 'The Divine Right to Rule'

{42} In 'Islam: Basis – Past – Present – Future'
Manfred Davidmann
ISBN 978-0-85192-053-5
see chapter 5: 'Compiling the Koran:
Hadiths (Traditions) State the Underlying Reality'

{43} In 'Islam: Basis – Past – Present – Future'
Manfred Davidmann
ISBN 978-0-85192-053-5
see chapter 6: 'Uthman's Rearrangement of the
Chronological (as revealed) Koran's Chapters'

{44} In 'Islam: Basis - Past - Present - Future'
Manfred Davidmann
ISBN 978-0-85192-053-5
see chapter 7: 'Prophet Mohammed's Word of
Allah and the Voice of the Ruling Elite'

{45} See chapter 15:
'Muslims and Jews'
Manfred Davidmann

{46} In 'The Real World in Which We Live:
The Social Rules and Social System under
Which We Suffer, Struggle, Survive and Prosper'
Manfred Davidmann
ISBN 978-0-85192-058-0
see chapter 8: 'Transfer Pricing and Taxation'

{47} In 'The Real World in Which We Live:
The Social Rules and Social System under
Which We Suffer, Struggle, Survive and Prosper'
Manfred Davidmann
ISBN 978-0-85192-058-0
see chapter 7: 'Exporting and Importing of
Employment and Unemployment'

{48} In 'The Real World in Which We Live:
The Social Rules and Social System under
Which We Suffer, Struggle, Survive and Prosper'
Manfred Davidmann
ISBN 978-0-85192-058-0
see chapter 6: 'Multinational Summits and
Agreements, Top-level Decision-making and
Democracy'

{49} Euphemism
http://euphemism.biography.ms/

{50} Euphemisms
http://info-pollution.com/euphemisms.htm

{51} Guide to English Usage

{52} 'Press Notices about the Works of Manfred
Davidmann'
www.solhaam.org

Additions by the Editor:

* See Manfred Davidmann's website 'www.solhaam.org'

** See 'www.solhaam.org/teachings/relsta5.html'

About the Author

Manfred Davidmann is an internationally well-known and respected scientist and consultant, and author of a number of books and reports which have had considerable impact. His work usually breaks new ground and opens up new understanding and is written in meaningful and easily understood language. Outstanding is that his work is generally accepted as factual, objective and unbiased.

His works have made known and publicised the human rights, the social laws and social system, and the intense worldwide struggle to achieve them, to achieve freedom, liberty, independence and a good and secure life, here and now in this life.

Here some of his works are described under the following headings

General Management (Middle, Senior and Top Level)

Community Conflicts and Confrontations

The Worldwide Struggle for a Better Life

Brain, Mind and Group Minds. Mental Health and Corresponding Social Organisations, of Individuals, People and Communities

Government and Religion, Church and State

Cooperatives and Cooperation

General Management (Middle, Senior and Top Level)

As said already, Manfred Davidmann is an internationally well-known and respected scientist and consultant, and author of a number of books and reports which have had considerable impact. His work usually breaks new ground and opens up new understanding and is written in meaningful and easily understood language. Outstanding is that his work is generally accepted as factual, objective and unbiased.

He brings to his tasks a rare combination of practical experience, knowledge and understanding backed by years spent training middle and top-level managers. Expert knowledge is expressed in clear and meaningful language.

What Manfred Davidmann has done in his work on the general management of enterprises and communities is to lay the foundation for, and develop, 'management science'. He developed and defined the scope and content of General Management, in these reports:

Directing and Managing Change

Organising

Motivation

Style of Management and Leadership

Role of Managers under Different Styles of Management

Work and Pay, Incomes and Differentials: Employer, Employee and Community

Using Words to Communicate Effectively

'Directing and Managing Change' (1979, 2006) {1}**
includes
adapting to change, deciding what needs to be done;
planning ahead, getting results, evaluating progress
and performance;
and appraisal interviews and target-setting meetings.

'Using Words to Communicate Effectively' (1998, 2006) (see chapter 6)*

shows how to communicate more effectively, covering aspects of thinking, writing, speaking and listening as well as formal and informal communications. Consists of guidelines found useful by practising middle and senior managers and by university students.

'Organising' (1981, 2006) {1}**
is a comprehensive review showing how to arrange matters so that people can work together successfully and well. It is about achieving effective co-operation and teamwork, particularly in large organisations where many experts have to work together in teams to enable aims and objectives to be achieved.

The most confused and intractable organisational problems tend to be about functional relationships and coordinating. Concerning these, the report's descriptions, definitions, specifications and examples, are outstanding.

'Motivation Summary' (1982, 1998) {4}**
In **'Motivation Summary'**, Manfred Davidmann summarises different motivation theories, draws on his earlier work including evidence from his U.K. study, and utilises material used by him for lecturing to degree-level students and for training experienced middle and senior managers.

'Style of Management and Leadership' (1981, 2006) {1}**
Manfred Davidmann's work **'Style of Management and Leadership'** is a landmark in management and community science and methodology. Over 770,000 copies have been downloaded from his website, worldwide, so far (April 2011).

'Role of Managers under Different Styles of Management' (1982, 1998) {1}**

is a short summary of the role of managers under authoritarian and participative styles of management. It also covers decision making and the basic characteristics of each style.

The term 'Participation', meaning by this 'participation in decision-making', was first coined, and defined, by Manfred Davidmann when he published his analysis and recommendations about the style of management, in 1981. His works on style of management and on participation in decision-making in management, leadership and government, are widely known, studied and applied, and sprouted a whole literature ranging from the scientific to misleading politically-motivated misrepresentations.

It was Manfred Davidmann who in 1981 formulated, clearly stated and then published ('Style of Management and Leadership', 1981) his principle that the real political struggle was not between political 'left' and 'right', but was for participation in decision-making, for the right to make the decisions.

Manfred Davidmann's concept of participative government and management, of participation in decision-making, has become a household word, in daily use when referring to government and management styles, worldwide. His concepts are applied all the way from village government and community projects to national policies and elections, are applied by cooperatives, companies and global corporations alike.

Clearly defined and described in 'Style of Management and Leadership' is the whole scale of style of management and organising, from fully authoritarian to fully participative. It applies to community organisations, commercial enterprises, political parties, whole countries. The social assumptions underlying each of the styles are given, as are problems they create, the symptoms by which they can be recognised, and the ways people work together or against each other within them.

The extent to which authority is balanced between top and bottom, and the corresponding style of management, are also discussed. This work pulls the diverse world-wide events in labour relations and in government/people confrontation into a meaningful, clear and highly significant picture of interrelated events fitting into a consistent pattern.

Community Conflicts and Confrontations

How local and national governments are managing our affairs is of crucial importance to every citizen. Government has to make ends meet, has to bring about a rising standard of secure living, social security and an increasing quality of life for its citizens.

"There can be ups and downs but", says Manfred Davidmann, "failure to make ends meet is just as directly and surely the result of bad leadership and management as it is in any commercial enterprise." This is a severe criticism also of the kind of experts and consultants used, and of the way they are used. "The quality of one's experts and whether and how their expertise is used, and applied, are of decisive importance."

Manfred Davidmann's report 'Work and Pay, Incomes and Differentials: Employer, Employee and Community' (1981, 2007) {2}** is a concise all-embracing review and analysis of the whole subject, in clear and easily understood language. What makes this report so special is that it covers incomes and differentials from the point of view of the owner or employer, from that of the individual and his family and from that of the community, discussing their interests and requirements.

When talking about pay, incomes and differentials we are dealing with matters which are at the centre of confrontation and conflict and around which rage controversy and strife. We are dealing with matters which determine how one man stands in relation to another, with something which depends on negotiation and bargaining between those who employ and those who are employed. The result is that almost all one sees about pay and differentials is biased towards one side or the other and both points of view are then equally misleading.

But Manfred Davidmann here provides the underlying knowledge and understanding for scientific determination and prediction of rates of pay, remuneration and differentials, of remuneration scales and of national patterns of pay and differentials.

These correlations and methods represent a major breakthrough and rates of pay, incomes and differentials can be assessed with a high degree of reliability. Now pay bargaining can include agreeing basic guide-lines of the kind described here as governing pay increases.

Illustrated are National Remuneration Scales which record the remuneration pattern for a group or profession and the position of every individual in it, showing also how income depends on age and degree of success. Illustrated also is the National Remuneration Pattern which is a precise pictorial record of the differentials within a country, from top to bottom, from young to old. Both are used to assess changes in pay, remuneration and differentials for individuals, groups and professions.

However, it is easier to tell the rich to share their wealth with the poor than to persuade them to actually do so. And companies, corporations and governments, owners, managers, experts and politicians, too often work for personal gain instead of serving employees, customers or citizens, exploiting instead of serving their community.

Just consider the following examples of corporate and individual antisocial practices.

One of the most controversial operations of multinationals, transfer pricing, has been clearly described and defined by Manfred Davidmann in his report 'Multinational Operations: Transfer Pricing and Taxation' (1991, 2006) {3}**.

The report showed that multinational companies were minimising their liability for corporation tax by transfer pricing, that is by making book entries which transfer profits to the country with the lowest corporation tax.

Say a multinational has increased its profits in such ways. As the government's expenses have not changed it must make up this shortfall elsewhere. From its other tax payers, say from its citizens. So its citizens pay more tax, the government can now spend the same amount as before, the multinational's profits have increased.

This tax avoidance is legal and governments have not legislated to prevent this practice.

The multinational, and this means the owners and directors of the multinational, are thus in effect taxing the country's citizens, its population, in this way increasing the multinational's profits and thus their own incomes and wealth.

A matter far removed from earning reasonable profits from providing needed quality goods and services at reasonable prices in open competition with other corporations.

Fifteen years ago, Manfred Davidmann coined the phrase 'Exporting Employment and Importing Unemployment', and pointed to, and warned about, the social and economic consequences of what is now often euphemistically called 'outsourcing' or 'globalisation'.

In his report 'Exporting and Importing of Employment and Unemployment' (1996, 2002) {3}** he pointed out that imports were being priced at what the market will bear, or just under, and that if the enormous profit margins were left uncontrolled, these would then cause production to move from high-wage to low-wage countries. The consequence is a lowering of the standard of living in high-wage countries to that in low-wage countries, instead of a raising of the standard of living in low-wage countries to that in high wage countries.

"Unemployment has reached an unacceptable level" says Manfred Davidmann. It is a principle of economics that social costs have to be paid by those causing them. But manufacturers and suppliers tend to increase their profits by passing on to the community the social costs of their operations, costs such as disposal of packaging and waste, or of polluting.

"The social costs of unemployment have to be paid by the enterprise which caused the unemployment in the first place" says Manfred Davidmann. "Social costs need to be allowed for when making decisions, need to be charged to the enterprise or organisation which is causing them. And this applies equally well to the social costs of redundancy and unemployment when transferring operations to countries with lower wages or fewer environmental safeguards."

It was Manfred Davidmann who twenty years ago demolished the then-current economic myths about 'Price Inflation' and 'Wage Inflation', and about inflation and unemployment.

In "**Inflation, Balance of Payments and Currency Exchange Rates**" (1981, 2006) {1}**, Manfred Davidmann explores how national and international accounts and accounting reflect the quality of management in national and local government, reflect multinational operations such as devaluation pricing, profits maximisation, transfer pricing, importing from low-wage countries, transferring work to low-wage countries. And he reviews different ways of balancing income and expenditure, causes of inflation, and tax avoidance.

In this report Manfred Davidmann reviews a country's ways out of a payments crisis and details the consequences of increasing interest rates, greater borrowing, selling assets or printing more money.

To give just a few examples, he:

> Shows how rising interest rates follow from balance of payments deficits.

> Shows how interest rates determine share prices and thus the extent to which pension funds are in surplus or underfunded.

> Shows how inflation affects currency exchange rates, trade and competing abroad.

Clear and meaningful language is backed by easily understood illustrations. And easy-to-follow diagrams illustrate the relationships.

The two coefficients of inequality between different countries, which Manfred Davidmann put forward in 1981 in this inflation report, are objective and effective measures of inequality and differentials.

The first he called 'Inequality between Countries'. The second, namely 'Relative Inequality between Countries', is numerically the same as the ratio between the GNP/person of the countries being compared. These measures of inequality are now in general use.

The Worldwide Struggle for a Better Life

In 'Motivation Summary' (1982, 1998) {4}**, Manfred Davidmann summarises different motivation theories, draws on his earlier work including evidence from the U.K. study, and utilises material used by him for lecturing to degree-level students and for training experienced middle and senior managers.

This chapter provides an objective, comprehensive and clear definition of 'motivation', of the factors which motivate and of what people are striving to achieve.

"Motivated behaviour is purposeful, directed towards some end" says Manfred Davidmann. "The driving force is need. The direction is towards perceived reward and away from perceived punishment."

And in the workplace one aims to achieve either job satisfaction or money rewards or both. "Motivation towards better performance depends on the satisfaction of needs for responsibility, achievement, recognition and growth."

One works to achieve that which one needs and which one does not have. "Attaining goals leads to feelings of self-respect, strength and confidence", and "persistent lack of rewards leads to a view of society as being hostile and unrewarding".

Manfred Davidmann's fundamental work on motivation, 'The Will to Work: What People Struggle to Achieve' (1981, 2006) {4}**, includes a detailed step-by-step listing of what people are struggling to achieve, their needs and wants, their achievements and objectives. It is a unique analysis of the worldwide struggle for a better life at all levels of life and development, in all countries.

What we see in the working environment is each person, family or community struggling to advance at their own level of development.

Manfred Davidmann here clearly defines and describes motivation, its basis and 'motivating'.

Starting by considering motivation from the point of view of the employer (productivity, remuneration, job satisfaction), this leads to considering what people want and what they struggle to achieve.

A key part of this chapter is community orientated, including a detailed step-by-step listing of what people are struggling to achieve, their needs and wants, their achievements and objectives.

It is a unique analysis of the worldwide struggle for a better life at all levels of life and development, in all countries. What we see in the working environment is each person, family or community struggling to advance at their own level of development.

This progression shows underdeveloped and developed people as they are, human beings at different stages of an identical struggle for a better life against those who wish to profit from their condition.

And you can assess how far the country/community you are living in has advanced in this struggle for independence and a good life for all, or where you are yourself on this scale.

Highlights are Figure 1 (Motivation of Directors) and Figure 3 (People's Needs and Wants, Achievements and Objectives: The Struggle for Independence and a Good Life).

In "**Family, Community, Sex and the Individual**" (1998, 2011) (see chapter 3)*, Manfred Davidmann exposes the causes of what seems to be a progressive breaking down of family life and of social strength.

Clearly described and defined is the role of the family under modern conditions, and the differences between the behaviour of human beings and that of the primitive animals from which human beings evolved. He illustrated the underlying basis of teamwork within the family, stating the various roles and responsibilities and functional relationships of its members for effective teamwork within the family.

He was the first to clearly describe and show, thirteen years ago, the effects of increasing life spans on the family, on its members and on their responsibilities.

We now live much longer and the time spent full-time at home looking after the family places women at a disadvantage when returning to work outside the family after the children have been brought up. So women need to be supported when returning to work.

And Manfred Davidmann showed that the family compensates women for the life-long effects of their contribution towards the upbringing of the children. It is the role of the spouse, of the husband, to continue to provide for the family. A life-long contribution from him which means she does not lose out for the rest of her life because she stayed at home to look after the children, the husband's input into the family balancing her input of bringing up the children and looking after the family's members.

This work also investigates the impact of casual sexual relations and its effects on individuals, family and community, on the social strength of individuals and communities.

And it examines and relates dominance and confrontation within the family to that in the working environment and considers oppression and exploitation within and outside the family.

Human rights are based on controlling primitive dominating behaviour, on concern, care and affection for our young and our families, for people and for our communities. Human rights express themselves in co-operation and teamwork between men and women to achieve a good life of high quality.

It is in democracies that a high standard of living has been achieved. In democracies people can struggle openly for a better life but we see that what has been gained has to be defended and extended.

This work is an unprecedented and comprehensive overview, states new insights, proves basic underlying causes.

The main report **What People are Struggling Against: How Society is Organised for Controlling and Exploiting People** (1998, 2002) {3}**, brings together key conclusions from four studies undertaken by Manfred Davidmann to obtain a better understanding of why people have to struggle throughout their adult lives, in all countries and organisations, at all levels, to maintain and improve their standard of living and quality of life. We know what people are struggling to achieve and so this study was undertaken to explore why people have to struggle by looking at what they are struggling against.

This work looks at the way 'Economics' is being used to misinform and mislead the general public, and looks at the role and vested interests of experts. It describes how companies (corporations) accumulate their capital and reserves from moneys taken from customers and how people's massive savings are placed under the control of others. And shows how taxpayers' moneys are used in different ways to enlarge the profits of companies.

It discusses and illustrates the internal struggles taking place in political parties and all other organisations, for achieving greater democracy and against those wishing to overpower democratic processes of decision-making.

In **'Democracy, Socialism and Communism: The Worldwide Struggle for a Better Life'** (2008) {4}** Manfred Davidmann outlined the battlefield in these terms:

Participative (democratic) organisation rests on the population electing representatives, on the basis of each person having one vote. Representatives are responsible to, and accountable to, the population for putting into effect policies decided by the population.

What underlies participative organisation (democracy) is decision-making by the people at the level of the people.

What needs to be stressed is that in a participative (democratic) organisation policies are decided by a well-informed population at the level of the population and that policies then become binding on management or government. It was Manfred Davidmann who formulated, clearly stated and then published ('Style of Management and Leadership', 1981) his principle that the real political struggle was not between political 'left' and 'right', but was for participation in decision-making, for the right to make the decisions.

Representatives, governments or government officials do not have the authority or right to reduce or sign away the participative (democratic) rights of the electors, of the population.

The real struggle is not between political left and right, but is a struggle for participation, that is for the right of the population to be well-informed and to make the decisions which then become binding on management or government, as outlined by Manfred Davidmann in **'Multinational Summits and Agreements, Top-level Decision-making and Democracy'** (2002) {3}**.

Brain, Mind and Group Minds. Mental Health and Corresponding Social Organisations, of Individuals, People and Communities.

In **'How the Human Brain Developed and How the Human Mind Works'** (1998, 2006) {4}**, Manfred Davidmann explains how the human brain evolved and functions, how the human mind works, and how brain and mind interact. This fundamental work provides fascinating insights clearly expressed in meaningful language, including a much clearer appreciation of the different functions of the two halves of the brain, and of the different kinds of sleep and memory.

The work showed how brain and mind determine what people do and how they do it, what people aim to achieve and how in the struggle for a better life we adapt to the world in which we live.

It proved that images penetrate deeply into the ancient and primitive parts of the human brain and how certain images can be "brutalising society, seemingly legalising, making acceptable, inconsiderate and unfeeling behaviour towards other people."

Relating the functioning of the brain to behavior, this report showed how human behavior is affected by the primitive instincts of our reptilian ancestors. It seems that instinctive behavior has to be controlled, and is modified according to the environment in which we find ourselves, in every generation, and that the mammalian and human parts of the brain play a major part in this.

Manfred Davidmann considers that humane behavior is based on feelings of care and affection for the young and for the family, and then for other people and the community. From this emerges a sense of social responsibility: People matter and are important, and need to be treated well.

A key finding of Manfred Davidmann's report is that the right hemisphere of the human brain is able to communicate by using images with the brain's older and more primitive component organs which have no verbal skills. And this enables us to communicate intentionally (that is "consciously") with our autonomic nervous system and by visualizing control of body functions and to affect our body's immune system. Clinical trials have shown remarkable success in areas such as the treatment of cancer and heart disease.

The day-night-day sleep pattern, the "DEEP sleep"/"REM sleep" sequence, and how the different halves of the brain communicate by means of images with the older parts of the brain, are correlated and illustrated. Manfred Davidmann makes the point that the brain paralyzes the body to enable dreaming to take place, that dreaming performs an essential function, and he explains the role and meaning of dreams and dreaming.

Manfred Davidmann considers that humane behavior is based on feelings of care and affection for the young and for the family, and then for other people and the community. From this emerges a sense of social responsibility: People matter and are important, and need to be treated well.

As a result of the work in this report, there emerged a much clearer appreciation of what happens during the course of a night's sleep, and clear explanations of the role of dreaming and the meaning of dreams.

The report explores the functioning and role of the two halves of the human brain and the relationship between them. It is the right half which usually communicates with the primitive parts of the human brain and this is related to the functioning of the autonomic nervous system and the immune system.

When Manfred Davidmann first announced his Group Mind Theory in 1973, this theory and his concepts and terms such as 'group minds', were completely new and unheard of. The second edition was published in 1998 and made available on the internet in 1999.

His "human group minds and how they function", that is the Group Mind Science he originated, are now widely quoted and discussed, have sprouted a whole literature about group minds ranging from publications of scientific institutions and in reference books, to unscientific misleading look-alikes about human minds.

In **'The Human Group Mind and How It Works'** (1973, 1978) {4}**, Manfred Davidmann outlines, describes, uncovers and proves the subconscious existence and workings of group minds by the extraordinary way in which they affect and determine what individuals and communities do. This is shown to explain how human communities and society are organised and function, countrywide and worldwide, and consequent confrontations and struggles from dictatorship to democracy. We are here looking at what motivates and drives human beings, seeing how the mind shapes the way in which we live, suffer, struggle and achieve.

Included are comprehensive but concise reviews of mental health and mental illness. There are sections which discuss how conflict arises within the mind, and the mind theories of Freud and of Jung are reviewed.

Manfred Davidmann's Group Mind Science is proved by the way in which it explains and predicts not only the mental problems of individuals but also society's social problems.

It predicts and explains the way in which society is organised as well as human activities and organisation, explains dominance, co-operation, non-conformity and conflict as well as why people are struggling and what they are struggling against.

The subconscious existence and workings of group minds become apparent by the extraordinary way in which they affect and determine what individuals and communities do. The chapters of this book which deal with how we live and struggle, with the way our communities and societies are organised and function, describe how our minds shape our lives, communities and society, and uncover the workings of group minds.

Manfred Davidmann's Group Mind Science represents substantial beneficial healing powers. Following the work of Freud and Jung, it is regarded as scientifically proved, as meaningful, objective and practical, as applying worldwide to all human beings in all societies and cultures and at all stages of development.

Manfred Davidmann's Group Mind Science is based on deep knowledge and understanding of the real world, and proved by the way in which it explains and predicts human activities and organisation as well as the mental problems of individuals and society's social problems. Its insights enable us to solve such problems effectively.

The work about 'The Human Group Mind', on how human minds work and operate, on human group minds, consists of four consecutive parts, as follows:

'The Human Group Mind and How It Works' (1973, 1998) {4}**

> The 'Group Mind' science is outlined and described. There are sections which discuss how conflict arises within the mind, mental health and illness, dominance, creativity and hearing voices.
>
> Shows how our minds shape our lives, communities and society.

'Manipulated Communities and Populations' (1973, 1998) {4}**

> The workings of group minds is shown to explain how human communities and society are organised and the consequent confrontations and struggles from dictatorship to democracy.
>
> Discusses how mass media are forming and manipulating public opinions and illustrates how writers and artists have been sensing and expressing the underlying subconscious reality.

'Manipulated Individuals' (1973, 1998) {4}**

> Shows how emotional unreasoning behaviour is being reinforced to make it easier to mislead and exploit.
>
> Reviews available information on incidence and causes of psychosomatic illnesses.

'Freedom, Liberty and Good Life: Overcoming Corrupt Manipulations' (1973, 2001) {4}**

> The Group Mind science of the way in which human minds work is proved by the way in which it explains and predicts human activities and organisation as well as mental problems of individuals and society's social problems. Its insights enable us to solve such problems effectively.

When individuals, communities and populations are manipulated, then behaviour is all-important. This report shows how we can overcome corrupt manipulations, how behaviour determines our standard of living and the quality of our lives, and describes the kind of behaviour and social organisation on which depend liberty, freedom and a good and secure life for all.

Government and Religion, Church and State

Manfred Davidmann's The God-given Human Rights, Social Laws and Social System (2003) (see chapter 2.1)* is a comprehensive statement of the God-given human rights and obligations which underlie freedom, liberty, independence and well-being. They underlie and determine a good life of high quality. People at all stages of development are struggling to achieve these rights and benefits, all over the planet.

Directly relevant to today's social and economic problems, these rights and obligations determine the quality of life in areas such as social and economic security, social responsibility and accountability, ownership and decision-making, government and management, humane behaviour, teamwork and trustful cooperation.

> These human rights, these social rules and this social system, are the very foundation of the three main religions of Judaism, Christianity and Islam.

> Manfred Davidmann discovered that what these religions have in common is that in each case a ruling elite succeeded in bypassing or overturning the religion's essential God-given benevolent social provisions and human rights, in this way exposing their communities and whole populations to oppression and exploitation.

What Manfred Davidmann has done with his works on the Pentateuch and the Bible, on religion and church-state relations, is to expose and correct the misinterpretations and mistranslations of the past. His works are major breakthroughs, constituting essential information for understanding the meaning and significance of the Pentateuch and the Bible.

The Pentateuch records and details the Social Cause-and-Effect Relationship, a fundamental scientific law which is stated as such and which was discovered by Manfred Davidmann. In his **'Struggle for Freedom: The Social Cause-and-Effect Relationship'** (1978, 2002) {5}** he shows that this law states that the consequences of keeping or not keeping the social laws are inescapable, that what happens to one is in the end the inevitable result of one's own behavior. It is stated to enable people to benefit from knowing the effects of their behaviour.

Ignorance of these rules of behavior is no excuse and the relationship applies to all. History and social science confirm it, the prophets knew and understood it and predicted accordingly. Jesus confirmed it; the Koran records Prophet Mohammed repeatedly confirming the Pentateuch, referring to it both as a guide and as a warning.

Whole communities prosper or suffer as a consequence of their collective behavior. Manfred Davidmann says, "The consequences of our behavior cannot be avoided but we can change the course of events by changing our behavior."

He states "A new factor has entered the equation. It is now possible for the first time in the history of human beings on this planet for just one or only a few socially irresponsible persons to do something or to introduce changes which could destroy us all or else make this planet uninhabitable for human beings."

The Ten Commandments are so important and are so well known because it is behaviour in accordance with these laws which is the basis for people trusting each other and so for people co-operating and working well with each other. They are listed in '**Struggle for Freedom: The Social Cause-and-Effect Relationship**' (1978, 2002) {5}** both in biblical language and in plain English.

It is the Ten Commandments as a whole which underlie freedom, independence and strength to oppose and resist oppression. Wherever there is any spiritual and material freedom today it exists because people followed these laws (rules) of behaviour and it exists to the extent to which they do so. In other words, following the provisions of the law results in freedom and ensures it, ensures strength and security.

History shows that in the past the people have been betrayed again and again, by non-observant leaderships no matter whether right or left and by so-called orthodox or fundamentalist leaderships who weakened the application of the law so as to be able to oppress the people in order to exploit them. It was those who did not follow the law who in the past grasped power and then weakened and defeated the hope for achieving freedom and a good life for the people and thus in due course for all humanity.

It is equally certain that the same battle is being fought today and it is just as certain that on the one hand is the opportunity to gain freedom while on the other hand our defeat can only result in mankind rapidly destroying itself.

To free ourselves from mental conditioning and brainwashing we have to follow the Ten Commandments and apply the social laws and the social system of the Pentateuch.

In **'Democracy, Socialism and Communism: The Worldwide Struggle for a Better Life'** (2008) {4}**, Manfred Davidmann exposes what people are struggling against, the secretive manipulations of bureaucracy, oppressors and exploiters.

He shows that underlying Judaism, Christianity and Islam are the same fundamental benevolent and egalitarian social laws and social system which also underlie Democracy, Socialism and Communism (See **'The God-given Human Rights, Social Laws and Social System'** (2003) above). He traces them to their origin and proves from contemporary written records that in each case the ruling and religious hierarchies (bureaucracies) soon bypassed or annulled the 'God-given' social laws and social system, replacing them with 'man-made', ruler- and hierarchy-serving obedience-demanding protest-silencing indoctrination.

It is these revisionist versions which are being taught and believed today and here we see clearly the causes of present controversies and conflicts between church and state, between beliefs and practice, in these religions.

This work also covers dominance and confrontation within the family and in the working environment, how men and women relate to each other, and the role of the family. The family is decisive in determining the quality of life; it is a source of strength and support in a time of need.

It shows how the media are being used for 'social engineering', a kind of brainwashing aimed at turning the struggle of the working population into 'self-defeating' directions, into 'scoring own goals'.

Manfred Davidmann's groundbreaking discoveries about Judaism, Christianity and Islam, published over twenty-five years, are acknowledged as major advances. And in his report "**Judaism, Christianity and Islam**" (2004) (see chapter 2.2)*, we see for the first time the complete sequence of consecutive events.

Manfred Davidmann has shown that underlying Judaism, Christianity and Islam are the Pentateuch's benevolent and egalitarian social laws and social system which include laws protecting the people by restraining the behaviour of their rulers. Those in positions of trust, responsibility or authority must not oppress people and the laws forbid personal gain from the misuse of wealth or position.

He not only proves the meaning and intent of Genesis, the first volume of the Pentateuch, but also exposes the mistranslations and political misrepresentations of the past. For example he established the meaning of the names of God which had been 'lost'.

Manfred Davidmann's work **'The Meaning of Genesis: Creation, Evolution and the Origin of Evil'** (2000) {6}** proves that there is no conflict or contradiction between Darwin's theory of evolution by natural selection and what is written in Genesis. Conflicts have arisen because some parts of Genesis have been mistranslated or misinterpreted.

The 'Creationism' hypothesis apparently assumes that the resulting erroneous text correctly states God's deeds. Following the publication of Manfred Davidmann's work, and of the publicity it generated, the 'Creationism' hypothesis was abandoned as untenable. But a similar hypothesis was then put forward called 'Intelligent Design' which apparently assumes that the same erroneous text could correctly state the deeds of some other supernatural being.

What Manfred Davidmann proves in **'The Meaning of Genesis: Creation, Evolution and the Origin of Evil'** (2000) is that Genesis clearly states the evolution from reptilian to mammalian instincts, feelings and behaviour and the evolution and behaviour of human beings from humanoids (animals resembling humans) through Homo erectus (early man) to Homo sapiens (human beings, ourselves).

For example, the allegory telling about Adam and Eve in the Garden of Eden describes the evolution of Homo sapiens (human beings, ourselves) from Homo erectus. Genesis records that childbirth became more difficult as a result of the increased brain size (evolution of neocortex) which enabled Homo sapiens to know the difference between good and evil and to choose between them. Also stated is the necessary division of work between the male and the female, as equals in different roles, in protecting and bringing up their children, and much more.

What Manfred Davidmann has done with his works on the Pentateuch and the Bible, on religion and church-state relations, is to expose and correct the misinterpretations and mistranslations of the past. His works are major breakthroughs, constituting essential information for understanding the meaning and significance of the Pentateuch and the Bible.

For example, in "**Meaning and Significance of the Names of God in Genesis**" (2000) (see chapter 10.1)*, Manfred Davidmann proved the meaning and significance of the different names of God which had been lost.

In "**Meaning and Intent of Genesis: Essential Notes on Hebrew Grammar**," (2000) (see chapter 10.2)* he stated the fundamental rules which were ignored at time of translation because required background knowledge was not available, with consequent mistranslations.

And in "**Bible Translations, Versions, Codes and Hidden Information in Bible and Talmud**" (2001) (see chapter 10.3)*, he showed how changes made in the past obscured the intended meaning.

In his book '**ISLAM: Basis - Past - Present - Future**', (2003, 2010) {7}** Manfred Davidmann assembles, evaluates and objectively records the events of the formative years which shaped Islam. He enables one to understand how Islam came to be and its present beliefs and practices, conflicts and confrontations.

Knowing about Prophet Mohammed's struggle for recognition of his mission and message, is of vital importance if one wishes to understand what Mohammed taught and the Koran. Just what upset the elite so thoroughly and persistently that it caused him and his followers to be harshly opposed and actively persecuted?

The events and struggles which took place after Mohammed's death, and how the Koran and Islam came to be, shaped Muslim belief and practice, formed Sunnism and Shiism, underlie today's conflicts and confrontations within Islam.

Cooperatives and Cooperation

When people are exploited and oppressed they co-operate with each other to escape from poverty, to overcome exploitation and oppression. As do people wishing to improve working conditions and the quality of their lives. They get together and form co-operatives.

Manfred Davidmann's book '**Cooperatives and Cooperation: Causes of Failure, Guidelines for Success**' (1973-2006, 2011) {8}** is based on and includes a series of eight studies of co-operatives and mutual societies which were undertaken to determine causes of failure and reasons for success, to see how these enterprises were controlled and managed, to learn from their mistakes, to understand why members of established co-ops are dissatisfied with what they are getting from their co-ops.

As a matter of principle, all profits (surplus) made by a co-operative or mutual society belongs to its members as individuals. Any profit which is retained and added to reserves is the total of amounts which in effect were deducted from the profit share of each individual member.

Manfred Davidmann showed with these case studies that, for example, co-ops and mutual societies retain much of the profits and that their members then cease to be entitled to them.

Component Case Studies

> Mutual Societies
>> Trustee Savings Bank
>> Credit Unions
>> Building Societies

> Consumer Co-ops
>> Co-operative Retail Services Ltd
>> Co-operative Wholesale Society Ltd
>>> The Co-operative Bank PLC
>> Co-operative Insurance Society Ltd

> Producer (Worker) Co-ops
>> John Lewis Partnership plc
>> Mondragon Co-operatives
>> Kibbutzim (Plural of 'kibbutz')

Additions by the Editor:

* Published in this book

** Published in the following books:

> {1}** 'Management and Leadership:
> Local, National, Multinational (Global),
> Principles and Practice'
> Manfred Davidmann
> ISBN 978-0-85192-057-3

> {2}** 'Messianic Struggle:
> The Worldwide Struggle for a Good and
> Secure Life for All, Here and Now'
> Manfred Davidmann
> ISBN 978-0-85192-059-7

> {3}** 'The Real World in Which We Live:
> The Social Rules and Social System under
> Which We Suffer, Struggle, Survive and Prosper'
> Manfred Davidmann
> ISBN 978-0-85192-058-0

{4}**   'The Human Mind and How it Works:
        Group Minds in Action:
        How the Human Group Mind Shapes
        the Quality of Our Life and Living'
        Manfred Davidmann
        ISBN 978-0-85192-055-9

{5}**   'Judaism: Basis - Past - Present - Future, Part 1'
        Manfred Davidmann
        ISBN 978-0-85192-060-3

{6}**   'God and People:
        The Social Laws and Social System Underlying
        Judaism, Christianity, Islam and Democracy'
        Manfred Davidmann
        ISBN 978-0-85192-054-2

{7}**   'Islam: Basis – Past – Present – Future'
        Manfred Davidmann
        ISBN 978-0-85192-053-5

{8}**   'Cooperatives and Cooperation:
        Causes of Failure, Guidelines for Success'
        Manfred Davidmann
        ISBN 978-0-85192-056-6

Manfred Davidmann

ISLAM: Basis – Past – Present- Future

Knowing about Prophet Mohammed's struggle for recognition of his mission and message, is of vital importance if one wishes to understand what Mohammed taught and the Koran. Just what upset the elite so thoroughly and persistently that it caused him and his followers to be harshly opposed and actively persecuted?

The events and struggles which took place after Mohammed's death, and how the Koran and Islam came to be, shaped Muslim belief and practice, formed Sunnism and Shiism, underlie today's conflicts and confrontations within Islam.

In this book Manfred Davidmann assembles, evaluates and objectively records the events of the formative years which shaped Islam. He enables one to understand how Islam came to be and its present beliefs and practices, conflicts and confrontations. Comprehensiveness of information, and depth of analysis, can be judged by the book's chapter headings:

> Prophet Mohammed's Struggle for a Better Life for All
>
> Text, Language, Dialect and Interpretation of the Koran
>
> The Divine Right to Rule
>
> Compiling the Koran: Hadiths (Traditions) State the Underlying Reality
>
> Caliph Uthman's Rearrangement of the 'as revealed' Koran's Chapters
>
> Prophet Mohammed's Word of Allah and the Voice of the Ruling Elite
>
> Muslims and Jews
>
> Church and State, Government and Religion
>> Judaism, Christianity and Islam
>> Religion, Government and Education

The book, and the earlier individual research reports which are included in it, contains not only Manfred Davidmann's clear and factual compilations about what actually happened after Mohammed's death, but also his comprehensive and detailed findings, definitions and conclusions about the '**Text, Language, Dialect and Interpretation of the Koran**' (2003), about how the Koran was compiled and about its contents. Published 2003, guided to some extent by some of the Koran's 'abbreviated letters'.

Manfred Davidmann

God and People:
The Social Laws and Social System Underlying Judaism, Christianity, Islam and Democracy

This book is a collection of works by Manfred Davidmann about the God-given human rights, social laws and social system, and about the worldwide struggle to achieve them, to achieve freedom, liberty, independence and a good and secure life, here and now in this life.

Manfred Davidmann not only proves the meaning and intent of Genesis, the first volume of the Pentateuch, but also exposes the mistranslations and political misrepresentations of the past. For example he establishes the meaning of the names of God which 'had been lost'.

Clearly described and defined is the role of the family under modern conditions, and the differences between the behaviour of human beings and that of the primitive animals from which human beings evolved.

The main chapter headings are:

> The Real World in which We Live
>
> The God-given Human Rights, Social Laws and Social System
>
> Struggle for Freedom, Liberty and Independence: The Social Cause-and-Effect Relationship
>
> Family and Community: Family, Sex and the Individual
>
> The Meaning of Genesis

Manfred Davidmann is an internationally well-known and respected scientist and consultant, and author of a number of books and reports which have had considerable impact. His work usually breaks new ground and opens up new understanding and is written in meaningful and easily understood language. Outstanding is that his work is generally accepted as factual, objective and unbiased.

Manfred Davidmann

THE HUMAN MIND AND HOW IT WORKS:
Group Minds in Action: How the Human Group Mind Shapes the Quality of Our Life and Living

Manfred Davidmann shows how the human brain evolved and functions, how the human mind works, and how brain and mind interact. This fundamental work provides fascinating insights clearly expressed in meaningful language, shows how brain and mind determine what people do and how they do it, what people aim to achieve and how in the struggle for a better life we adapt to the world in which we live.

The chapters of this book which deal with how our communities and societies are organised and function, describe how our group minds shape our lives, communities and society, explain the consequent confrontations and struggles from dictatorship to democracy.

Relating the functioning of the brain to behaviour, this work shows how human behavior is affected by the primitive instincts of our reptilian ancestors. There are sections which discuss how conflict arises within the mind, mental health and illness, dominance, creativity and hearing voices.

Comprehensiveness of information, and depth of analysis, can be judged by the book's chapter headings:

> The Human Brain and the Human Mind
> > How the Human Brain Developed and How the Human Mind Works
>
> The Human Group Mind
> > The Human Group Mind and How It Works
> > Manipulated Communities and Populations
> > Manipulated Individuals
> > Freedom, Liberty and Good Life: Overcoming Corrupt Manipulations
>
> What People Struggle to Achieve
> > Motivation Summary
> > What People are Struggling Against: How Society is Organised for Controlling and Exploiting People
> > The Will to Work: What People Struggle to Achieve
>
> Worldwide Struggle
> > Democracy, Socialism and Communism: The Worldwide Struggle for a Better Life

Manfred Davidmann

Cooperatives and Cooperation:
Causes of Failure, Guidelines for Success

When people are exploited and oppressed they cooperate with each other to escape from poverty, to overcome exploitation and oppression. As do people wishing to improve working conditions and the quality of their lives. They get together and form cooperatives.

Different forms of cooperatives tackle different kinds of problems. What they have in common is that they serve their members and the community, aiming to improve the quality of life for their members.

As a matter of principle, all profit (surplus) made by a cooperative or mutual society belongs to its members as individuals. Any profit which is retained and added to reserves is the total of amounts which in effect were deducted from the profit share of each individual member.

This book is based on a series of eight studies of cooperatives and mutual societies which were undertaken to determine causes of failure and reasons for success, to see how these enterprises were controlled and managed, to learn from their mistakes.

Its conclusions and recommendations are relevant and cover fundamental and practical problems of coops and mutual societies, of members, of direction, management and control.

Manfred Davidmann showed with these case studies that, for example, coops and mutual societies retain much of the profits and that their members then cease to be entitled to them.

> Component Case Studies
>> Mutual Societies
>>> Trustee Savings Bank
>>> Credit Unions
>>> Building Societies
>> Consumer Coops
>>> Cooperative Retail Services Ltd
>>> Cooperative Wholesale Society Ltd
>>>> The Cooperative Bank PLC
>>>> Cooperative Insurance Society Ltd
>> Producer (Worker) Coops
>>> John Lewis Partnership plc
>>> Mondragon Cooperatives
>>> Kibbutzim (Plural of 'kibbutz')

Manfred Davidmann

Management and Leadership:
Local, National, Multinational (Global),
Principles and Practice

The term 'Participation', meaning by this 'participation in decision-making', was first coined, and defined, by Manfred Davidmann when he published his analysis and recommendations about the style of management. His works on style of management and on participation in decision-making in management, leadership and government, are widely known, studied and applied.

Manfred Davidmann brings to his tasks a rare combination of practical experience, knowledge and understanding backed by years spent training middle and top-level managers. Expert knowledge is expressed in clear and meaningful language and easy-to-follow diagrams illustrate the relationships.

The main chapter headings are:

Style of Management and Leadership

Motivation

Directing and Managing Change

Organising

Work and Pay

Inflation, Balance of Payments and Currency Exchange Rates

Using Words to Communicate Effectively

How local and national governments are managing our affairs is of crucial importance to every citizen. Government has to make ends meet, has to bring about a rising standard of secure living, social security and an increasing quality of life for its citizens.

"There can be ups and downs but", says Manfred Davidmann, "failure to make ends meet is just as directly and surely the result of bad leadership and management as it is in any commercial enterprise."

Manfred Davidmann reviews ways of balancing income and expenditure, causes of inflation, and tax avoidance, reviews ways out of a payments crisis and details the consequences of increasing interest rates, greater borrowing, selling assets or printing more money.

One works to achieve that which one needs and which one does not have. "Attaining goals leads to feelings of self-respect, strength and confidence", and "persistent lack of rewards leads to a view of society as being hostile and unrewarding".

311

Manfred Davidmann

The Real World in Which We Live:
The Social Rules and Social System under Which We Suffer, Struggle, Survive and Prosper

This community orientated book brings together studies undertaken by Manfred Davidmann to obtain a better understanding of why people have to struggle throughout their adult lives, in all countries and organisations, at all levels, to maintain and improve their standard of living and quality of life. Manfred Davidmann says: "We know what people are struggling to achieve and so these studies explore why people have to struggle by looking at what they are struggling against".

He discusses and illustrates the internal struggles taking place in political parties and all other organisations for achieving greater democracy and against those wishing to overpower democratic processes of decision-making.

And Manfred Davidmann here clearly defines and describes motivation, its basis and 'motivating'. He includes a detailed step-by-step listing of what people are struggling to achieve, their needs and wants, their achievements and objectives.

The depth of his analysis can be judged by the main chapter headings:

Ownership and Limited Liability

Community and Public Ownership

Ownership and Deciding Policy: Companies, Shareholders, Directors and Community

Multinational Summits and Agreements, Top-level Decision-making and Democracy

Exporting and Importing of Employment and Unemployment

Transfer Pricing and Taxation

Creating, Patenting and Marketing of New Forms of Life

What People are Struggling Against: How Society is Organised for Controlling and Exploiting People

Democracy Under Attack: Top-level Leadership and Decision-making

Taxing the Population for Private Profit

Corrupted Economics and Misguided (Misleading) Experts

Using Words to Communicate Effectively

The Will to Work: What People Struggle to Achieve

Manfred Davidmann says: "Decision-taking by leaderships has to be replaced by decision-making at the level of the people. The real struggle is not between political left and right, but is a struggle for participation (the right to make decisions)".

Manfred Davidmann

Messianic Struggle:
The Worldwide Struggle for a Good and Secure Life for All, Here and Now

Manfred Davidmann's fundamental works about management principles and leadership, community economics and needs, profit motivation and social costs, and participation in decision-making at all levels are major advances in human knowledge and key findings.

The author exposes humanity's hidden core confrontations, the source of oppression and enslavement, the role of biblical prophets and their warnings, how religious teachings were distorted, and he states the scientific benevolent social laws of behaviour and community organisation.

Following Manfred Davidmann's publications and recommendations, people are struggling now worldwide for a better life, for the right to make the decisions, for social security, for equality, freedom and independence, for socially responsible and humane behaviour, and the survival of humanity on this planet.

Comprehensiveness of information, and depth of analysis, can be judged by the book's chapter headings:

> Social Responsibility, Profits and Social Accountability. Incidents, Disasters and Catastrophes. The Worldwide Struggle for Social Accountability. Community Aims and Community Leadership.

> Work and Pay, Incomes and Differentials: Employer, Employee and Community

> The Right to Strike

> Reorganising the National Health Service: An Evaluation of the Griffiths Report

> Community Economics: Principles

> Social Responsibility and Accountability: Summary

> The World at War! Multinational (Global) Operations, and Government Of, By, and For the People: Democracy Under Attack: The Struggle for the Right to take the Decisions, and for Social Accountability

> The choice is yours: Unemployment, Charitable Social Security and Today's Religious Teachings or High Standard of Living, Satisfying Work and a Good Life, as God-given rights

> Creationism and Intelligent Design, Evolution, Education or Indoctrination

The Way Ahead: Policies for a Better Future

The Global (Worldwide) Struggle for a Better Life and The Root of all Evil, the Source of All Good, and the Messianic Struggle

Faith and Trust in God, No Matter by What Name called

Manfred Davidmann

Judaism: Basis – Past – Present - Future
Part 1

A major review and analysis by Manfred Davidmann of the essential but little-known social laws and social system of the Pentateuch (Torah) and of the fundamental scientific Social Cause-and-Effect Relationship which applies to all people everywhere at all times, and of Jewish history, finding the causes of subsequent defeat of the people and loss of country. The author provides a fully documented record of previously undiscovered material in the Talmud about Hillel. And he describes the struggles within Judaism which accompanied the birth of Rabbinical Judaism and how the Talmud recorded events.

Manfred Davidmann provides the required background knowledge of the essential core of Jewish belief and practice for drawing the only possible conclusion that the procedure called 'Prosbul' is contrary to the laws and intent of the Torah. He then annuls the Prosbul.

He shows that there are two separate root causes of antisemitism which one would normally not consider.

And he proves that the right to the land in which one lives, that is the strength and success of a people, depends on how people behave towards each other.

Comprehensiveness of information, and depth of analysis, can be judged by the book's chapter headings:

Struggle for Freedom: The Social Cause-and-Effect Relationship

History Speaks: Monarchy, Exile and Maccabees

At the Time of Jesus, This is What Actually Happened in Israel: The Truth about Hillel and his Times

One Law for All: Freedom Now, Freedom for Ever

Jewish Belief and Practice

Causes of Antisemitism

The Right to the Land of Israel